As one of the world's longest e
and best-known trav
Thomas Cook are the expert

For more than 13
guidebooks have unlocked
of destinations around the world,
sharing with travellers a wealth of
experience and a passion for travel.

**Rely on Thomas Cook as your
travelling companion on your next trip
and benefit from our unique heritage.**

Thomas Cook **driving** guides

CATALONIA &
THE SPANISH PYRENEES

Tony Kelly

Written and researched by Tony Kelly, updated by Josephine Quintero

Published by Thomas Cook Publishing
A division of Thomas Cook Tour Operations Limited
Company registration no. 3772199 England
The Thomas Cook Business Park, Unit 9, Coningsby Road,
Peterborough PE3 8SB, United Kingdom
Email: books@thomascook.com, Tel: + 44 (0) 1733 416477
www.thomascookpublishing.com

Produced by Cambridge Publishing Management Limited
Burr Elm Court, Main Street, Caldecote CB23 7NU
www.cambridgepm.co.uk

ISBN: 978-1-84848-377-4

© 2005, 2007, 2009 Thomas Cook Publishing
This fourth edition © 2011
Text © Thomas Cook Publishing
Maps © Thomas Cook Publishing/PCGraphics (UK) Limited

Series Editor: Karen Beaulah
Production/DTP: Steven Collins

Printed and bound in India by Replika Press Pvt Ltd

Cover photography © Terence Waeland/Alamy

About the author

Tony Kelly became a travel writer after teaching English in China and Sudan, but he did not really discover Spain until a walking holiday in Mallorca in 1995. Since then he has made many visits to the country, writing guidebooks to Mallorca, Menorca and the Costa Brava, and developing a particular affinity with Spain's Catalan-speaking regions. Although he is not averse to the odd afternoon on the beach, his real interest is in seeking out those hidden parts of Catalonia where he can get beneath the skin of the local character. Some of his most memorable experiences while researching this book were a night in a hilltop castle and another at the monastery of Montserrat, a meeting with Salvador Dalí's electrician and a walk in the snow in the Aigüestortes park. He also took the opportunity of a first visit to the Basque Country and a return to La Rioja to indulge his passion for the local wine. Among his other interests are George Orwell (whose earlier visit to Catalonia, in very different circumstances, was a constant source of inspiration), golf, walking, Manchester United and the songs of Jacques Brel. He writes regularly on travel for newspapers and magazines and has won awards for his writing from the British Guild of Travel Writers and the Mallorca Tourist Board. He lives near Cambridge, eastern England, with his wife and son.

Acknowledgements

Tony Kelly would like to thank the Paradores de Turismo, for generously inviting him to stay in their *paradors* in Cardona and La Seu d'Urgell. These state-run hotels, many of them in beautiful and historic buildings, are the best places to stay if you want Spanish atmosphere and regional cuisine at a reasonable, though hardly a budget, price. He would also like to thank Holiday Autos in the UK for supplying the cars in which he completed some 5000km of research, and the many Spanish drivers who, despite several near misses, failed to drive him off the road. Above all he would like to thank Kate, who put up with his long absences with extraordinary patience and without whose support this book would never have been completed.

Contents

About driving guides

Thomas Cook's driving guides are designed to provide you with a comprehensive but flexible reference source to guide you as you tour a country or region by car. This guide divides Catalonia into touring areas – one per chapter. Major cultural centres or cities form chapters in their own right. Each chapter contains enough attractions to provide at least a day's worth of activities – often more.

Ratings

To make it easier for you to plan your time and decide what to see, every area is rated according to its attractions in categories such as Architecture, Entertainment and Children.

Chapter contents

Every chapter has an introduction summing up the main attractions of the area, and a ratings box, which will highlight the area's strengths and weaknesses – some areas may be more attractive to families travelling with children, others to wine-lovers or people interested in finding castles, churches, nature reserves or good beaches.

Each chapter is then divided into an alphabetical gazetteer, and a suggested tour. You can select whether you just want to visit a particular sight or attraction, choosing from those described in the gazetteer, or whether you want to tour the area comprehensively. If the latter, you can construct your own itinerary, or follow the author's suggested tour, which comes at the end of every area chapter.

The gazetteer

The gazetteer section describes all the major attractions in the area – the villages, towns, historic sites, nature reserves, parks or museums that you are most likely to want to see. Maps of the area highlight all the places mentioned in the text. Using this comprehensive overview of the area, you may choose just to visit one or two sights.

One way to use the guide is simply to find individual sights that interest you, using the index or overview map, and read what our author has to say about them. This will help you decide whether to

Symbol Key

- **❶** Tourist Information Centre
- **❷** Advice on arriving or departing
- **❸** Parking locations
- **❹** Advice on getting around
- **❺** Directions
- **❻** Sights and attractions
- **❼** Accommodation
- **❽** Eating
- **❾** Shopping
- **❿** Sport
- **⓫** Entertainment

Practical information

The practical information in the page margins, or sidebars, will help you locate the services you need as an independent traveller – including the tourist information centre, car parks and public transport facilities. You will also find the opening times of sights, museums, churches and other attractions, as well as useful tips on shopping, market days, cultural events, entertainment, festivals and sports facilities.

visit the sight. If you do, you will find plenty of practical information, such as the street address, the telephone number for enquiries and opening times.

Alternatively, you can choose a hotel, perhaps with the help of the accommodation recommendations contained in this guide. You can then turn to the overall map on pages 10–11 to help you work out which chapters in the book describe those cities and regions that lie closest to your chosen touring base.

Driving tours

The suggested tour is just that – a suggestion, with plenty of optional detours and one or two ideas for making your own discoveries, under the heading *Also worth exploring*. The routes are designed to link the attractions described in the gazetteer section, and to cover outstandingly scenic coastal, mountain and rural landscapes. The total distance is given for each tour, as is the time it will take you to drive the complete route, but bear in mind that this indication is just for the driving time: you will need to add on extra time for visiting attractions along the way.

Many of the routes are circular, so that you can join them at any point. Where the nature of the terrain dictates that the route has to be linear, the route can either be followed out and back, or you can use it as a link route, to get from one area in the book to another.

As you follow the route descriptions, you will find names picked out in bold capital letters – this means that the place is described fully in the gazetteer. Other names picked out in bold indicate additional villages or attractions worth a brief stop along the route.

Accommodation and food

In every chapter you will find lodging and eating recommendations for individual towns, or for the area as a whole. These are designed to cover a range of price brackets and concentrate on more characterful small or individualistic hotels and restaurants. In addition, you will find information in the *Travel facts* chapter on chain hotels, with an address to which you can write for a guide, map or directory. The price indications used in the guide have the following meanings:

€   budget level
€€   typical/average prices
€€€   de luxe

Page 40

Santander

Page 58

Page 48

Bilbao

Llodio   Durango

Page 76

Page 66

Donostia-San
Sebastian

Tolosa

Vitoria-
Gasteiz

Miranda
de Ebro

Page 86

Haro

Burgos

Page 96

Pamplona-Iruña

Estella

Tafalla

Calahorra

Page 114

Jaca

Ejea de los
Caballeros

Huesca

Tudela

Soria

Aranda de Duero

Page 106

Zaragoza

Calatayud

Torrijo

Guadalajara

Madrid   Sacedon

Teruel

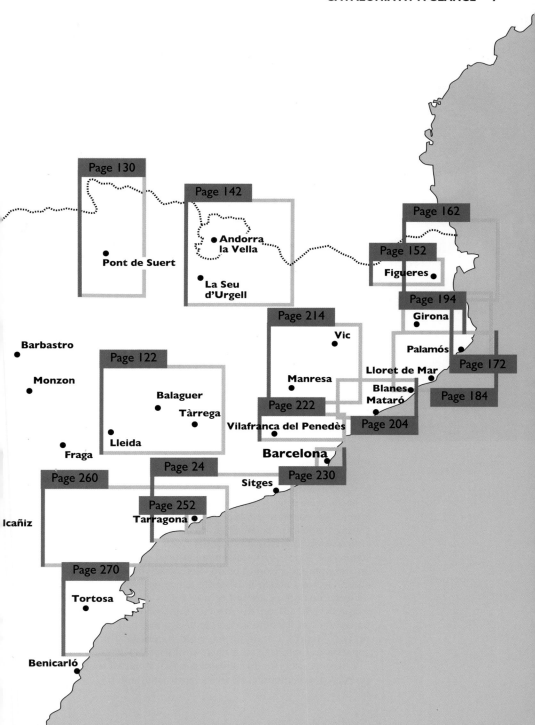

Page 130

Page 142

Page 162

Page 152

● Andorra
  la Vella

Figueres ●

Pont de Suert ●

● La Seu
  d'Urgell

Page 194

Girona ●

Page 214

Vic ●

Palamós ●

Barbastro
●

Page 122

Manresa ●

Lloret de Mar ●

Page 172

Monzon
●

Balaguer ●

Blanes ●

Page 184

Tàrrega ●

Page 222

Mataró ●

Lleida ●

Vilafranca del Penedès ●

Page 204

Fraga
●

Barcelona

Page 24

Page 230

Page 260

Sitges ●

Icañiz

Page 252

Tarragona ●

Page 270

Tortosa ●

Benicarló
●

Above
Dalí museum, Figueres

Introduction

The clichéd Spanish images of bullfighting, flamenco and gypsies have little in common with the true culture of Catalonia. Instead, when you think of Catalonia, you think of dancers holding hands in a ring; of green mountains, icy peaks and rugged coves; of the creativity which has produced singers like Montserrat Caballé and artists like Joan Miró and Salvador Dalí. You think of Barcelona, the genius of its Modernista architects and the way in which it has reinvented itself as a proud regional capital for the 21st century.

Catalonia, in the far northeast of Spain, has always been a place apart. The Catalans have a reputation for being serious, conservative and businesslike in comparison with the flamboyance of their Spanish neighbours. As anyone who has witnessed a Catalan festival will tell you, this is not entirely fair. The Catalans certainly know how to throw a good party, but they will be back at work the next day. The concept of *mañana*, the idea that you should never put off till tomorrow what could be put off till next week, is barely known here. Perhaps that is why Catalonia was the engine of Spain's industrial revolution and continues to be one of the wealthiest regions in Spain.

Catalonia looks outwards, to Europe, as much as in to the Iberian peninsula. In part, this is a result of its history and geography. The Romans launched their conquest of Spain by landing in Catalonia and establishing their capital at Tarragona. Romanesque art crossed into Spain over the Catalan and Aragonese Pyrenees. In the Middle Ages, Catalonia was a major Mediterranean power, its territory extending to Sicily and Naples. It should come as no surprise that Spain's large-scale tourist industry began in Catalonia, as tourists discovered the Costa Brava beaches in the 1950s. This was, after all, merely a continuation of Catalonia's long tradition of forging links with the outside world.

At the same time, of course, Catalonia is very much a part of modern Spain. Not everyone is happy about this, but most Catalans accept it. During the Franco dictatorship, the Catalan language was banned and expressions of regional solidarity such as the *sardana* dance were suppressed. Since 1979, Catalonia has been given a new lease of life as an autonomous region of Spain. Democracy brought a new awareness and a vibrant Catalan renaissance as young people rediscovered their heritage. Bookshops are full of novels in Catalan and the language is frequently heard on the streets. Boosted by the 1992 Olympics, Barcelona has become a confident city and a rival for the Spanish capital, Madrid. Catalonia has used its political muscle to extract concessions for the region from governments of left and right.

Catalonia may be officially a region, but it has all the trappings of a country. It has mountains, rivers, great cities and a coast. Each of its four provinces has its own distinct character. Most people live in and around Barcelona, in the industrial and commercial heartland. Girona has the Costa Brava beaches, a stunningly beautiful coastline and several solid and very Catalan towns. Tarragona has beaches, Roman remains, vineyards, castles and one of Europe's top theme parks. Lleida, the only landlocked province, is perhaps the most Catalan of all, stretching from the Ebro valley to the high Pyrenees.

Because many visitors use them as entry points to Spain, the scope of this book stretches to the Atlantic ports of Santander and Bilbao, with suggested routes from there to Catalonia. The book takes as its northern boundary the Spanish border with France – though it would be possible to argue, historically and culturally, that Catalonia does not actually stop there. As a general rule, the southern boundary is the River Ebro, which begins in the Cantabrian mountains and flows into the sea near Tarragona. The Bilbao to Barcelona motorway follows the Ebro for much of its course; if you really want to, you can drive between the two cities in a day. Alternatively, you can take your time, travelling across the mountainous regions of the Basque Country, La Rioja, Navarra and Aragón, each with its own rich history and culture and varying degrees of independence within the Spanish state. The constant backdrop to your journey will be the Pyrenees, 400km long and 3,000m high, a huge mountain range which has always provided a natural barrier between the Iberian peninsula and the rest of mainland Europe.

The routes in this book have been chosen to avoid motorways wherever possible and to follow the scenic back roads that reveal so much of the Catalan and Spanish character. Most of them are between 100km and 200km long, and can be completed in less than half a day.

Below
Pottery in Pals

They are designed, though, to be taken slowly, over one day or even two, giving yourself time to appreciate the towns and villages, the castles and Romanesque churches, to stop for a picnic in the countryside or a long seafood lunch by the beach. There is no need to follow them slavishly. Armed with a good map, one of the great thrills of Catalonia is in wandering off the beaten track, following that hidden valley just to see where it leads, and allowing yourself to discover that small village in the mountains with just a handful of houses, a solid stone church and a welcoming café in the main square.

Travel facts

Accommodation

Hotels in Spain are graded by the government, from one to five stars according to their facilities. Lesser categories are *hostals*, graded one to three stars, and *pensiones*, graded one to two. The Catalan government has a simpler system, with just two categories, hotels and *pensions*. The latter have fewer facilities but may be just as comfortable. Any establishment graded with two stars or more is likely to have rooms with private bathrooms. The Spanish tourist board publishes an annual *Guía Oficial de Hoteles*, with full listings for each province. It is widely available at bookshops and airports.

Paradors are a chain of state-run hotels, many in historic buildings or areas of scenic interest. Most have a great deal of character, with antique furniture and regional cuisine. There are *paradors* in Catalonia at Cardona, Vic, Aiguablava, Tortosa, La Seu d'Urgell, and at Vielha and Artíes in the Vall d'Aran. There are also *paradors* in Santo Domingo de la Calzada and La Calahorra in La Rioja, Olite in Navarra, Sos del Rey Católico and Bielsa in Huesca, Hondarribia and Argómaniz in the Basque Country, and Santillana del Mar and Limpias in Cantabria. These can make excellent bases for a touring holiday, with a couple of nights in each one. *Paradors* can be booked through a central reservation office in Madrid (*tel: 90 254 7979; email: info@parador.es; www.parador.es*) or before departure in London (*tel: 020 7616 0300; email: paradors@keytel.co.uk; www.keytel.co.uk*). Out of season, there are often substantial discounts available for senior citizens.

The majority of Spain's **campsites** are in Catalonia, mostly beside the coast. Again these are classified by the government, from first to third class. Most first-class sites offer excellent facilities. Campsites are listed in the *Guía Oficial de Campings*. You can book online at *www.campingsonline.com/espana*

Agrotourism is a fast-growing area, and local tourist offices keep lists of *casas rurales* (*casas de pagès* in Catalonia) and working farms where you can spend the night. Some of these houses are also available to rent on a self-catering basis. Look out for signs for *casa rural*, *agrotarismo* or (in the Basque Country) *nekazalturismoa*. Cases Rurals de Catalunya (*www.casesrurals.com*) lists *cases rurales* in the province.

The price indications in this book refer to a double room in autumn:
€   budget level
€€   typical/average prices
€€€ de luxe

Above
Bermeo windows

Addresses

If you see *s/n* in a Spanish address, this means *sin número* – without number.

Airports

The main international airport for Catalonia is El Prat at Barcelona. It has three terminals and excellent facilities, including numerous car-hire outlets. There are also smaller airports at Girona, Reus and Zaragoza, which handle budget scheduled flights and charter flights in summer. Bilbao has its own international airport. Spain's national carrier, Iberia, operates domestic flights between Barcelona, Bilbao and cities across Spain.

Children

Spain is a very child-friendly country, and children are welcome at all but the smartest restaurants. For specific child-centred activities, head for the coast, where there are plenty of safe beaches, play areas, fun-fairs and water parks. Remember that small children are particularly vulnerable to the sun. Look out for hazards such as swimming pools, and never let children play in or near the sea if the coastguard's red warning flag is flying.

Climate

Even in summer, the climate can vary wildly between the mountains and the coast. Most areas of Catalonia enjoy a Mediterranean climate, with mild winters, hot summers and long hours of sunshine from May through to October. Up in the Pyrenees, the snow persists until June and the weather can never be guaranteed. In general, the ski season lasts from December to April, spring and autumn are good times for walking, while July and August are too hot to do very much at all. On the north coast, Cantabria and the Basque Country have a cooler Atlantic climate, with long winters and heavy rainfall. The *tramuntana*, particularly prevalent on the Costa Brava, is a fierce, cold north wind, much feared by sailors and fishermen, which can strike at any time and last for several days.

Currency

Spain's currency is the euro, available in coins from 1 cent to 2 euros and in banknotes from 5 to 500 euros. Major credit cards are widely accepted and Spain has one of the world's highest densities of automatic teller machines (ATM), meaning there is one on nearly every corner in urban areas. Traveller's cheques and foreign currency can be changed at banks and hotels.

Customs regulations

Visitors arriving from countries outside the European Union may bring in one litre of wine, one litre of spirits, 200 cigarettes or 50 cigars, and 50g of perfume. Within the European Union, any amount of goods may be brought in provided they are for personal use.

Pets will require a general health certificate and proof of vaccination against rabies, issued by a vet in your home country before departure.

Below
Calella de la Palafrugell

Eating and drinking

Electricity

Electrical appliances run on 220–225 volts AC, using standard European round-pinned plugs. Visitors from the UK require an adaptor and US visitors may need a transformer for appliances operating on 100–120 volts.

Entry formalities

Citizens of European Union countries may visit Spain without restrictions, provided they hold a valid passport or national identity card. All other visitors require a passport. Citizens of the USA, Canada, Australia and New Zealand do not need a visa for visits of less than 90 days. South African citizens require a visa, issued by the Spanish Embassy. Under the European Union's Schengen Agreement, people travelling between France or Portugal and Spain by road are not usually required to show their passports, though you must still have one.

Spanish mealtimes are considerably later than elsewhere, with most restaurants opening for lunch between around 1300 and 1500, and dinner from about 2100. Breakfast is a light snack, perhaps coffee and a pastry or a mid-morning sandwich taken at about 1100. Between mealtimes, you can graze on *tapas*, small portions of food which are displayed beneath the counter at bars and heated up in a microwave. The Spanish do not think of *tapas* as a meal, and though several portions can make an enjoyable spread, it is an expensive way of filling up. The best value is usually the *menú del día*, a three-course set meal, with wine or water included, which most restaurants offer at lunchtime. For regional food specialities, *see* **Food**.

The price indications for restaurants in this book are for a three-course meal without wine:
€   budget level
€€   typical/average prices
€€€   de luxe

Most meals are accompanied by wine (*see* **Wine**, *page 21*), though you can usually order lager-type beer. Mineral water is widely available, either still (*agua sin gas*) or sparkling (*con gas*). Two popular soft drinks are *granizado*, a mixture of crushed ice with sweetened orange or lemon juice, and *horchata*, made from the milk of tiger-nuts. Coffee is usually drunk strong and black, as an espresso (*café solo*) or with a little bit of milk (*cortado*), though you can also ask for it to be made in a large cup with hot milk (*café con leche*), which is how the Spanish drink it at breakfast. Tea is less common, though herb teas such as camomile (*manzanilla*) and peppermint (*poliomenta*) are popular. Coffee can be accompanied by one of the many varieties of Spanish brandy, such as Fundador, Soberano and Carlos I. *Sangría* is a chilled summer punch of red wine, brandy, fresh fruit and lemonade, popular in tourist areas and on the coast, while *patxaran* is a Basque liqueur which is rather like a sloe gin.

Above
Pa amb tomàquet

Information

Left
San Sebastián café

Festivals

Every town and village in Catalonia has its annual festival, held on the feast day of the patron saint and combining religious celebrations with a large dose of pre-Christian ritual. Common features include giants, devils, fireworks, stick dances and mock battles between Moors and Christians or other representations of good and evil. Two uniquely Catalan traditions, often seen at festivals, are the *sardana* dance (*see page 219*) and the building of human *castells* (*see page 266*). Fire is another recurring theme, especially on the night of Sant Joan (23 June), when bonfires are lit all over Catalonia and beacons light up the summits of the Pyrenees. Other festivals celebrated across the region are the pre-Lenten Carnival (*see page 249*), the feast of Catalonia's patron saint, St George (23 April), and La Diada, Catalonia's national day (11 September).

Food

The cooking of Spain is regional cuisine, rooted in the soil and in peasant traditions. The Basques, with their history of seafaring, have a heavy emphasis on fish with classic dishes such as *kokotxa* (hake throat), *bacalao pil-pil* (salt cod in a light garlic sauce) and *bacalao a la vizcaina* (salt cod with peppers). In La Rioja, Navarra and Aragón, roast and grilled meat, heavy casseroles and vegetable dishes are accompanied by the robust local red wines. Catalonia has developed its own unique cuisine known as *mar i muntanya* ('sea and mountains'), combining chicken with lobster, rabbit with prawns, or pigs' trotters with snails. Seafood is excellent all along the coast, while inland specialities include *botifarra*, *fuet* and *longanissa* sausages. In Tarragona province, the *calçotada* is a spring feast based on barbecued spring onions (*see Valls, page 265*), and *xató* is a seasonal spicy salad containing tuna, anchovies and cod. One Catalan snack which is popular everywhere is *pa amb tomàquet*, crusty bread rubbed with tomato and drizzled with olive oil, then topped with anything from sliced ham to a slab of *tortilla* (Spanish potato omelette).

Health

Insurance

It is essential to take out a comprehensive travel insurance policy, covering accidents, theft and personal liability. Be aware that many policies exclude cover for hazardous pursuits, such as rafting, scuba diving and winter sports. Motorists need to be fully covered (see **Driver's guide**, *page 22*).

There are no major health hazards in Spain, though travellers should ensure that they are covered by adequate health insurance. Citizens of European Union countries should take a European Health Insurance Card, which entitles them to free basic health care. This is available free from *www.ehic.org.uk*, by phoning *0845 606 2030*, or from post offices. The biggest danger is the sun; it is sensible to cover up with a strong sunscreen at first, to wear a hat and to avoid the midday sun. Tap water is safe to drink, though mineral water is widely available and cheap.

Pharmacies can easily be identified by a large green cross displayed in the street. Outside normal hours, a notice on the door of each pharmacy gives the address of the nearest duty chemist. If you do need to consult a doctor, ask at your hotel. In an emergency, dial *112*.

Maps

The most useful maps for touring are the 1:400 000 Michelin maps, which are updated regularly and widely available in Spain and elsewhere. Map 573 covers the Basque Country, Navarra and La Rioja; map 574 covers Catalonia, Aragón and the Pyrenees. Tourist offices can usually supply you with a free city map (*un plano*). Detailed walking maps are available locally in popular trekking areas, such as the Montseny mountains and the Pyrenees.

Note that many road numbers in Spain have been changed in the last few years, so buy an up-to-date map that shows the new road numbers.

Museums

Most museums close on Sunday afternoons and all day on Monday. Check the individual entries in this book, but note that opening times are subject to change.

National parks

There are national parks at Aigüestortes in the Catalan Pyrenees (*see page 132*) and at Ordesa in the Aragonese Pyrenees (*see page 119*). These parks are open to visitors, but there are restrictions on hunting, fishing and camping in the interests of conservation. Other protected areas include the Montseny mountains (*see pages 204–13*), the Ebro Delta (*see page 272*) and the Medes islands (*see page 177*).

Opening times

- **Shops** are generally open from around 0900 to 1400 and 1700 to 2000 on weekdays and 0900 to 1300 on Saturday mornings, though supermarkets and shops in tourist resorts may stay open throughout the day and on Sundays. Markets generally take place in the morning, from around 0800 to 1400; indoor markets in the larger towns and cities are also open in the evening.
- **Banks** are open from 0830 to 1400, Monday to Saturday, though most close on Saturday mornings between June and September.
- **Post offices** in the larger towns may be open from 0830 to 2000, but most are only open on weekday mornings. Outside these hours, stamps can be bought at tobacconists.
- **Tourist offices** generally follow shopping hours, though some are open throughout the day, especially in summer. Many offices have reduced opening hours in winter.

Left
Bilbao's Guggenheim Museum

Public transport

A wide network of local bus routes connects the main towns of Catalonia; in summer, there are additional services to and from the coastal resorts. For day trips to Barcelona and the other large cities, it is usually easier to base yourself outside the city and travel in by bus than to take a car into the city. Train services are generally efficient, especially on the coastal route from Barcelona to Tarragona and on the main line north to Girona and Figueres. This line forms part of the rail link between Barcelona and Paris and is earmarked for high-speed development.

- **Restaurants** typically open from around 1300 for lunch and 2100 for dinner. Restaurants in the tourist resorts on the coast have largely adapted to northern European times. Bars are open throughout the day.
- **Petrol stations** are open from around 0700 to 2100 daily, or in some cases for 24 hours. A number of petrol stations accept out-of-hours automated credit card payments.
- **Churches** are generally open in the mornings, but some are open for services only. You can check the times of services on the door.

Postal services

Stamps (*sellos* in Spanish, *segells* in Catalan) can be bought at post offices, tobacconists, news kiosks and some shops which sell postcards. Mail can be posted at post offices (*correus*) or in the yellow postboxes on the street.

Public holidays

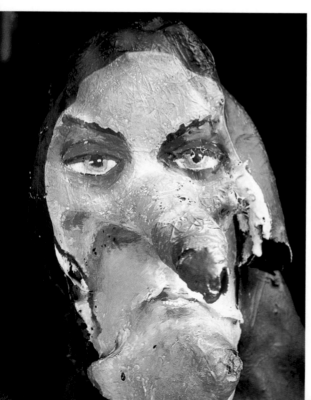

The following are public holidays throughout Spain:

1 Jan New Year's Day
6 Jan Epiphany
Mar/Apr Good Friday
1 May Labour Day
15 Aug Assumption of the Virgin
12 Oct National Day (*Día de la Hispanidad*)
1 Nov All Saints' Day
6 Dec Constitution Day
8 Dec Immaculate Conception
25 Dec Christmas Day (*Navidad*)

The following are public holidays in Catalonia:
24 Jun St John's Day
11 Sept Catalan National Day (*La Diada*)

In addition, there are various regional and local holidays. Two which are widely observed outside Catalonia are Maundy Thursday (the day before Good Friday) and the feast of St James on 25 July. Banks, shops and offices are closed on these days. If a holiday falls at a weekend, an extra day may be taken in lieu; if it falls on a Tuesday or Thursday, it may be used as an excuse for a long holiday weekend.

Shopping

Most shops are open from around 0900 to 1400 and 1700 to 2000 on weekdays and 0900 to 1300 on Saturdays. Good buys include leather, ceramics, shoes, South American clothes and jewellery, Spanish and Latin music, wine, brandy and food items such as olive oil, saffron, sausages and cured ham. Spain's biggest department store, **El Corte Inglés**, has branches in Barcelona, Pamplona, Bilbao and Zaragoza, all open from 1000 to 2200 Monday to Saturday. Large supermarkets, such as Carrefour, Supersol and Intermarché, are often found on the outskirts of towns and tend to be open from 1000 to 2100 Monday to Saturday and on Sunday mornings.

ETA

At the time of writing, the terrorist group ETA maintains its long-standing dispute with the Spanish government over the status of the Basque Country, although tourists are usually not targeted and a ceasefire, announced in September 2010, is still in force.

Reading

- Hemingway, Ernest, *Fiesta: The Sun Also Rises* (1926): the novel that told the world about the bull-running festival at Pamplona.
- Hopkins, Adam, *Spanish Journeys* (1992): a *tour de force* of Spanish history and art, explored through a series of journeys. There are detailed explorations of Goya and of the Civil War collectives in Aragón.
- Hughes, Robert, *Barcelona* (1993): the definitive account of Barcelona's history, from the Bronze Age until recent times.
- Lewis, Norman, *Voices of the Old Sea* (1984): an elegiac, semi-fictional account of three years in the death of a Catalan fishing village, as tourism overwhelmed the Costa Brava in the 1950s.
- Morris, Jan, *Spain* (1964): although it was written 40 years ago, this remains the freshest, most readable introduction to the country by one of the great travel writers of the age.
- Orwell, George, *Homage to Catalonia* (1938): Orwell's classic account of fighting on the Republican side in Catalonia during the Spanish Civil War.
- Tóibín, Colm, *Homage to Barcelona* (1990): this vivid personal account of modern Barcelona captures the mood of post-Franco confidence sweeping the city.
- Zafón, Carlos Ruiz, *Shadow of the Wine* (2001): an international bestseller, this complex thriller, written by Barcelona-born Zafón, is set in the city after the Spanish Civil War. The equally-awaited prequel, *The Angel's Game* (2009) follows a young writer who is approached by a mysterious figure.

Safety and security

The levels of crime in Catalonia are no higher than elsewhere, but it makes sense to take a few simple precautions. You should always leave your valuables in a safe at your hotel, including copies of your passport and driving licence if you need to have these with you. Theft from cars is common, and all valuables and luggage should be locked out of sight in the boot. Foreign-registered cars, and those which are obviously hire cars, can be particularly at risk. In Barcelona and other large cities, be on your guard for pickpockets and anyone who tries to divert your attention, for example by selling you flowers or pointing out a stain on your shirt. If you are unfortunate enough to be involved in an incident, telephone the police on *091* or the general emergency number *112*. You will also need to make a personal visit to the police station in order to obtain from them a copy of the report, required by your insurance company for any claims you may wish to make. For help in replacing a stolen passport you should contact your nearest consulate.

Left
Festive mask

Telephones

Although most public telephones take coins, the easiest way to make a call is by using a phonecard (*tarjeta telefónica*), available from post offices and tobacconists for €6 or €10. For international calls, dial 00 followed by the country code (UK = 44, Ireland = 353, USA/Canada = 1) and then the local number. Be aware that most hotels levy a supplement on calls made from your room.

You can also buy a pre-paid SIM card for around €30.

When phoning Spain from abroad, the international code is +34.

Time

Spain is one hour ahead of GMT in winter and two hours ahead in summer, from the last Sunday in March to the last Sunday in October.

Sport

The biggest spectator sport is football, with FC Barcelona (*see page 232*) a Catalan passion. Big matches are screened live on Spanish television and there is always an eager crowd watching in the bars. Most matches are played on Sunday afternoons between September and June. Tickets are hard to come by for the big games, though you should be able to see Barcelona's other team, Espanyol, who play in the Olympic stadium on Montjuïc. You can also see *Primera División* football in Bilbao (Athletic Bilbao) and Santander (Racing Santander).

Bullfighting is not generally considered a sport, still less an act of cruelty; look in the papers and you will find it on the arts pages. It has never been as popular in Catalonia as elsewhere. There are major bullrings in Barcelona, Zaragoza and Pamplona, famous for the 'running of the bulls'. If you want to see a fight, look out for posters advertising events in spring and summer.

Tipping

Restaurant bills include a service charge but it is usual to leave a modest extra tip of around 5 to 10 per cent for good service. In bars you usually pay for all drinks when you leave and it is customary to leave some small change on the counter. For taxi drivers round up the bill to the nearest whole number. Chambermaids, porters, tour guides and coach drivers are always happy to receive a tip.

Toilets

In many parts of Spain there is a shortage of public toilets, but it is nearly always acceptable to go into a bar – though the price of a coffee will save any potential embarrassment. It is always a good idea to make the most of the facilities on visits to department stores, supermarkets and museums.

Travellers with disabilities

Facilities for people with disabilities are improving all the time in Spain, and new buildings are equipped with wheelchair access, but many museums, churches and historical sights are still inaccessible. Hotels vary widely in their accessibility and it is important to check when you book. The seafront promenades at most coastal towns are extremely wheelchair-friendly.

What to pack

Formal dress is rarely necessary except at the smartest hotels. If you plan to eat out at some of the more expensive restaurants, men may feel more comfortable in a jacket and tie. Most of the time, the Spanish dress smartly but informally. On the beaches in summer, just about anything goes, though beachwear is not considered acceptable elsewhere and a sarong is useful for covering up. It is wise to take a small first-aid kit, including insect repellent and sunscreen, though these are also available locally. You could also consider taking an electric anti-mosquito device, together with tablets. A tube of concentrated 'travel wash' detergent is useful for washing out clothes in hotels.

Wine

The regions covered in this book include several of Spain's leading wine-producing areas. The most famous wine region is La Rioja (*see page 86*), where a number of *bodegas* can be visited. Good red wines are also produced in neighbouring Navarra and particularly in Aragón, where the Somontano district, around Barbastro, has established a growing reputation. Catalonia's main wine-producing area is the Penedès, the birthplace of *cava* (*see page 225*), though other denominations worth looking for are Empordà, Costers del Segre, Terra Alta and especially Priorat, known for its full-bodied, strong red wines.

Quality wines are generally distinguished by the letters DO (*denominación de origen*) on the label. Wines labelled *crianza*, *reserva* or *gran reserva* have been aged for stipulated periods and are usually more complex. Most Spanish people drink red wine with their meal, or occasionally rosé, whatever they are eating. For something very different, try *txakoli*, a fizzy, slightly tart white wine produced on the Basque coast.

Right
Mas Oliver *cava* hails from
Sant Sadurní d'Anoia in the
Alt Penedes region

Driver's guide

Members of affiliated motoring organisations, such as the AA and RAC, may use the services of the Real Automóvil Club de España, RACE (*tel: 902 404545, emergency breakdown assistance: 902 404545; www.race.es*).

Autoroutes

The Spanish motorway system has been subject to massive expansion throughout Spain, a process that is still ongoing and greatly facilitating motoring around the country.

Major centres are connected by *autovías* and *autopistas* (toll motorways). The letter N signifies a *carretera nacional* (national route). Tolls (*peaje*) must be paid on many motorways. A fixed-price toll is payable on some small stretches of motorway, but the usual system is to pick up a ticket when you drive on and pay when you leave according to the distance travelled. Tolls can be paid by cash or credit card. If you want to avoid tolls, there are usually signs directing you to a slower and generally more scenic route. A toll is also payable for the following tunnels: the Cadi tunnel, between Berga and Bellver de Cerdanya; the Garaf tunnel between Barcelona and Sitges; and the Vallvidrera tunnel near Barcelona.

Accidents

Drivers involved in an accident are required to mark the presence of their vehicle by placing two warning triangles, one 50m in front of the car and another 50m behind and wear a fluorescent orange waistcoat (supplied in all rental cars). If possible, you should move your car into a lay-by or on to the hard shoulder, and arrange for it to be moved by the rescue services. In the case of injuries or damage to vehicles you should attend to the injured, request the assistance of the rescue services and call the police immediately on *112*.

After an accident, make sure you take down the name, address, registration number and insurance details of any other party, preferably on the standard European Accident Statement form which your insurer should be able to provide. The advantage of this form is that it is identical in every language, so both parties understand that they are answering the same questions. If the other driver refuses to co-operate, call the police – there are SOS telephone posts situated every 2km on motorways and dual carriageways.

Breakdowns

Anyone taking their own car to Spain should take out European breakdown cover. You will be provided with a 24-hour contact number for use in case of breakdown. If you need emergency medical service call *091*, reporting the number from which you are calling and giving your location and emergency needs. Car-hire firms have their own breakdown arrangements. As with accidents, it is essential to mark the presence of your vehicle on the road by using two warning triangles. The towing of one vehicle by another, unless it is a breakdown truck, is only allowed in exceptional circumstances in order to move the broken-down vehicle to safety.

Caravans and camper vans

Many of the mountain roads in Catalonia are narrow and twisting, making them difficult to manoeuvre in a long vehicle. If you do bring a caravan, the maximum permitted dimensions of a private vehicle, including a trailer or caravan, are 12m long, 4m high and 2.5m wide. Vehicles towing caravans are required to observe lower speed limits (*see page 26*). Make sure that your caravan braking system is properly adjusted and that all the lights of the caravan or trailer are

Documents

Drivers are required at all times to carry a driving licence, car registration document and third-party insurance certificate. Citizens of European Union countries may use their standard paper or card licence, but those holding older licences and travellers from non-EU countries will require an international driving licence, available from motoring organisations. You are also required to carry a passport or national identity card. It is a good idea to carry a copy of the European Accident Statement, available from your insurer for use in the event of an accident.

Insurance

Third-party insurance cover is compulsory in Spain, though you should take out full comprehensive insurance. A Green Card, or international insurance certificate, is accepted as evidence that your cover extends to Spain. Apply to your insurance company several weeks before you travel. Although it is no longer a legal requirement, your insurance company may also issue a bail bond, which prevents the police from impounding your vehicle or property following an accident. In the past, a number of foreign drivers have ended up in prison as a result of not obtaining a bail bond. As well as motor insurance, it is essential to take out a comprehensive travel insurance policy, covering accidents, theft and personal liability.

functioning. Check also that both tyres on the caravan are of the same size and type and in good order.

When travelling with a caravan try to avoid overtaking other vehicles if possible and do not overtake more than two vehicles in one stretch. Always keep a good distance between vehicles. Should you need to stop, pull up off the carriageway and on to the hard shoulder. If you can, drive off the road altogether.

Campsites are plentiful in the area contained within this guide and are divided into three categories, first, second and third. There are numerous sites close to the sea, while many more are located in beautiful surroundings near natural parks.

The majority of campsites have electrical hook-up points and plug-in water supplies, making caravan touring a comfortable option. There are strict regulations with regard to off-site camping. This is allowed only in isolated areas and permission is required from the local police and the landowner, if there are not more than three caravans/tents or ten campers in one place. Several websites provide information about caravanning in Spain including *www.vayacamping.net*

Driving in Catalonia and the Spanish Pyrenees

Roads are generally in good condition, though the mountain passes in the Pyrenees are frequently closed by snow in winter. The main types of road are motorways (*autopistas*), toll-free dual carriageways (*autovías*), national carriageways (*carreteras nacionales*, prefaced with N) and regional roads (*carreteras comarcales,* prefaced with C or with the first two letters of the province). Many mountain roads require a high degree of concentration because of the large number of hairpin bends.

Toll roads in Catalonia include the A2, which stretches from Barcelona west to Lleida and beyond, and the A7, a major motorway that runs from the French border south to Valencia, via Girona, Barcelona and Tarragona.

Note that the majority of road signs and place names in Catalonia are now in Catalan. In the Basque Country they generally appear in both Basque and Castilian (Spanish).

Driving rules

Traffic drives on the right in Spain with overtaking on the left. The majority of main roads are designated as priority roads and these are most often indicated by a sign showing a yellow diamond on a white background.

Where a minor road intersects a major road you should see the sign 'Stop' or 'Ceda el Paso'. When roads that intersect have equal classification, with no signs given, priority is given to traffic coming from the right. If you are in any doubt, the safest bet is always to give way to all traffic coming from your right.

Drinking and driving

The blood-alcohol limit is 0.05 per cent, which is strictly enforced. The limit for drivers with less than two years' experience is 0.03 per cent. You can be subject to random breath tests at any time and driving over the limit can result in a substantial fine, suspension of your licence or even imprisonment. Motorists involved in an accident or who infringe any driving regulations will be given alcohol and drug tests. Failure to comply can result in the immobilisation of the vehicle, payment for the offence and withdrawal of your licence. Alcoholic drinks in Spain tend to be strong and measures generous, so the only sensible action is never to drive after drinking alcohol.

Essentials

By law, drivers must carry two warning triangles, a spare set of bulbs and fuses, a spare tyre and a reflective vest for roadside emergencies which must be kept in the passenger compartment, not the boot. A first-aid kit is also advised. Drivers who wear glasses are required to carry a spare set. Foreign vehicles must display a nationality sticker. In winter, snow chains are essential for driving in the Pyrenees.

Petrol

Petrol	– gasolina
Unleaded	– sin plomo
Normal	– 95 octane
Super	– 98 octane
Diesel	– gasoleo

Vehicles already on roundabouts have the right of way. When entering a roundabout you must give way to traffic from the left. Take care when negotiating traffic islands as many drivers may not indicate the exit they are going to take. Note also that some exits leading from an island have a zebra crossing on them.

Driving in bus, taxi or cycle lanes, shown by a line running parallel to the kerb, could result in an on-the-spot fine if seen by a policeman, unless it's a question of avoiding an obstruction or accident.

Fuel

It is technically an offence to run out of fuel, so it is important to top up regularly. Petrol prices vary continuously and from one supplier to the other, but are generally considerably cheaper than in the UK. Most petrol stations are operated by Spanish companies, such as Campsa, Cepsa and Repsol. Self-service stations are becoming more widespread, but attendants are still the norm. You should ask for the tank to be filled (*lleno*) or quote an amount in euros. While credit cards are widely accepted at service stations, with automated credit card payment also possible in most stations, you must also be prepared to pay in cash.

Most petrol stations stay open from early morning to late in the evening and many remain open 24 hours on motorways and main highways. But they can be few and far between in rural areas, so make sure you have filled up.

Information

Many Spanish road numbers have been changed in the last few years. This driving guide uses the new numbers. On the maps, national road numbers (prefaced with N on road signs) are shown in white against a red background; regional road numbers (prefaced with C or the first two letters of the province) are shown in black on a white background.

If you intend exploring independently, make sure you take up-to-date maps with you. The Michelin Spain and Portugal map is useful for the whole country, while the regional Michelin maps Cataluña/Catalunya, Aragón, Andorra, and the País Vasco/Euskadi, Navarra, La Rioja provide good coverage for the areas contained within this guide.

The Ministerio de Fomento issues an atlas of all the roads in Spain, the *Mapa Oficial de Carreteras*, which can be purchased in many Spanish bookshops. Maps can also be obtained from Spanish tourist offices abroad or within Spain.

Fines

Because of the high incidence of road accidents, fines for a variety of traffic offences are strictly enforced. These can include speeding, overtaking without signalling or not wearing a seat belt. Non-resident offenders are usually issued with on-the-spot fines. Failure to pay can result in your car being impounded or immobilised.

Speed limits are shown in black figures on a white background, encircled by a red rim. Be aware that these tend to be more strictly enforced in towns and resorts. Radar controls are in use throughout the country and speed limits are also enforced by motorcycle traffic police.

Fines depend upon the type of offence committed, whether considered to be minor, serious or very serious. A very serious offence can carry a substantial fine.

Complaints regarding traffic fines, such as a very high fine, should be referred to the provincial traffic office where the fine was issued, as shown on the ticket. Make sure you receive a receipt for any payments you have to make.

TELE RUTA

For traffic and weather information check the local papers or the recorded information service in Spanish (*tel: TELE RUTA, freephone within Spain 900 123505*).

Parking

Parking can be a nightmare in many Spanish cities, and it is not uncommon to spend up to an hour driving around looking for somewhere to park. Most towns and cities have a restricted parking area in the centre, with pay-and-display spaces marked out by blue lines. These generally operate during business hours, from around 0800 to 1400 and 1600 to 2000 Monday to Saturday, with a time limit of two hours. For longer periods, you need to find a space outside the centre or follow signs to one of the underground car parks. These are generally convenient, central and secure, but can work out very expensive, especially overnight.

When booking hotels, especially in cities, make sure to ask about parking. It is by no means guaranteed that hotels will have car-parking facilities for their guests. In many cases, such facilities are non-existent; more commonly, there is a garage which you pay to use.

In small towns and villages with little in the way of parking facilities, it's often advisable to park just outside and explore on foot, rather than try to negotiate the narrow streets, many of which are one-way or pedestrianised.

Police

The Spanish police are divided into three different branches. Each town and city has its *policía local*, usually dressed in blue, whose duties include dealing with urban traffic. The *policía nacional*, though less visible, deal with serious crimes and will probably be your first point of contact in an emergency. Most highway patrols are carried out by the *guardia civil*, a constant presence on Spanish roads and easily recognised by their olive green uniforms. To make matters more complicated, the Basque Country and Catalonia have their own autonomous versions of the *policía nacional*. In Catalonia these are known as the *Mossos d'Esquadra*. In any emergency, you can call the police on *091* or the general emergency number on *112*.

The *guardia civil* can impose on-the-spot fines for speeding and other offences. If you do not pay, your car may be impounded.

Those witnessing an accident are obliged to stop, tend to the victims and call the emergency services.

Security

Theft from cars is a common occurrence, especially in Barcelona and other big cities, and foreign-registered vehicles are particularly at risk. You should always lock all luggage and valuables out of sight in the boot, and never leave anything on display inside the car. If possible, remove or disable any radios or audio equipment whenever you leave the car.

Lights

Sidelights and dipped headlights should be used between sunset and sunrise, in poor visibility and in tunnels. Full headlights are prohibited in built-up areas. Motorcyclists must use dipped headlights throughout the day, but other vehicles should not use them unless it is necessary. Rear fog lamps are only to be used in the event of very poor visibility.

All motorists are required to carry a spare set of light bulbs. Right-hand drive vehicles will need to have their headlights adjusted using headlamp converters which can be bought at motoring shops and ferry ports.

Mobile phones

The use of mobile phones and any other communication apparatus is forbidden at all times when driving unless the vehicle is fitted with a hands-free unit.

Seat belts

The driver and front seat passenger must wear seat belts. Rear seat passengers are also required to do so if belts are fitted. Children under 12 may not travel in the front unless using an approved restraint system. The police will levy large on-the-spot fines for any infringement.

Never leave the keys inside the car, for example, at petrol stations or while you are unloading your luggage at a hotel. Always keep your essential documents with you, and remove them each time you get out of the car. If possible, you should keep photocopies in a safe place, such as at your hotel.

Should you find yourself the victim of a crime, contact the police as soon as possible, on *091* or *112* (emergencies), and make sure you obtain a copy of the report, which will be required by your insurers.

Speed limits

The following speed limits apply across Spain, unless otherwise indicated:
- Motorways 120kph
- Dual carriageways 100kph
- Other roads 90kph
- Built-up areas 50kph

Cars with caravans or trailers are required to observe lower speed limits of 80kph on motorways and dual carriageways and 70kph on other roads. The speed limit in Andorra is 90kph on main roads and 10kph in built-up areas.

Road signs

The majority of road signs follow international convention and are easily recognised. You may also see the following:

aparcamiento parking
calzada detoriorada bad road
calzada estrecha narrow road
cambio de sentido change direction
ceda el paso give way
cruce peligroso dangerous crossroad
cuidado drive with care
curva peligrosa dangerous bend
despacio slow
desvío/desviación detour
dirección única one-way street
estaciónamiento prohibido no parking
gasolinera petrol station
mantenga su derecha keep right
mantenga su izquierda keep left
obras roadworks
peaje toll
peligro danger
prioridad a la derecha priority to the right
prioridad a la izquierda priority to the left
prohibido el paso road closed
salida exit

SPANISH ROAD SIGNS

RESTRICTION SIGNS

No right turn

Minimum
Speed Limit

No motor
vehicles

No stopping at
any time

WARNING SIGNS

Signal lights
ahead

Roundabout
ahead

Guarded railroad
crossing

Double bend,
first curving to
the right

PRECEDENCE SIGNS

Oncoming traffic
must wait

Give way

Crossroads

You have
right of way

GENERAL SIGNS

Pedestrian
crossing

Snow chains
required

Parking

No through
road

Above
Nationalist flag

Getting to Catalonia

If you are planning a driving tour of Catalonia and northeast Spain, you have four basic options. You can drive your own car to Spain; you can take your car on a ferry; you can take it on the Motorail service; or you can fly to Spain and hire a car when you get there.

Each of these has its advantages and disadvantages, and the decision will come down to a combination of factors including cost, time and your proposed itinerary. Many people feel happier driving their own car, but the car may not be equipped for left-hand driving, and in the event of mechanical problems it may not be easy to get spare parts. You also need to take out additional breakdown cover. On top of all this, foreign-registered cars are frequently targeted by thieves. You may decide that taking your car is not worth the trouble.

With hire cars, by contrast, any problems are taken out of your hands. Most hire cars are new, efficient and economical to run, and in the event of accident or breakdown the hire company will supply you with a replacement car. This is obviously a more expensive option, but over relatively short periods the advantages might well outweigh the drawbacks.

The whole question of cost is a complicated one. It is by no means certain that the cheapest option is to travel overland by car. The cost of petrol, motorway tolls and overnight accommodation in France has to be offset against the cost of a plane or ferry ticket. The price of tickets fluctuates wildly according to demand and season. A number of no-frills airlines offer cheap scheduled flights from London to Barcelona, and outside the peak summer season there may be good flight-only deals available on charter flights. Some of the high-street packages for off-season deals are so cheap that they are worth taking for the flight alone, even if you have no intention of using the accommodation. The disadvantage is that you are tied to a fixed period, usually of one or two weeks. It may be better to go for a more flexible fly-drive deal with car hire included, or to book your flight and car hire independently.

By car

From the UK, there are regular ferry crossings to several ports in northern France, including Calais, Caen, Cherbourg and Le Havre. The easiest way of taking a car to France is on the Le Shuttle train service through the Channel Tunnel. The trains, adapted to take cars in double-decker wagons, leave the terminal at Folkestone up to four times an hour, taking around 35 minutes to reach Calais. Tickets can be booked in advance (*tel: 08705 35 35 35; www.eurotunnel.com*), which is advisable during the summer months.

Slip roads at Calais lead directly on to the French motorway network, from where there are two main routes south to Spain. Both routes follow the A26 and A1 towards Paris, where you need to take the ring road to join the A10. The routes diverge near the town of Orléans. The A10 continues through Tours and Poitiers on its way to the west coast, then travels south to Bordeaux. From here the N10 leads to Biarritz, and you enter Spain at Irun, close to the Basque city of San Sebastián. For a more direct route to Catalonia, head south from Orléans on the A71, continuing to Clermont-Ferrand and from there to Perpignan. From Perpignan, a motorway leads to Barcelona, entering Spain at the border post of La Jonquera.

Each of these journeys is well over 1,000km and, while they can just about be done in a day, it is not to be recommended. The French motorway system is well served by good-value, comfortable hotels where you can break up your journey. Alternatively, if you have the time, you can travel slowly across France, avoiding tolls and taking one of the scenic routes to Spain across the Pyrenees.

By ferry or Motorail

Below
San Sebastián harbour

Two ferry routes connect the UK to northern Spain. Brittany Ferries (*www.brittany-ferries.co.uk*) operates car ferries from Plymouth to Santander, and Plymouth to Bilbao. The journeys take between 24 and 36 hours. Many passengers find the choppy waters of the Bay of Biscay particularly uncomfortable. One option, combining the overland and ferry routes, is to take the ferry to Santander or Bilbao, drive across Catalonia and return through France.

An alternative is to have your car transported on French Motorail (*tel: 0844 484050; www.raileurope.co.uk*) from Calais to Perpignan, near the Catalan border. You leave Calais in the early morning and can enjoy dinner the same day on the Costa Brava. Departures from Paris offer a wider choice of destinations within France.

By air

For shorter visits, you might want to consider a fly-drive holiday, beginning in Barcelona or Bilbao. Barcelona is the main entry point to Catalonia and the second international airport of Spain, with daily scheduled flights to London and to major European and North American cities.

Large carriers include British Airways, KLM and the Spanish airline, Iberia, but it is worth looking around at other airlines. In the UK, easyJet (*www.easyjet.com*) offers low-cost scheduled flights from London Gatwick, Luton and Stansted to Barcelona and Bilbao, Ryanair (*www.ryanair.com*) has cheap flights from Stansted to Girona and Reus, and BMI (*www.bmibaby.com*) has flights from various airports in the Midlands, as well as Cardiff and Belfast.

Setting the scene

History

The history of modern Catalonia begins in AD 878, when Guifré el Pilós (Wilfred the Hairy) became the first Count of Barcelona, ruling over an area from Barcelona to the Pyrenees. According to tradition, it was as Wilfred lay wounded in battle that his lieutenant Charles the Bald dipped his fingers in Wilfred's blood and wiped them across his golden shield, thus creating the red and gold stripes of the Catalan flag.

Wilfred had managed to unite the various factions of the southern Pyrenees, following the Christian Reconquest of northern Catalonia from the Moors. In 988, Wilfred's great-great-grandson, Borrell II, broke off the ties of servitude to the Frankish king and established Barcelona as an independent region. To Catalan nationalists, this is seen as the birth date of Catalonia.

Above
Romanesque architecture in Santillana del Mar

The region had already been inhabited for thousands of years. Prehistoric man has left rock carvings and burial chambers, though nothing as spectacular as the caves at Altamira in Cantabria (*see page 42*). By the 7th century BC, Iberian settlers had established their civilisation, with the development of a written language and towns such as Ullastret. The Greeks set up trading posts on the coast at Empúries and Roses, and the Carthaginians founded Barcelona in around 230 BC.

The Romans landed at Empúries in 218 BC to begin their conquest of the Iberian peninsula. Olives and vines were introduced, and before long much of Spain was being governed from Tarragona, the capital of the province of Hispania Citerior. By the 5th century AD, the decline of the Roman empire left Spain in the hands of the Visigoths, former allies of Rome, who briefly established their capital at Barcelona.

The Moorish occupation of Spain began in 711 and lasted for more than 700 years. As the Reconquest began, much of Catalonia quickly capitulated; Girona was captured by Charlemagne in 785 and Barcelona by his son Louis in 801. In the aftermath of such victories, Catalonia became a buffer zone between the French and Moorish lands, allowing Wilfred the Hairy to establish his power base.

His dynasty ruled for more than 500 years. In 1137, Count Ramón Berenguer IV married the infant Petronilla of Aragón, uniting the two houses and paving the way for Catalonia's Mediterranean expansion. Ramón completed the Catalan Reconquest, wresting the southern territories of 'New Catalonia' from the Moors and building the great Cistercian monasteries near Tarragona. Over the next three centuries, Catalan-Aragonese conquests included the Balearics, Valencia, Sicily,

Above
The medieval town walls of
Montblanc

Corsica, Sardinia, Athens and Naples. Catalan was established as the official language and the first Catalan literature was published. The *Corts Catalans*, Europe's first form of parliamentary government, was set up with representatives of the people, the clergy and the nobility, and the *Generalitat* (Catalan government) was established under Pedro IV. This period has come to be known as Catalonia's Golden Age.

The marriage of Fernando of Aragón to Isabel of Castile (the so-called 'Catholic Monarchs') in 1469 brought the kingdom of Aragón to an end and ushered in a period of decline for Catalonia. The final defeat of the Moors, who lost Granada in 1492, led to the unification of Spain. The Inquisition was set up and the Jews were expelled, from Catalonia and elsewhere. In the same year, Christopher Columbus discovered America and Spain's maritime focus shifted away from the Mediterranean towards the New World across the Atlantic. Catalonia retained its own language, currency and government, but increasingly power was concentrated in Castile, now governed by the Habsburg dynasty of the Holy Roman Emperors.

In 1640, the first open confrontation occurred with the revolt of *els segadors* ('the reapers') against Spanish rule. These farmers have become Catalan folk heroes, recalled in the Catalan national anthem, which calls on the people to defend their rights. The revolt occurred during Spain's 30-year war with France; Catalonia declared itself independent and threw itself under the protection of the French king, finally surrendering in 1652. The Treaty of the Pyrenees in 1659 ended the war and resulted in the loss of much of the Cerdanya to France.

Catalonia picked the wrong side during the War of the Spanish Succession, which resulted in victory for the Bourbon king Felipe V in 1714. As punishment for supporting the claims of the Austrian pretender, Felipe imposed a series of repressive measures on Catalonia. Its political and judicial systems were dismantled, its language banned and its universities suppressed. At the same time, Barcelona was growing into a significant port as the ban on Catalonia trading with the Americas was relaxed.

There was more trouble ahead in the 19th century, when Napoleon's troops occupied Catalonia during the Peninsular War. Despite their history, the Catalans rallied to the Bourbon cause and Girona was heroically defended during a seven-month siege. The restoration of the Bourbon monarchy in 1814 was followed by the Carlist wars, the result of continuing disputes over the succession which dragged on for most of the 19th century.

Catalonia was at the forefront of the industrial revolution, which by the mid-19th century had made it the wealthiest region in Spain. The cork and wine industries flourished, and Spain's first railway opened in Barcelona. This was accompanied by a return of Catalan nationalism and by the cultural movement known as the *Renaixença* (Renaissance), which had at its heart the revival of the Catalan language. Among the new ideas which emerged out of this period was the growth of the Modernisme architectural movement.

The 20th century was a period of turmoil in Catalonia as in the rest of Spain. In 1931, following the fall of the dictator Primo de Rivera, Catalonia declared itself a republic. In 1936, after victory for the left-wing Popular Front parties in the Spanish general election, the *Generalitat* was restored under the presidency of Lluís Companys. This was too much for General Franco, commander of a military garrison in Morocco, who launched the rebellion which became the Spanish Civil War.

Below
Henry Moore sculpture in the European Nations Park, Guernica

The Catalan town

Almost every town and village is centred around a *plaça major* (*plaza mayor* in Spanish), a main square which acts as a focal point for the community. The *plaça major* probably owes its origins to the Roman forum, an open space with porticos around the sides where business was transacted and the main functions of government and justice carried out. The town hall (*ajuntament*) is generally situated on the main square; the parish church may be there, too. The square is usually surrounded by a covered arcade, providing shelter for market stalls and cafés and relief from the sun and rain. In the past, the *plaça major* would serve as a bullring, and it is still likely to be the venue for markets, fiestas, *sardana* dancing and other public events.

Above right
Dalí museum, Figueres

Barcelona remained in government hands, becoming the Republican capital; thousands of international volunteers, including the writer George Orwell, flocked to the city to join the militias which they saw as fighting for the cause of freedom. Orwell has described how the militias ended up fighting among themselves, with Communists set against anarchists and only Franco's Nationalists benefiting. The war lasted for three years, causing hundreds of thousands of deaths and witnessing countless horrors, among them the introduction of saturation bombing at the Basque town of Guernica (*see page 60*). The final battle, the Battle of the Ebro, at Tortosa in 1938, was perhaps the bloodiest of all. Barcelona fell in 1939 and thousands of Catalans fled into France as Franco seized power across Spain. President of Catalonia Lluís Companys was captured and executed on Franco's orders in 1940.

The Franco era (1939–75) saw repression throughout Spain and an attempt to centralise power in an alliance of church and state. Inevitably there were reprisals against Catalonia for its support of the Republicans during the Civil War. The Catalan language was banned, along with expressions of Catalan solidarity including the *sardana* dance. Catalonia was used as a testing ground for mass tourism, with concrete resorts springing up on the Costa Brava and little thought given to the long-term impact.

Although an underground Catalan nationalist movement always existed, it never resorted to violence in the same way as the Basque group ETA, who were responsible for the murder of Franco's prime minister in 1973. Typical of the Catalan opposition was Jordi Pujol, imprisoned for singing the unofficial 'national anthem' during a visit by Franco to Barcelona in 1960. Twenty years later, Jordi Pujol was elected President of Catalonia.

In a third restoration of the Bourbon monarchy, Franco appointed King Juan Carlos as his chosen successor. Franco died in 1975 and the king surprised many by his commitment to democracy. A new constitution granted limited regional autonomy, and in 1979 the people of Catalonia voted in a referendum to approve the new statute of autonomy.

Catalan was reinstated as an official language, and a Law of Language Normalisation passed in an effort to encourage its

The Basques

The Basques are often described as the oldest race in Europe. Their origins are lost in ancient history, but it appears that they were living on the European continent well before the arrival of the Indo-Europeans and are therefore the closest that Europe has to an indigenous population. Their language, Euskara, is like no other and probably dates from aboriginal times. It is spoken by about a third of the population of the Basque Country and is the main language in rural areas. Although many Basques are happy to belong to Spain, Basque nationalism is a potent force, expressed by the long terrorist campaign of ETA (Euskadi Ta Askatasuna, which means 'The Basque Country and Freedom'). The group's political wing, Batasuna, has been declared illegal by the Spanish government, although the party doesn't accept the decree. ETA and its supporters believe in a wider Basque nation, Euskal Herria, which extends into Navarra and modern-day France (see page 84).

widespread use. Street signs have gradually been replaced in Catalan; it is the principal language of education and (apart from in Barcelona, with its sizeable non-Catalan population) it is once again the language heard on the streets.

Spain, meanwhile, has not only survived but has prospered since the transition to democracy. An attempted coup in 1981, hatched in Catalonia by rebel army officers, soon failed when it became clear that it did not have the support of the king. The election of a Socialist government the following year, with barely a murmur from the military, was an indication that democracy had taken root. In 1986, Spain joined the European Community (now the European Union), a clear sign that it had entered the European mainstream. Fourteen years of socialism were followed by eight years of a centre-right coalition. In 2004, however, the socialists returned to power, gaining an unexpected victory, under the leadership of José Luis Rodríguez Zapatero.

After 20 years as an autonomous region, Catalonia has grown up. The initial euphoria has been replaced by a degree of cautious maturity – though most visitors are still struck by the mood of optimism and the unmistakable sense of building a new society. Literature and the arts are flourishing, and the second Catalan Renaissance has extended into areas from architecture to cuisine. Since the 1992 Olympics, Barcelona has become a confident, modern city and a fine advertisement for the region. In common with the rest of Spain, Catalonia and the other regions covered in this book are coping with the challenges posed by decades of rapid economic growth, particularly the environmental impact of mass tourism and the growth of cities, and the transformation of Spain from a generator of migrant labour for the countries of northern Europe to one dependent on migrant workers from Africa and South America.

Politics and government

The central government may be in Madrid, but Spain is a highly evolved state. This book visits 6 of the 17 *comunidades autónomas* (autonomous regions) into which the country is divided: Cantabria, the Basque Country (País Vasco or Euskadi), Navarra, La Rioja, Aragón and Catalonia (Catalunya). Most regions are subdivided into provinces and these, in turn, organised into local districts called *comarcas* (*comarques* in Catalonia).

Each regional government has its own prime minister (president) drawn from a parliament in which various political parties, national and local, are represented. Its work is financed by a combination of regional and national taxes.

Because of their distinct cultures and languages, two regions have somewhat greater autonomy than others. Catalonia is made up of the provinces of Barcelona, Girona, Lleida and Tarragona and its capital is Barcelona. The Basque Country is made up of Vizcaya/Bizkaia,

Above
Tarragona

Guipuzcoa/Gipuzkoa and Alava provinces with Vitoria-Gasteiz as its capital. The governments of these two regions have wide-ranging responsibilities for health, social security, transport, tourism, culture, local government and public works as well as some executive powers relating to education and the environment. Responsibility for policing is shared with central government. The other regions of Spain have slightly fewer autonomous powers.

Catalonia and the Basque Country are technically regions of a nation state but many Catalans and Basques consider themselves as nations within a nation. There is some pressure for independence – particularly in the Basque Country – which has been eased by the devolution system and recognition of the local languages. The relationship between central government and these two regions sometimes causes political tension and resentment from people living elsewhere in Spain.

The Spanish state retains control over defence, foreign affairs and the economy; the latter suffering a serious crisis in 2010, with 20 per cent nationwide unemployment. King Juan Carlos I is the head of state. The leader of the government is the prime minister, currently José Luis Rodríguez Zapatero, who is responsible to the two-house Cortes Generales (parliament).

Art and architecture

The principal architectural movements of western Europe, most notably Romanesque and Gothic, crossed into Catalonia and northeast Spain over the Pyrenees. Each of these movements developed a distinct Catalan/Spanish style, taking account of local traditions and climate. Churches were built with walls of solid stone, with the minimum number of windows in order to lessen the impact of the sun; public buildings invariably needed a patio, with porticos to provide shade. As well as absorbing outside influences, each of the Spanish regions has developed its own vernacular architectural styles, such as the solid, stone-built farmhouses known as *masías* in Catalonia and *etxea* in the Basque Country. Catalonia's unique contribution to architecture has been the Modernisme movement, a Catalan version of art nouveau made famous by Antoni Gaudí's works in Barcelona.

Romanesque art crossed the Pyrenees with the medieval pilgrims to Santiago, and reached its peak in Catalonia, Aragón and Navarra between the 11th and 13th centuries. Essentially a style of religious architecture, it is distinguished by its solid, sober forms, its round arches, multiple apses and the tall, slender bell towers of its churches. Some of the finest examples are found in the isolated valleys of the Catalan Pyrenees, as well as along the pilgrim route at Jaca and Estella. Also of note are the cathedral at La Seu d'Urgell and the carved portal of the monastery of Santa María at Ripoll. Many Romanesque churches were adorned with frescoes, strongly influenced by the Byzantine style from eastern Europe. Some of these frescoes are now on display in the Museu Nacional d'Art de Catalunya in Barcelona, which has one of the finest collections of Romanesque art in the world.

Gothic art was imported from France during the 13th century and remained the predominant style for some 300 years. This is the style most closely associated with Catalonia's Golden Age, seen in the cathedrals and civil palaces of Barcelona and Girona. In contrast to the simplicity of Romanesque, Gothic art was elaborate and ambitious, with pointed arches, ornamental tracery and huge churches supported by flying buttresses. Stained glass was prominent, rose windows were a common feature, and altarpieces were painted or sculpted with rich, colourful expression. Some of the best-known Gothic religious painters in Spain, such as Ferrer Bassa, Lluís Borrassà, Pere and Jaume Serra, Bernat Martorell and Jaume Huguet, were Catalans.

Mudéjar is the name given to a style of architecture which combined both Gothic and Islamic elements. It was developed by Muslim craftsmen under Christian occupation, and is distinguished by its ornamental designs in brick and ceramics. Some of the finest Mudéjar buildings in Spain can be seen in Zaragoza.

Renaissance architecture arrived from Italy in the 16th century, but soon developed a distinctive Spanish style, known as Plateresque

---

The *rambla*

A feature of every town is its *rambla*, an avenue traditionally laid out along the course of a dried-up riverbed. This is the setting for the early evening *passeig* (*paseo* in Spanish), a ritual promenade which is not often seen except on Sundays and public holidays. As in other Mediterranean countries, this is an opportunity to dress up, gossip, flirt, see and be seen, or simply take a welcome dose of fresh air once the heat of the day relents. The most famous *rambla* of all is Las Ramblas in Barcelona, where the two-way traffic of people goes on 24 hours a day.

because its fine detail was reminiscent of silverwork. The Renaissance was a deliberate attempt to mimic the style of ancient Rome, with a return of round arches and classical columns. Elaborate Renaissance altarpieces (*retablos*) were carved in alabaster and decorated with gold leaf. One of the masters of this technique was Damián Forment, whose work can be seen in Zaragoza, Huesca and Poblet.

Baroque, the dominant form of the 17th and 18th centuries, was characterised by extravagance, with twisting columns and dense ornamental façades. Its Spanish expression became known as Churrigueresque, after a well-known family of architects. The basilica dedicated to St Ignatius of Loyola in the Basque Country is a good example of the style.

Modernisme (Catalan modernism), which developed in the late 19th century, was a uniquely Catalan movement though it had its equivalents in other cultures – Art Nouveau in France, *Jugendstil* in Germany, Modern Style in Britain and the USA. In Catalonia, Modernisme was closely linked with Catalan nationalism and the literary and artistic renaissance which had begun in the mid-19th century. The movement embraced painters (Ramón Casas, Santiago Rusiñol), sculptors (Josep Llimona, Miquel Blay) and even furniture makers (Gaspar Homar), but its most enduring impact has been in the field of architecture, where its exponents, such as Gaudí and Domènech i Montaner, took materials such as wrought iron, brick and industrial glass and used them to re-create classic forms. Barcelona alone has more than 1,000 classified Modernista buildings, though others can be seen in Girona, Lleida, Olot, Reus and the holiday resort of Sitges. In keeping with its democratic origins, Modernista architecture can be found in everything from opera houses and hospitals to apartment blocks, wine cellars and shops.

Highlights

The top 10 sights of Catalonia
- Barcelona – the Ramblas and Gothic quarter (*see page 233*)
- Barcelona's Modernista architecture (*see page 237*)
- The monastery at Montserrat (*see pages 222–4*)
- The Roman remains at Tarragona (*see pages 252–6*)
- The old town of Girona (*see pages 194–203*)
- The mountain scenery of the Pyrenees (*see pages 130–41*)
- The Romanesque churches of the Vall de Boí (*see pages 137–8*)
- The coastal scenery of the Costa Brava (*see pages 172–93*)
- The medieval town of Besalú (*see pages 153–4*)
- The Teatre-Museu Dalí at Figueres (*see pages 166–7*)

The top 10 sights outside Catalonia
- The prehistoric cave paintings at Altamira (*see page 42*)
- The Guggenheim Museum at Bilbao (*see pages 50–51*)
- The Oak of Guernica (*see page 61*)
- La Concha beach, San Sebastián (*see pages 66–7*)
- The basilica of Santuario de Loiola (*see page 79*)
- The vineyards of La Rioja (*see pages 86–95*)
- The Romanesque architecture of Estella (*see pages 96–8*)
- Monastery of San Frande la Peria (*see pages 118–19*)
- The Mudéjar architecture and Aljafería palace at Zaragoza (*see pages 108–11*)
- The mountain scenery of the Aragonese Pyrenees (*see pages 114–21*)

Below
Tarragona's Roman theatre

Five places to see ancient art
- The prehistoric cave paintings at Altamira (*see page 42*)
- The Greek and Roman towns at Empúries (*see page 176*)
- The Iberian settlement at Ullastret (*see page 181*)
- The Roman amphitheatre at Tarragona (*see page 252*)
- The archaeological museum at Tarragona (*see page 254*)

Five places to see Romanesque and Gothic art
- Museu Nacional d'Art de Catalunya, Barcelona (*see page 235*)
- Museo Diocesano, Jaca (*see page 117*)
- Museu Diocesà, Solsona (*see page 217*)
- Museu Episcopal, Vic (*see page 218*)
- Museu d'Art, Girona (*see page 197*)

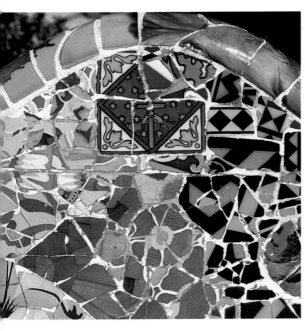

Above
Mosaic detail, Parc Güell, Barcelona

Five places to see modern art
- Museo Guggenheim, Bilbao (*see pages 50–51*)
- Museu Picasso, Barcelona (*see page 236*)
- Fundació Joan Miró, Barcelona (*see page 235*)
- Teatre-Museu Dalí, Figueres (*see pages 166–7*)
- Museu de Montserrat, Montserrat (*see page 224*)

Five good specialist museums
- Museo del Vino, Haro (wine) (*see page 86*)
- Museu del Joguet, Figueres (toys) (*see page 167*)
- Museu del Ganivet, Solsona (knives) (*see page 217*)
- Museu de l'Art de la Pell, Vic (leather) (*see page 218*)
- Museu del Futbol Club Barcelona, Barcelona (football) (*see page 232*)

Five good days out with children
- Port Aventura theme park (*see pages 245–6*)
- The funfair at Tibidabo, Barcelona (*see page 233*)
- The aquarium at Barcelona (*see page 234*)
- The zoo at Barcelona (*see page 236*)
- Waterworld, Lloret de Mar (*see page 187*)

Five scenic drives
- The northern Cantabrian coastline around Cabo de Ajo (*see pages 46–47*)
- Vielha to Sort over the Bonaigua pass (*see pages 138–41*)
- The circuit of the Aragonese Pyrenees from Huesca to Jaca (*see pages 120–21*)
- The circuit of the Serra de Montseny (*see pages 210–13*)
- The Costa Brava corniche from Tossa de Mar to Sant Feliu de Guíxols (*see page 192–3*)

Five places to see wildlife
- Parque Nacional de Ordesa, Aragonese Pyrenees (*see page 119*)
- Parc Nacional d'Aigüestortes, Catalan Pyrenees (*see pages 132–4*)
- The Medes islands (*see page 177*)
- The Serra de Montseny (*see pages 204–13*)
- The Ebro Delta (*see pages 272–3*)

The Cantabrian coast

Ratings

Beaches	●●●● ○
History	●●●● ○
Villages	●●●● ○
Children	●●● ○ ○
Churches	●●● ○ ○
Museums	●●● ○ ○
Scenery	●●● ○ ○
Watersports	●●● ○ ○

For visitors arriving on the ferry from Britain, the Cantabrian coast provides their first glimpse of Spain – and to many it comes as a surprise. Between Santander and Bilbao there are sandy beaches, rugged capes and sweeping bays where rivers empty into the sea, backed by a green, pastoral landscape which supports Spain's largest dairy industry. Not for nothing is this region known as 'Green Spain'. The rains which water the lush Cantabrian farmland mean that winters here can be long, cold and damp, but in summer the coast is swarming with holidaymakers – especially the provincial capital Santander, a fashionable place once favoured by the Spanish royals. Fishing ports and bathing resorts spread out along the coast, while just inland lie one of Spain's prettiest villages and the most remarkable of its prehistoric sites.

CABO DE AJO

Beaches

Of several beaches along this stretch of coastline, the best are at **Noja**, a popular summer resort thought to have been named after Noah – whose ark was once said to have been washed up on this shore.

The spur of land that juts into the sea between the bays of Santander and Santoña reaches its zenith at Cabo de Ajo, where a solitary lighthouse marks the northernmost point of the Cantabrian coastline. There are marvellous views of this spot from the drive across the cape, especially on the high section between Galizano and Ajo. Near here, a side turning leads to the **Iglesia de Santa María de Bareyo**, a 12th-century Romanesque church with a Visigothic font, situated on a hill overlooking the Ajo river.

CASTRO URDIALES

ⓘ *Avda de la Constitución 1; tel: 942 871512; email: turismocastro@cantabria.org; www.castro-urdiales.net*

ⓐ A weekly market takes place on Thursday mornings.

This sturdy fishing port and summer resort sits on a rocky promontory overlooking the bay. Behind the harbour, narrow medieval streets lead up to the cathedral-like **Iglesia de Santa María de la Asunción**, perhaps the finest Gothic church in Cantabria. If you manage to get inside, look for the standard flown by Christian forces at the battle of Las Navas de Tolosa in 1212 – the battle which marked the final defeat of the Moors in northern Spain.

Beside the church, a ruined castle built by the Knights Templar now shelters a lighthouse. The seafront promenade here makes a delightful place to stroll, with glass-fronted houses, lively restaurants and bars, and fishing boats moored in the picturesque harbour.

Accommodation and food in Castro Urdiales

La Sota € *Calle La Correría 1; tel: 942 871188; fax: 942 871284.* If you want to stay in the heart of the old town, this simple, family-run hotel is a good bet.

Las Rocas €€ *Avda de la Playa; tel: 942 860400; fax: 942 861382; www.lasrocashotel.com.* The town's top hotel, by the beach with a full range of facilities.

Mesón El Segoviano €€€ *Calle La Correría 19; tel: 942 861859.* Roast suckling pig and other hearty Castilian meat dishes are the specialities at this bustling waterfront restaurant.

Mesón Marinero €€€ *Calle La Correría 23; tel: 942 860005; www.mesonmarinero.com.* This seafood paradise beneath the arches of the

Opposite
Harbour at Cabo de Ajo

main square features the freshest local fish as well as paella and other rice dishes. The upstairs restaurant overlooks the port, or you can feast on fish *tapas* at the downstairs bar.

Cuevas de Altamira

Museo de Altamira
€ *Tel: 942 818815;*
http://museodealtamira.
mcu.es. Open May–Oct
Tue–Sat 0930–2000,
Sun 0930–1500; Nov–Apr
Tue–Sat 0930–1800,
Sun 0930–1500. The caves
are only open with prior
booking. There is a waiting
list to get inside and
applications should be made
far in advance. Apply in
writing to **Centro de**
Investigación y Mueso
de Altamira, *39330*
Santillana del Mar, Cantabria.

The archaeologist Marcelino de Sautuola stumbled across this remarkable discovery in 1879 when his nine-year-old daughter pointed out some primitive rock paintings on the roof of a cave. Yet such was the initial scepticism of his critics that few were prepared to believe he had unearthed a treasure of palaeolithic art. Subsequent investigation has revealed that the paintings date back to at least 12,000 BC, making them the most significant example of prehistoric art in Spain. The largest chamber, 18m long with a vivid polychrome ceiling portraying startlingly realistic images of bison, horses and wild boar, has been called the Sistine Chapel of Ancient Art. Entry to the caves is restricted to a few visitors a day, but many others come just to feel the atmosphere of the place and to see the video of the paintings in the accompanying **museum**. A copy of the famous ceiling is on display in the National Archaeological Museum in Madrid.

Laredo

Alameda de Miramar;
tel/fax: 942 611096;
email: laredo@cantabria.org;
www.turismodecantabria.com

One of Cantabria's most colourful festivals, the **Batalla de Flores**, takes place in Laredo on the last Friday in August, when floats decorated with flowers are paraded through the streets and the people indulge in a riotous flower-throwing 'battle'.

The busiest resort on the Emerald Coast has been a Roman seaport, a medieval seat of power and a base for the Spanish Armada, but these days Laredo is better known as a holiday centre, much favoured by the French. The Pueblo Viejo ('Old Town'), above the harbour, is little changed since the 13th century, but the 5km stretch of beach, though it retains some wild elements at its northern end, is increasingly backed by modern apartments and urbanisation.

Accommodation and food in Laredo

Casa Felipe €€ *Tercera Travesía José Antonio 5; tel: 942 603212.* Excellent regional Cantabrian fare and bar, specialising in fresh fish and seafood.

Miramar €€ *Alto de Laredo; tel: 942 610367; fax: 942 611692;*

Right
Galleons in Santander's Parque de la Magdalena

www.hmiramarlaredo.com. Just outside Laredo on the old road to Bilbao, this comfortable hotel features a swimming pool, a private car park and panoramic windows with great sea views.

SANTANDER

❶ *Jardines de Pereda (tel: 942 203000; email: turismo@ayto-santander.es; www.ayto-santander.es).* There is also a tourist information kiosk at El Sardinero, opposite the Gran Casino, in summer and in *Mercado del Este, Hernan Cortés 4 (tel: 942 310708; email: afitur@cantabria.org).*

P Parking in Santander can be a real headache in summer. There is a large car park at the southern end of El Sardinero, but this fills very quickly. In the centre, short-term parking is available along Paseo de Pereda, or follow signs to one of the underground car parks.

❷ Boat tours of the bay depart regularly in summer from the jetty beside the Pereda gardens. There are also ferries throughout the year to Pedreña and Somo, whose beaches face Santander across the bay. You can buy tickets at the Reginas kiosk on the waterfront.

❸ **Catedral** *Plaza del Obispo José E. Eguino; tel: 942 226024. Open Mon–Fri 1000–1300, 1600–2000, Sat 1000–1330, 1630–2000, Sun 0800–1400, 1700–2100. Free.*

The first port of call for many visitors to Spain is a mixture of modern provincial capital, fading *belle époque* resort, and a busy ferry and fishing port with a fair amount of charm. Although Santander has been occupied since Roman times and was once an important trading centre and seaport for the medieval kingdom of Castile, the town reached its heyday in the early 20th century when Alfonso XIII would come here to take the waters.

Much of the so-called old town is surprisingly modern, the result of rebuilding after a massive fire in 1941 which destroyed most of the city centre. The oldest remaining structure is the **Catedral**, though even this was gutted and had to be rebuilt. All that remains of the original church is the early Gothic crypt (where a glass floor reveals fragments of a much earlier Roman building) and a section of the 14th-century cloisters.

The town centre is dominated by two large squares. The delightful Plaza Porticada, surrounded by arcades, is the venue for several of the events during Santander's music and dance festival each summer. A few streets away, Plaza del Generalísimo is rather less appealing, with a statue of General Franco still standing in front of the town hall. Between and behind the two lies a network of pedestrian shopping streets, a busy indoor market and Santander's main museum, the **Museo de Bellas Artes**, with its collections of contemporary and Cantabrian realist paintings, as well as a portrait of Fernando VII by Goya. Adjoining the museum, the **Biblioteca y Casa Museo Menéndez Pelayo** contains more than 40,000 books, including rare manuscripts, in the library of Spain's greatest literary historian, a native of Santander.

The ferry station is situated on the waterfront between the fishing harbour and the leisure port, close to the Jardines de Pereda where boats leave in summer for cruises of Santander Bay. The gardens mark the start of a waterfront walk which eventually leads to two more museums. The **Museo Municipal de Arqueología y Prehistoria** contains exhibitions on Cantabrian archaeology and ancient history, while the star exhibit at the **Museo Marítimo del Cantábrico** is the skeleton of a 24m whale.

The headland at the north end of Santander Bay is now the **Parque de la Magdalena**, a popular summer playground with a beach, a tourist train circuit and a mini-zoo where polar bears and lions do their best to entertain the day-trippers. The royal palace here, built in 1912 and funded by popular subscription as a gift to Alfonso XIII, is now a prestigious international summer university. From the park,

Museo de Bellas Artes *Calle de Rubio; tel: 942 239485. Open Mon–Fri 1030–1300, 1730–2000, Sat 1000–1300. Free.*

Biblioteca y Casa Museo Menéndez Pelayo *Calle de Rubio 6; tel: 942 234534. Guided tours Mon–Fri, every 30 minutes from 0900–1130. Free.*

Museo Marítimo del Cantábrico *Calle San Martín de Bajamar s/n; tel: 942 274962. Open Tue–Sun, summer 1000–1930, winter 1000–1800. Admission charged.*

Parque de la Magdalena *Open daily 0800–2000. Free.*

Parque de Mataleñas *Avda del Faro. Open daily 0800–2000. Free.*

For a quick snack, head for **Café Cibeles Plaza**, near the town hall on Plaza del Ayuntamiento.

The **Festival Internacional de Santander** takes place in August, featuring jazz, opera and ballet, and a host of other events. Tickets and information are available from the Palacio de Festivales. Tel: 942 210508; www.palaciofestivales.com

you can walk to **El Sardinero**, Santander's longest beach, backed by elegant buildings including the recently restored Gran Casino.

The coast road continues northwards, passing a **golf course** on its way to **Faro de Cabo Mayor**, where the cliffs beside the lighthouse offer impressive views over the Cantabrian Sea.

It is possible to walk to Faro de Cabo Mayor, following a footpath which leaves from the north end of El Sardinero beach. The walk leads over a headland with magnificent sea views, passing through the **Parque de Mataleñas** where there is a small wildlife park and a lake which attracts aquatic birds. A second path to the right leads down to the remote Mataleñas beach. The walk to the lighthouse and back will take about two hours.

Accommodation and food in Santander

Asador Lechazo Aranda €€ *Calle Tetuán 15; tel: 942 214823.* Roast lamb and suckling pig are on the menu at this Castilian roast house in the streets behind the yacht harbour.

Bodega del Riojano €€ *Calle Río de la Pila 5; tel: 942 216750; email: comercial@grupocabomayor.com.* The painted wine barrels are the best-known feature at this classic *bodega,* serving Riojan cuisine and *tapas* in a dark old wine cellar.

Las Brisas €€ *Calle La Braña 14; tel: 942 275011; fax: 942 281173; email: abrisas@cantabria.org; www.hotellasbrisas.net.* Charming, small cottage-style hotel in the backstreets behind the El Sardinero beach.

Hotel Central €€ *Calle General Mola 5; tel: 942 222400; fax: 942 363829; email: hotelcentral@elcentral.com; www.elcentral.com.* The Sardinero district can be crowded in summer and deserted in winter, so you may prefer this stylish, cosy hotel in the city centre – though parking can be a problem.

La Cúpula €€€ *Plaza de Italia; tel: 942 274300.* The terrace tables here, overlooking El Sardinero beach, are unquestionably the best setting in which to enjoy a feast of fresh fish and seafood specialities.

Gran Hotel Sardinero €€€ *Plaza de Italia 1; tel: 942 271100; fax: 942 271698; email: hotelsardinero@gruposardinero.com; www.gruposardinero.com.* A large, old-style hotel perfectly located right beside the casino and facing El Sardinero beach.

Hotel Real €€€ *Paseo Pérez Galdos 28; tel: 942 272550; fax: 942 274573; email: realsantander@husa.es; www.hotelreal.es.* This Modernist palace, built in the late 19th century, remains the city's best hotel, combining elegance and luxury with spectacular views over the bay.

Zacarías €€€ *Calle Hernán Cortés 38; tel: 942 212333.* This busy downtown restaurant serves some of the most authentic Cantabrian cuisine, with a wide range of fish *tapas* as well as more complete meals.

SANTILLANA DEL MAR

ⓘ *Jesus Otero 20; tel: 942 818812; email: santillana@ cantabria.org*

ⓘ **Colegiata and Museo Diocesano €**
Tel: 942 840317. Open Tue–Sat 1000–1330, 1600–1830 (mid-Jun–Sept 1000–1330, 1600–1930). Closed in Feb and on Wed in winter.

This village of golden stone houses, the setting for the 18th-century French romance *Gil Blas de Santillana*, has often been described as the prettiest village in Spain. Two main streets of Renaissance mansions, with wrought-iron balconies, wooden galleries and coats of arms above the doors, converge at the **Colegiata**, a 12th-century church built to house the relics of Santa Juliana, who was martyred in Asia Minor in the 6th century. The saint's 15th-century sarcophagus sits in the centre of the nave, and the Romanesque cloisters feature exquisitely sculpted capitals. The ticket to the Colegiata also gives access to the **Museo Diocesano**, with a collection of sacred art in a former convent. Until tourism took over, Santillana was largely a farming village, and you can still see the cattle byres built into the ground floors of the seignorial mansions (known as *casonas*).

Accommodation and food in Santillana del Mar

Altamira €€ *Calle Canton 1; tel: 942 818025; fax: 942 840136; www.hotelaltamira.com.* This restored 17th-century mansion is now a charming hotel, whose restaurant has established a reputation as one of the best in the village.

Los Blasones €€ *Plaza de la Gándara 8; tel: 942 818070.* The top restaurant in the village features hearty northern fare, from roast meats to Asturian bean stews.

Los Infantes €€ *Avda Le Dorat 1; tel: 942 818100; fax: 942 840103; email: hinfantes@mundivia.es; www.hotel-santillana.com.* A solid stone façade adorned with the arms of the Calderon family leads into this intimate town-house hotel, with a restaurant serving Cantabrian mountain cuisine.

Parador de Santillana Gil Blas €€€ *Plaza Ramón Pelayo 8; tel: 942 028028; fax: 942 818391; email: santillana@parador.es; www.parador.es.* Set in a 17th-century ancestral home with creepers climbing up the walls, this beautiful inn is filled with antiques and works of art. The restaurant features Cantabrian specialities and highland stews.

Left
Santander's El Sardinero beach

SANTOÑA

New World map

Juan de la Cosa's map of the New World is now on display at the Naval Museum in Madrid.

The fishing port facing Laredo across the bay was once a significant naval base and the home town of the cartographer Juan de la Cosa, who accompanied Columbus on one of his first voyages to America and produced the earliest known **map of the New World**. Besides being a summer resort, Santoña is at the edge of an important wildlife area, where winter wildfowl and waders can be seen among the marshland and estuary dunes.

Suggested tour

Hotel Juan de la Cosa €€ *Playa de Berria 14; tel: 942 661238; fax: 942 661632; www.hoteljuandelacosa.com.* This comfortable beach hotel just north of Santoña features an indoor pool, an exercise room and a terrace restaurant with sea views.

Total distance: The main route from Santander to Castro Urdiales is around 85km; the return to Santander by motorway adds a further 70km.

Time: The entire round trip can be completed in around 2½ hours, but the roads can get very crowded in summer and it is best to allow a leisurely day – with time for a long lunch by one of the fishing harbours or an afternoon on the beach.

Links: From Laredo and Castro Urdiales, the A8 motorway continues to Bilbao (*see pages 48–57*), linking the Cantabrian coast to the main routes to Catalonia from northern Spain.

From the ferry terminal at **SANTANDER ❶**, follow the signs out of the city and on to the A8 motorway towards Bilbao. When you reach exit 7, 10km from Santander, leave the motorway and take the CA141 to **Pedreña** and **Somo**, following a broad sweep around Santander Bay with views of the city across the water. After Somo, the road turns inland to cross the green, rural landscape of the Ajo peninsula. Shortly

Left
Castro Urdiales

before Ajo you climb to a pass where you can park beside the mirador for views down over the coastline and **CABO DE AJO** ❷. Continuing along this road, there are several opportunities to visit the beaches at **Isla** and **Noja** before reaching the small town of **Argoños**, where you can make a brief diversion to **SANTOÑA** ❸ or turn right to reach **Gama**.

Alternatively, after leaving Santander, continue on the motorway to exit 13A, then pass through the town of **Solares** and turn left on to the N634 to Bilbao. This road runs parallel to the motorway but passes through a number of small towns such as **Hoznayo** and **Beranga**, whose tempting wayside inns would make good lunch stops. A large roadside ceramics emporium, 18km from Solares, signals the approach to Gama.

From Gama, the N634 continues for a further 12km to **LAREDO** ❹, where it twists back inland before returning to the coast at **Islares**, a tiny village with a beautiful beach beneath the cliffs. From here the road hugs the coast all the way to **CASTRO URDIALES** ❺. From Castro Urdiales you can continue on the N634 and the A8 to Bilbao or return quickly to Santander via the toll-free motorway.

Also worth exploring

The CA131 coast road from Santillana del Mar leads to a couple of interesting resorts. **Comillas**, 16km west of Santillana, was once the favoured resort of the Barcelona aristocracy and it is one of the few places outside Catalonia where you can see *modernista* architecture – including a fantasy of a summer palace by Antoni Gaudí, now a restaurant. **San Vicente de la Barquera**, a further 11km west, is an attractive fishing port dominated by a 13th-century church and linked by a long causeway to its beach.

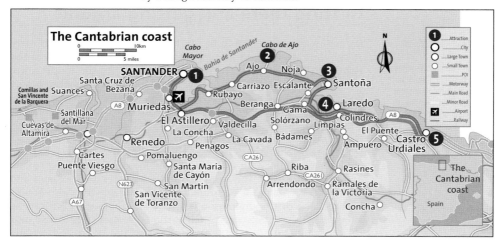

Bilbao

Ratings

Architecture	●●●●●
Bars	●●●●○
Museums	●●●●○
Restaurants	●●●●○
Parks	●●●○○
Shopping	●●●○○
Children	●●○○○
Climate	●○○○○

The largest city in the Basque Country has undergone a renaissance, having boldly reinvented itself for a new millennium. For years a byword for heavy industry, with its iron mines, steelworks and shipyards, Bilbao was facing a lingering decline until it decided to give itself a new, post-industrial image. Leading architects from Spain and beyond were commissioned to design striking modern buildings: among these are the new airport terminal and glass-decked footbridge over the River Nervión, created by Santiago Calatrava, the modern Metro system designed by Sir Norman Foster and the Cesar Pelli development of the old shipyards into a riverside park. At the heart of this renaissance, however, is the Guggenheim Museum, the opening of which in 1997 has given a cultural and economic boost to the entire region. Tourism is booming and the Guggenheim is established as one of the most visited museums in Spain. In just a few years, Bilbao has been turned from a symbol of industrial decay into one of the artistic hot spots of Europe.

Getting there and getting around

ℹ *Plaza del Ensanche; tel: 944 795760; email: bit@ayto.bilbao.net; www.bilbao.net.* There are also tourist information offices in Plaza Arriaga, at Sondika airport and outside the Museo Guggenheim.

If you are arriving at Bilbao by air, buses leave Sondika airport every 40 minutes for the short journey into the city, terminating at the bus station on Paseo del Arenal. This is convenient for the tourist office and the Casco Viejo, but if you are staying in the Ensanche you may do better to take a taxi. If you plan on spending a couple of days in Bilbao before moving on, don't pick up your hire car just yet; instead, arrange to have it delivered to your hotel or collect it from the airport when you leave.

Arriving on the ferry or by car from elsewhere in Spain, you have no choice but to bring a car into the city and face up to the huge parking and traffic problems. The best bet is to find a hotel with a garage and leave your car there for the duration of your stay. Otherwise, follow signs to one of the underground car parks where your car can be stored expensively but safely. There is some free parking available near the Guggenheim Museum and some beside the river on Paseo del

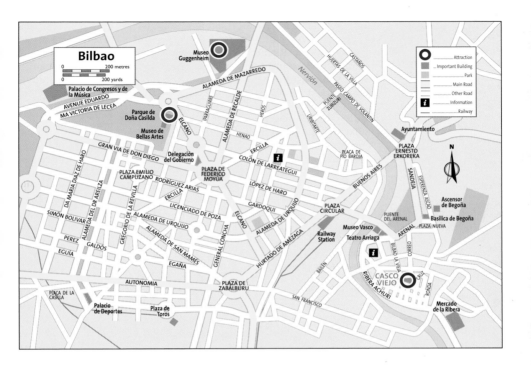

Arenal, but you will be very lucky to get a space. Driving in Bilbao is a nightmare best avoided – use taxis, local buses or the excellent new Metro system.

Sights

Casco Viejo (Old Town)

The city may have greatly expanded beyond its 14th-century origins, but the heart of Bilbao remains this medieval enclave on the right bank of the river. From Plaza Nueva, an arcaded square lined with *tapas* bars, the pedestrian shopping streets converge on the Catedral de Santiago, begun in the 14th century in Gothic style. South of the cathedral, the atmospheric Siete Calles ('Seven Streets'), the original centre of Bilbao, lead to **Mercado de la Ribera**, an Art Deco market hall spread over three floors, with fruit and flowers on the top floor, meat and cheese downstairs and a fish market in the basement.

On the edge of the old town, the **Museo Vasco**, housed in a 17th-century convent, is devoted to Basque history and ethnography, with displays on traditional industries including seafaring, fishing and

Casco Viejo

Broadly speaking, Casco Viejo refers to the area on the right bank of the Nervión, while the more modern districts on the left bank, reached by the Puente del Arenal, are collectively known as the Ensanche, or 'extension'.

Museo Vasco €
Plaza Miguel Unamuno
4; tel: 944 155423;
www.euskal-museoa.org.
Open Tue–Sat 1100–1700,
Sun 1100–1400. Free Thur.

Museo de Bellas Artes
€ Plaza del Museo 2;
tel: 944 396060;
www.museobilbao.com.
Open Tue–Sun 1000–2000.
Free Wed.

Plentzia

A popular day out from
Bilbao is to take the
Metro to the end of the
line at Plentzia, a former
fishing port with an
excellent surfing beach.

**Museo
Guggenheim €€**
Avda Abandoibarra 2;
tel: 944 359080;
www.guggenheim-bilbao.es.
Open Tue–Sun 1000–2000.
Nearest Metro: Moyua. Free
guided tours of the
museum take place twice
daily in Basque, Spanish and
English. Book in advance at
the information desk near
the entrance. Tickets for
the museum are valid all
day and allow you to leave
and re-enter as often as
you like – so you can break
up your visit with a walk
along the waterfront or a
stroll around the Parque de
Doña Casilda. The museum
has an excellent café
serving sandwiches and
bar snacks, and also a
restaurant (tel: 944 239333;
reservations advised) offering
contemporary Spanish and
Basque cuisine.

Right
The Guggenheim Museum

pottery. A large gallery on the top floor is given over to a scale model of the province of Vizcaya. The museum is interesting as an introduction to Basque life, but to get the most out of it you really need to understand the captions, which are in Basque and Spanish only. The most impressive exhibit is the Idol of Mikeldi, a primitive, stone-carved animal figure in the centre of the cloister.

Museo de Bellas Artes

Bilbao's fine arts museum, on the edge of **Parque de Doña Casilda**, contains Spanish paintings from the 12th to the 20th centuries including works by El Greco, Morales and Zurbarán, and a series of portraits by Goya. There is a particularly strong collection of 19th- and 20th-century Basque art, with Ignacio de Zuloaga, Juan de Echevarría and Aurelio Arteta all well represented. The museum also incorporates the collection of the former Modern Art Museum, with works by foreign artists including Gauguin and Bacon as well as the Basque sculptor Eduardo Chillida.

Museo Guggenheim

In the early 1990s, as Bilbao was searching for its big idea, the New York-based Solomon R Guggenheim Foundation was also looking for a new European home in which to display its expanding collection of modern art. The result was a partnership that has produced one of the most remarkable architectural achievements of recent years. Frank Gehry's masterpiece is destined to rank alongside the Empire State Building and the Sydney Opera House as one of the most influential buildings of the 20th century. A triumph of titanium, glass and limestone in organic, free-flowing forms, it deserves to be seen from every angle and in every possible light.

From across the river it resembles a ship with billowing sails; from Calle Iparraguirre it rises like a futuristic dream above the solid banks and apartment buildings, with a surrealistic touch added by Jeff Koons' playful floral sculpture of a giant puppy standing guard outside. Inside, the central atrium is filled with natural light, the huge windows forming a symbolic link between the city, the river and the university on the far bank.

With so much emphasis on the architecture, many visitors have little time for the art itself, which is a pity. The exhibits are constantly changing, and much space is given over to temporary exhibitions, but the focus of the permanent collection is firmly on the second half of the 20th century. Two large-scale installations commissioned especially for the museum are *Snake* by Richard Serra, a sculpture created out of three huge pieces of steel and placed at the centre of a 170m-long gallery, and *Untitled* by Jenny Holzer, a meditation on sex, death and AIDS through the medium of electronic signboards transmitting a series of short, poignant messages in English, Spanish and Basque. One day, it is hoped, the museum may be able to display Picasso's *Guernica* (see page 61).

Accommodation and food

For good-value and filling meals, check out the various bars specialising in *cazuelitas* along Calle del Perro in the Casco Viejo. A *cazuelita* is a cooking pot designed for one person and is a good way of trying Basque classics such as *bacalao pil-pil* or *bacalao a la vizcaína* at a reasonable price.

Ortua € *Alameda de Mazarredo 18; tel: 944 245102*. Simple but filling vegetarian lunches, a short walk from the Guggenheim Museum.

Arriaga €€ *Calle de la Ribera 3; tel: 944 790001; fax: 944 790516; www.hotelarriaga.es*. A traditional Spanish parlour hotel on the edge of the old town, with clean, comfortable rooms and good views over the river.

Rio-Oja €€ *Calle del Perro 4; tel: 944 150871*. This deeply traditional restaurant serves squid in its own ink and all variety of carnivorous fare, prepared in typical dishes from the Riojan region. It's perfect for a filling lunch, but turn up early or be prepared to queue.

Silken Indautxu €€ *Plaza Bombero Etxanix s/n; tel: 944 440004; fax: 944 221331; email: reservas@hotelindautxu.com; www.hotelindautxu.com*. Another good choice, this castle-like building is now a comfortable and stylish hotel with modern facilities.

Sirimiri €€ *Plaza de la Encarnación 3; tel: 944 330759; fax: 944 330875; email: hsirimiri@luskalnet.net; www.hotelsirimiri.com*. This small, modern hotel is situated in an attractive old town square near the river.

Víctor Montes €€ *Plaza Nueva 8; tel: 944 157067; www.victormontesbilbao.com*. This busy Art Nouveau wine bar in the heart of the old town is one of the best places to try *pintxos* (Basque titbits). There is also a more formal restaurant upstairs, specialising in seafood.

Carlton €€€ *Plaza Moyúa 2; tel: 944 162200; fax: 944 164628; email: carlton@aranzazu-hoteles.com; www.aranzazu-hoteles.com*. This fine old building on a central square was the Basque Republican headquarters during the Civil War and was later used by Franco's chief of staff in Bilbao. For a combination of modern luxury with historical atmosphere, this is hard to beat.

Etxanobe €€€ *Calle Abandoibarra 4; tel: 944 421071*. Fine upscale restaurant for varied tastes, where chefs Fernando Canales and Mikel Población prepare fresh seafood and land fare with both traditional Basque and a modern twist.

Goizeko Kabi €€€ *Particular de Estraunza 4; tel: 944 211129; www.goizekocatering.com*. Chef·Aitor Elola has gained a Michelin star for his innovative versions of classic dishes, such as potato stuffed with crab and gazpacho mayonnaise, or steak roasted in olive oil.

Gorrotxa €€€ *Alameda de Urquijo 30; tel: 944 434937; www.gorrotxa.es*. This restaurant, unexpectedly situated inside a modern shopping arcade filled with designer bars, serves elaborate, very traditional Basque dishes and is popular with bankers and politicians.

López de Haro €€€ *Calle Obispo Orueta 2; tel: 944 235500; fax: 944 234500; email: lh@hotellopezdeharo.com; www.hotellopezdeharo.com.* Named after the founder of Bilbao, this intimate five-star hotel, close to the Guggenheim Museum, is popular with architects and designers who flock to the city.

Mandoia €€€ *Calle del Perro 3; tel: 944 150228.* Classical and modern Basque cuisine at a stylish *asador* ('roast house') in the old town, with its own lobster hatchery.

Zortziko €€€ *Alameda de Mazarredo 17; tel: 944 239743.* Daniel García's creative modern Basque cuisine has been rewarded with a Michelin star. A signature dish is his salt cod and truffle risotto.

Bars and cafés

The tradition of nibbling at *pintxos* – miniature snacks served on tiny pieces of bread – is very much alive in Bilbao and in the early evening many of the bars are packed with people eating *pintxos* and drinking wine before heading home to dinner. The *pintxos* are laid out along the counter for customers to help themselves and the bill is calculated by counting up the number of cocktail sticks on your plate. The best hunting-grounds are the Casco Viejo, particularly Plaza Nueva and Calle Somera, and the area of the Ensanche between Gran Vía López de Haro and Alameda de Urquijo, especially on Calle Diputación. Of several good bars on this street, two of the best are **Lekeitio**, whose speciality is a three-tiered 'country omelette', and **El Globo**, with a wide array of unusual *pintxos* based on Basque sausages and seafood.

Above
Traditional fiesta

Bilbao has several old-fashioned cafés which make popular meeting-places for anything from breakfast to afternoon tea to late-night drinks. **Café Boulevard**, opposite the Arriaga theatre on Paseo del Arenal, is the oldest coffee shop in the city, founded in 1871 and decorated in art deco style. Across the bridge, **La Granja** on Plaza Circular is lively on weekend evenings, while **Café New York** on Calle Buenos Aires, with its murals and wood panelling, exudes old-world style. Not far from here, **Café Iruña**, facing the Albia gardens on Calle Colón de Larreátegui, is the most spectacular of all, a fantasy of Moorish rosewood and tiles designed in Mudéjar style in 1903 and containing both coffee lounge and a busy early-evening *tapas* bar.

The British connection

The British influence is strong in Bilbao and dates back more than 100 years. Many British engineers came to work in the steel-making industry, and the first football match in Bilbao was played between a team of British sailors and local stevedores. **Athletic Bilbao**, founded in 1898, was modelled on British teams and still retains its English name – though only Basques are allowed to play for the club. Another sign of British influence is **La Bilbaina**, a private gentlemen's club overlooking the river, with a billiard room, a library, English furniture and an 'English bar'.

◐ Teatro Arriaga
Plaza del Arriaga 1;
tel: 944 792036;
www.teatroarriaga.com

Palacio de Congresos y de la Música *Avda Abandoibarra 4*; tel: 944 035000.

Kafe Antzokia *Calle San Vicente 2*; tel: 944 244625. Live bands at weekends.

Dubliners *Plaza Moyúa 6*; tel: 944 240223. *Open daily 0800–0200.*

Bilbaina Jazz Club *Calle Navarra*; tel: 944 231407.

◉ Athletic Bilbao
Tel: 944 240877;
www.athletic-club.net

Frontón Club Deportivo
Alameda de Recalde 28;
tel: 944 231109.

Entertainment and nightlife

You can find out what's on by looking in local newspapers or in the free quarterly guide to Bilbao (*Bilbao Guía-Gida-Guide*), available at tourist offices and hotels, which has listings (in English and Spanish) of theatres, clubs and bars. Look out for performances of theatre, music and ballet at the **Teatro Arriaga**, a neoclassical pile beside the river, built in 1890 and named in honour of local composer Juan Crisóstomo Arriaga, who was known as 'the Spanish Mozart' and had written a number of symphonies before his death at the age of 19. The second major performance venue, the **Palacio de Congresos y de la Música**, opened in 1999 in a stunning new building on the waterfront and is home to both the Bilbao Symphony Orchestra and the winter opera season.

Nightlife starts late and mostly consists of bar-hopping. The bars of the Casco Viejo, and of Calle Licenziado Poza in the Ensanche, are particularly lively, especially on football nights. Several of the most fashionable bars are situated in the Galerías Urquijo shopping mall on Alameda de Urquijo, a good place for a late-night *copas* ('drinks') crawl. For live music, check out **Kafe Antzokia** on Calle San Vicente, **Dubliners** Irish pub on Plaza Moyúa, or the Thursday-night jazz at **Bilbaina Jazz Club**.

To catch the Basque fervour for sport, try to take in a match at the Campo de San Mamés, the football stadium commonly known as 'the cathedral'. **Athletic Bilbao** play here in the Spanish *Primera División*; matches are generally on Sunday afternoons between September and June. The local *pelota* club, **Frontón Club Deportivo**, has matches all year, a boxing ring and a covered swimming pool.

Shopping

The biggest department stores, including **El Corte Inglés**, are spread out along Gran Vía López de Haro, the main street of the Ensanche. Gran Vía is also home to numerous fashion boutiques, which spill over into the surrounding streets. Close to the Guggenheim Museum, **Basandere** (*Calle Iparraguirre 4*) is a classy souvenir shop featuring Basque berets, music, food, wine and folk art, while **Kukuxumusu** (*Rodriguez Arias 27*) is a great place for T-shirts and accessories with distinctive cartoon designs. The pedestrian streets of the Casco Viejo are great for strolling and window-shopping – look out for **Boinas Elosegui**, an old-fashioned hat shop on Calle Victor.

Just outside Bilbao on the A8 towards Santander, **Max Center** (*www.maxcenter.com*) is a huge shopping mall with a hypermarket and more than 150 shops.

Suggested walk

Time: The walk can be completed in around 2 or 3 hours but is probably best spread over a day, with stops in museums, cafés and parks along the way.

Begin at the **Teatro Arriaga** ❶ beside the river on the edge of the old town. From here, cross the **Puente del Arenal** ❷ to reach the Ensanche, the modern business district built around the turn of the 20th century. As you walk up Calle Navarra, look out for **La Bilbaina**, an English-style gentlemen's club reached by an alley to the left. This is still the place where Bilbao's business deals are struck and where the sons and daughters of Bilbao's society families are married.

Plaza Circular is presided over by a statue of Bilbao's founder, Diego López de Haro. Look out, too, for the sleek, bubble-like Metro entrance designed by the British architect Sir Norman Foster, one of several so-called *fosteritos* around the city. Continue along **Gran Vía López de Haro** ❸, Bilbao's main shopping street, until you reach Plaza Moyúa, a busy road junction dominated by the Hotel Carlton. From here, a right fork along Calle Elcano, pausing to glance at the view of the Guggenheim Museum down Calle Iparraguirre, leads to the **MUSEO DE BELLAS ARTES** ❹.

Behind the museum, **Parque de Doña Casilda** is one of the city's most pleasant green spaces, a good place for a picnic or a stroll among the fountains. At the far end of the park, the **Palacio de Congresos y de la Música** ❺ marks the start of a waterfront development which has transformed the derelict shipyards of the Abandoibarra flats into a showcase for modern architecture. A riverside footpath makes it possible to walk from here all the way back to Puente del Arenal along the river.

Follow the river around behind the **MUSEO GUGGENHEIM** ❻ and continue to **Puente Zubizuri** ❼, a slender-arched, stylish white footbridge designed by Santiago Calatrava. Cross this bridge to reach the right bank, where a brief diversion leads to the **Funicular de Artxanda**, a cable railway offering panoramic views of Bilbao.

Stay on the river bank as it returns towards the old town, passing the **town hall (Ayuntamiento)** ❽ on your left. After crossing the roundabout, keep left on Calle Esperanza. Just before the end of this street, hidden behind an entrance at No 6, an elevator, **Ascensor de Begoña** ❾, transports you to a hilltop for splendid views of the city. A short walk from the upper terminus leads to the **Basilica de Begoña**, built in the 16th century. You can return to the Casco Viejo by elevator or walk down the Mallona steps.

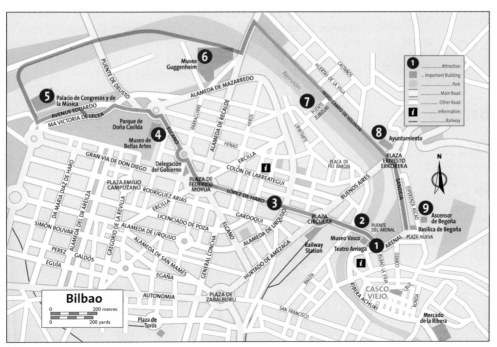

The Vizcayan coast

Ratings

Basque culture	●●●●○
Food	●●●●○
Scenery	●●●●○
Villages	●●●●○
Beaches	●●●○○
Children	●●●○○
History	●●●○○
Museums	●●●○○

Leaving behind the heavily populated, industrial outskirts of Bilbao, you soon reach a jagged coastline where the villages shelter inside hidden coves and the cliffs almost lean into the sea. The Basque identity is strong here, seen in the Basque flags flying from town halls and the fishing boats painted in the Basque colours of red and green. The harbours are picturesque but these are working ports, with some of the busiest fishing fleets on the north coast feeding the appetites of diners in Bilbao, San Sebastián and beyond. Behind the coast, a region of dense beech and oak forests gives way to the Duranguesado, a rural, almost alpine landscape dotted with solid, stone-built *caserios* or farmhouses. This is the province of Vizcaya (Bizkaia in the Basque language and hence Biscay in English), whose symbolic spiritual centre, the town of Guernica, was immortalised by Picasso in his eponymous painting.

BERMEO

ℹ *Calle Lamera; tel: 946 179154; www.bermeo.org*

🏛 **Museo del Pescador** *Torre Ercila, Plaza Torrentero 1; tel: 946 881171. Open Tue–Sat 1000–1400, 1600–1900, Sun 1000–1415. Free.*

The former provincial seat of Vizcaya is now an important fishing port whose harbour is filled with gaily painted boats. The history of the local fishing fleet is told in an interesting museum, **Museo del Pescador**, housed in a 16th-century granite tower beside the old jetty.

Right
Fishing boats at Bermeo

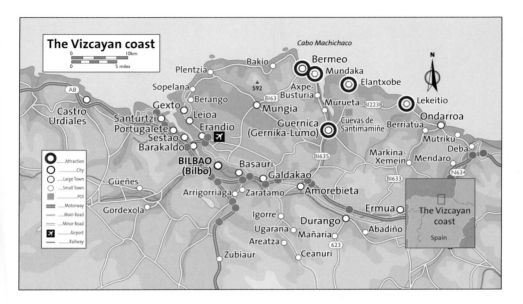

The Vizcayan coast

The streets of the old quarter around the harbour are full of Basque character – the scent of grilled fish drifts out of back-alley bars where the conversation is likely to be in Euskara (the Basque language) rather than in Spanish. Not far from Bermeo, reached by the coastal corniche, **Bakio** is another small fishing village with beautiful beaches and a nice line in fizzy red *txakoli* wine.

Accommodation and food in Bermeo and vicinity

**Hostería del Señorio de Bizkaia € *Calle José María Cirarda 4, Bakio; tel/fax: 946 194725; email: hostbizkaia@hosteriasreales.com.* This stone house with balconies overlooking the beach must be one of the most charming places to stay on the Basque coast. The restaurant features Basque and Spanish cooking and there is also an intimate bar. The shady gardens are a delight.

**Jokin €€€ *Calle Eupeme Deuna 13; tel: 946 884089; www. restaurantejokin.com.* One of the best of Bermeo's fish restaurants, with great views from a terrace overlooking the harbour.

ELANTXOBE

The houses of Elantxobe hug the mountainside on the steep cliffs of Cabo Ogoño and cascade down to the small fishing port at the centre of this attractive village. There are two fine beaches near here – Playa de Laga, at the foot of the cliffs, and Playa de Laida, at the mouth of the Guernica estuary.

Accommodation and food in Elantxobe

Arboliz € *Calle Arboliz 12, Ibarrangelu; tel: 946 276283.* Simple, rustic inn on a promontory overlooking the coast. There are just six rooms, some of which have balconies.

GERNIKA-LUMO (GUERNICA)

🛈 *Artekalea 8;*
tel: 946 255892;
email: turismo@gernika-
lumo.net;
www.gernika-lumo.net

Below
The Guernica Oak

This small town is of enormous symbolic significance for Basques. For centuries the representatives of the various communities in Vizcaya would meet in Guernica under an oak tree, continuing a form of democracy practised since ancient times. The feudal lords of Vizcaya, and later the kings of Spain, came to Guernica where they would swear to uphold the *fueros*, the traditional rights of the Basque people which were finally abolished in 1876.

After the outbreak of the Civil War in 1936, the Basque government declared autonomy and its president was sworn in at Guernica in October. This was the prelude to one of the most shocking war crimes the world has ever seen. On a busy market day in April 1937, warplanes of Hitler's Condor Legion – the Germans were close allies of Franco – attacked Guernica with three hours of saturation bombing, killing at least 200 people and reducing the town to rubble. Remarkably, although 99 per cent of the buildings were destroyed, the Tree of Guernica was unscathed – allowing Franco's soldiers to pose for photographers as the defenders of Basque tradition.

The bombing might have passed unnoticed into history were it not for Picasso's painting (*see opposite*). Instead, Guernica has become a byword for the inhumanity and horrors of war. A fascinating exhibition at the **Museo de la Paz de Gernika** (Guernica Peace Museum) describes the background to the

Museo de la Paz de Gernika € *Foru Plaza 1; tel: 946 270213; www. peacemuseumguernica.org. Open Tue–Sat 1000–1400, 1600–1900 (1000–2000 in summer), Sun 1000–1500.*

Casa de Juntas *Allende Salazar Etorbidea; tel: 946 251138. Open daily 1000–1400, 1600–1800 (till 1900 in summer). Free.*

Museo Euskal Herria € *Allende Salazar Etorbidea; tel: 946 255451. Open Tue–Sat 1000–1400, 1600–1900, Sun 1100–1500.*

Parque de los Pueblos de Europa *Open daily 1000–1900 (1000–2100 in summer).*

A **market** is held every Monday and on Saturdays June to December at the Plaza de Gernika, Calle Don Tello, near the train and bus station. A major agricultural fair takes place on the last Monday of October. During the months of June to October, there is a special artisan market on the first Saturday of the month. There are also events on 26 April each year to mark the anniversary of the bombing of Guernica.

bombing, the devastating effects, the reconstruction of the town and the myths which have grown up around it.

The neoclassical **Casa de Juntas**, built in 1826, was reconvened as the Vizcayan Assembly House in 1979; when it is not in use you can visit the assembly chamber and a large hall containing a museum of Basque history and a stained-glass ceiling depicting the sacred oak. The tree itself, the **Arbol de Gernika**, stands in the garden and is still used for oath-taking by newly elected presidents of the Basque government. The tree is a direct descendant of an older, petrified oak, which is preserved in a small rotunda. A third sapling was planted in 1979 on the occasion of the restoration of the Vizcayan assembly.

On the same street, the **Museo Euskal Herria**, housed in a baroque palace, features Basque furniture, paintings and historical records. Behind the museum, the **Parque de los Pueblos de Europa** is an attractively landscaped park with sculptures on the theme of peace by Eduardo Chillida and Henry Moore.

Accommodation and food in Guernica

Boliña € *Barrenkalle 3, tel: 946 250300; fax: 946 250304; www.hotelbolina.net.* This modern hotel is both central and comfortable, and has an excellent restaurant.

Gernika € *Calle Carlos Gangoiti 17; tel: 946 250350; fax: 946 255874; email: h-gernika@hotel-gernika.com; www.hotel-gernika.com.* Two-star hotel in a quiet area on the edge of town.

Zallo Barri €€ *Calle Juan Calzada 79; tel: 946 251800; www.zallobarri.com.* This roast house and grill serves classic Basque dishes with a modern touch. The specialities include grilled sea bass and there is also a bar with a wide array of snacks.

Picasso's *Guernica*

Arguably the single best-known work of art of the 20th century was commissioned by the Spanish Republican government for the International Exposition in Paris in 1937. Angered by the attack on Guernica, Picasso responded with a devastating black-and-white critique of the atrocities of war, expressed through shocking and barely understood imagery. Critics labelled the painting propaganda rather than art, but it has since been recognised as a masterpiece. According to Picasso's wishes, *Guernica* hung for many years in the Museum of Modern Art in New York and was only returned to Spain after Franco's death. The painting, somewhat controversially, is currently on display in the Reina Sofía gallery in Madrid but there have been repeated calls for it to be transferred to the Basque Country – perhaps to the new Guggenheim Museum in Bilbao.

LEKEITIO

🛈 *Independentzia*
   Enparantza;
tel: 946 844017;
email: turismo@learjai.com;
www.learjai.com

Festivals

Lekeitio plays host to two of Vizcaya's most traditional festivals. On 29 June, the feast of **San Pedro**, patron saint of fishermen, is celebrated with a special dance known as the *kaizarranka*.

San Antolin, in the first week of September, is also known as the *fiesta del ganso* ('goose festival') because of the bizarre contests involving dead geese being suspended over the estuary.

This picturesque fishing port sits at the mouth of a deeply indented bay, facing the islet of San Nicolás which is joined to the mainland at low tide. The old part of town, around the harbour, is dominated by the late Gothic **Iglesia de Santa María de la Asunción**, with flying buttresses, a baroque belfry and a 16th-century Flemish altarpiece. The cobbled streets around here shelter numerous fine palaces and mansions, as well as several excellent fish restaurants. Lekeitio, with its two sandy beaches, once rivalled San Sebastián (*see pages 66–75*) as a royal summer residence, and it was while staying here in 1868 that Queen Isabel II was surprised by a rebellion and forced to flee into exile in France.

Accommodation and food in Lekeitio

Piñupe € *Avda Pascual Abaroa 10; tel: 946 842984; fax: 946 840772.* This small, simple hotel makes a comfortable mid-range choice.

Emperatriz Zita €€ *Avda Santa Elena; tel: 946 842655; fax: 946 243500; www.aisiahoteles.com.* The top hotel in the resort has excellent health facilities, including thalassotherapy, a sauna, a gym and an indoor pool. It also offers good views over the beach and the port.

Kaia €€ *Txatxo Kaia 5; tel: 946 840204.* One of the better restaurants on the harbour side; enjoy elegant décor and sea views while indulging in excellent fresh seafood dishes.

MUNDAKA

ℹ *Kepa Deuna;*
tel: 946 177201;
www.mundaka.org

Opposite
Mending the nets, Lekeitio

This estuary town to the north of Guernica is a mecca for surfers the world over, particularly during the early autumn when the Atlantic rollers are at their best. The town stands at the head of a great expanse of sandflats which attracts a wide variety of plant and bird life. The whole area was declared a biosphere reserve by UNESCO in 1984 and is now a protected natural park. From a viewpoint in Mundaka there are good views across the estuary to Cabo Ogoño, the highest point on the Basque coast. Ferries make the short trip across the estuary in summer, taking day-trippers to Laida beach.

Accommodation and food in Mundaka

El Puerto € *Calle Portu Kalea 1; tel: 946 876725; fax: 946 876726; www.hotelelpuerto.com.* This two-storey fisherman's house, delightfully converted into a small hotel, is very popular with surfers.

Atalaya €€ *Calle Itxaropen Kalea 1; tel: 946 177000; fax: 946 876899; www.atalayahotel.es.* A Modernist hotel on the water's edge with glass galleries all around, and good views of the estuary and fishing port from its comfortable, well-furnished rooms.

Casino de Mundaka €€ *Kepa Deunaten 1; tel: 946 876005.* Enjoy fresh fish overlooking the beach in a 19th-century building which once housed a fish market.

Suggested tour

Total distance: 180km. The detour to Elantxobe adds a further 16km.

Time: The coast road can be slow going, especially in summer, so you need to allow around 4 hours in total.

Links: From Ondarroa the coast road continues through Deba to San Sebastián (*see pages 66–75*), linking up with the tour of Gipuzkoa (*see pages 82–85*) at Zumaia.

Leave **Bilbao** ➊ (*see pages 48–57*) on the right bank of the river. Shortly after passing opposite the Guggenheim Museum, look for the right fork, signposted towards Getxo and Plentzia. Continue to follow signs to these two places as you negotiate Bilbao's bewildering system of ring roads and motorways. **Getxo** is more or less a suburb of Bilbao, but with a pleasant seafront promenade and an attractive old harbour. In recent years the town has established a reputation for its many music festivals, featuring jazz, blues, folk and classical music, running from July through to November.

① Cuevas de Santimamiñe €
Tel: 946 511657; email: santimamine@bizkaia.net. Open Tue–Sun, visits by appointment only.

⑪ A good restaurant close to the caves is **Lezika €€**, where Basque classics such as red beans with chorizo and hake in parsley sauce are served up on the terrace of an 18th-century country house. There are several good walks in the forest near here.

Below
Bermeo

At **Plentzia ②**, a popular yachting resort, look out for the Metro station signalling the end of the line from Bilbao and the smart new pedestrian bridge across the estuary. Cross the road bridge and turn left through the town centre to reach the wide beach where surfers gather at weekends. At the far end of the beach, turn right and follow signs to Bakio. The road crosses green hills towards **Arminza**, whose small rocky beach signals the start of a spectacular coastal drive, climbing through pine woods and on to the clifftop. Shortly after **Bakio**, a pretty fishing village, park at the mirador where you can look down over a rugged islet topped by the chapel of **San Juan de Gaztelugache**. If you are feeling energetic you can walk down to the chapel, reached by a footbridge and a great many steps.

The road now descends to **BERMEO ③**. Passing the harbour, continue towards **Mundaka**. As the route heads inland, you are rewarded with dramatic views of the estuary across the sandflats to your left and mountains looming in the distance ahead. As you enter **GUERNICA ④**, turn sharp left on to the BI638, following signs for Lekeitio. At **Kortezubi**, an interesting diversion leads to the **Cuevas de Santimamiñe**, where cave paintings more than 13,000 years old, featuring bison and other animals, were discovered in 1917. The caves, which also contain some remarkable stalactites and stalagmites, can only be visited on a guided tour. The nearby **Bosque Pintado de Oma** is another unusual attraction, a forest of painted pine trees which is the work of the Basque artist Agustín Ibarrola. Back on the main road, continue to the next village, **Gautegiz Arteaga**, dominated by a 19th-century castle.

Detour: From Gautegiz Arteaga, turn left on to a minor road which follows the right bank of the Mundaka estuary. The road passes the beaches at **Laida** and **Laga** and the base of **Cabo Ogoño** before passing close to

**Museo Simón
Bolívar** *Calle Beko,
Bolibar; tel: 946 164114.
Open Mon–Fri 1000–1300,
Sat & Sun 1200–1400. Free.*

Elantxobe. From here it follows the coast, passing the small fishing village of **Ea** before rejoining the main route near Lekeitio.

Alternatively, stay on the BI638 as it climbs into a thickly wooded landscape with distant views of the coast before descending to the harbour at **LEKEITIO ⑤**. From here it continues along the clifftop, with more dramatic coastal views and distant glimpses of the Pyrenees, to reach **Ondarroa**, a fishing port at the mouth of the Artibai river in a wide bay protected by low green hills. Fish-canning and salting are big industries here and the deep-sea fishing fleet is the largest on the Basque coast.

Now turn inland on the BI633 to reach **Markina-Xemein ⑥**, a small town dubbed the 'university of *pelota*' because of the number of champions it has produced. A chapel here, San Miguel de Arretxinaga, contains a remarkable altar consisting of three huge boulders said to have been dragged there by a giant. Shortly after Markina, turn right on to the BI224, passing the hamlet of **Bolibar**, once the home of the ancestors of the South American revolutionary Simón Bolívar. There is a statue of Bolívar in the village square and a **small museum** devoted to his life.

At the next crossroads, turn left on to the twisting BI3231 to reach the **Balcón de Vizcaya**, a viewpoint offering spectacular vistas of the forested mountain landscape. The road now drops gradually until it reaches the BI635, where a left turn leads quickly to the N634 and a swift return to Bilbao.

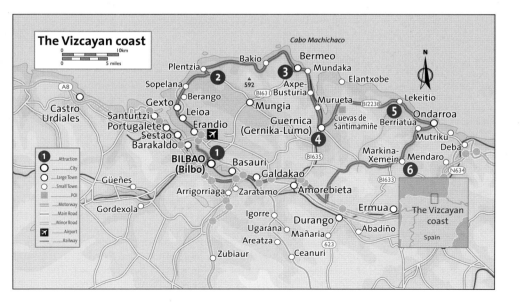

Donostia-San Sebastián

Ratings

Bars	●●●●●
Beaches	●●●●●
Restaurants	●●●●●
Children	●●●●○
Entertainment	●●●●○
Festivals	●●●●○
Walking	●●●●○
Museums	●●○○○

Donostia-San Sebastián is the pearl of the Basque coast. Beautifully situated on a crescent bay at the mouth of the River Urumea, its shell-shaped beach, set between two green hills, is protected from the harsh Atlantic winds by the calming presence of the Isla de Santa Clara just offshore. First popularised by the Spanish royals who came to take the waters in the 19th century – it was recommended by Isabel II's physician as a cure for a skin complaint – the resort reached its heyday in the belle époque era immediately before World War I, when the Spanish aristocracy would stay at its lavish hotels, moving between beach, casino, racecourse and opera house. Such decadence belies a violent history – this border town has been destroyed by fire at least a dozen times.

Getting there

ℹ️ *Calle Reina Regente 3; tel: 943 481166; email: cat@donostia.org; www.sansebastianturismo.com.* The city tourist office is a good source of information on events. In summer there are two more offices, one on Plaza Pío XII and the other one at the Alderdi Eder gardens.

The airport for Donostia-San Sebastián is at Hondarribia, 22km away and mainly used for internal flights to Madrid. Donostia-San Sebastián can also be reached by train from Barcelona or Biarritz, although from Biarritz you usually have to change trains at Hendaye/Irun.

Sights

P Parking is restricted in the city centre so use one of the underground car parks beneath Paseo de la Concha, Alameda del Boulevard and the cathedral square.

La Concha

The name of this beach means 'seashell' and it is easy to see why as you gaze down from above at a wide arc of golden sand, perfectly situated inside a sheltered, shell-shaped bay. In summer there is barely enough room to put out a deckchair; in winter the beach takes on a different character as the locals come out to play football on the sand and couples take romantic moonlit walks beside the sea. The beach promenade, Paseo de la Concha, with its white railings, Edwardian

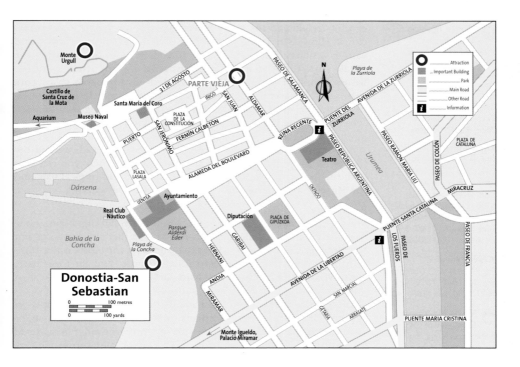

Donostia-San Sebastian

0   100 metres
0   100 yards

Between June and September, motorboats depart regularly from a jetty near the east end of La Concha for the **Isla de Santa Clara**, a rocky island with a miniature dock which is known as 'San Sebastián's fourth beach'.

Palacio de Miramar The gardens can be visited free of charge. Open daily 0900–2100, summer; 1000–1700, winter.

lampposts and tamarind trees, is the focal point of Donostia-San Sebastián. During the early evening the entire population of the city seems to put on its best casuals for a stroll here and an aperitif at one of the beachfront cafés.

The promenade runs out at the **Palacio Miramar**, a summer palace built in Queen Anne style for Maria Cristina of Habsburg by the English architect Selden Wornum in 1893. Beneath the palace gardens, a tunnel leads to Ondarreta beach, in reality a continuation of La Concha. At the far end of Ondarreta is an extraordinary sculpture, *El Peine de Viento* ('Comb of the Wind'), consisting of several pieces of twisted metal built into the rocks by local sculptor Eduardo Chillida. The appeal of the sculpture lies in the way in which it is exposed to the elements, especially at high tide as the waves shoot up over the rocks. Nearby, a rickety 1912 funicular leads up to **Monte Igueldo** for panoramic views over the bay. Local families head up here at weekends to enjoy the old-fashioned funfair, with its dodgems, house of horror and a roller coaster perched precariously on the edge of the cliffs.

Monte Urgull
The hillock which stands guard over the entrance to the harbour is crowned by a modern statue of Christ as well as the ruins of a 12th-century fortress, **Castillo de Santa Cruz de la Mota**. The castle boasts

ⓘ Monte Igueldo €
The funicular operates every day in summer 1000–2200; in winter it varies a lot. *www.monteigueldo.es*

Castillo de Santa Cruz de la Mota €
Open daily 0900–dusk.

Aquarium €€€ *Palacio del Mar; tel: 943 440099; www.aquariumss.com. Open summer Mon–Fri 1000–2000, Sat & Sun 1000–2100 (Easter, Jul & Aug daily 1000–2100); winter Mon–Fri 1000–1900, Sat & Sun 1000–2000.*

Museo Naval €
Tel: 943 430051. Open Tue–Sat 1000–1330, 1600–1930, Sun 1100–1400.

⬤ Vinos Martinez
Calle Narrika 29, in the Parte Vieja, is a delightful family-run wine shop selling local wine, cider and liqueurs as well as cheese and other Basque delicacies.

exhibits related to the city's history (formerly housed in the now-closed Museo San Telmo), including costumes, old photographs and various artifacts. The exhibits also include a series of murals by the Catalan artist José María Sert depicting the historic struggles of the Basque people. The walk up to the castle leads through a shady park with several peaceful spots such as the **Cementerio de los Ingleses**, where the graves of English soldiers who died liberating Donostia-San Sebastián during the Carlist wars in 1836 stand on a hillside looking out to sea.

A promenade, Paseo Nuevo, constructed in 1919, leads around the foot of Monte Urgull, ending beside the harbour where you can visit both the **Aquarium**, with displays of marine life and tropical fish, and the **Museo Naval**, devoted to the history of Basque seafaring.

Parte Vieja

Much of Donostia-San Sebastián was burnt down by Anglo-Portuguese troops during the Napoleonic wars in 1813, so the 'old quarter' is not actually that old. Of the buildings that survived, the oldest is the 16th-century Gothic church-fortress of San Vicente. Not far from here, **Santa María del Coro** has a fine baroque façade and an altar where an image of the Virgin of the Choir, patroness of the city, is venerated.

The greatest pleasure to be had in the Parte Vieja is simply in strolling the maze of narrow streets, with their old-fashioned shops and numerous *tapas* bars. The streets converge on **Plaza de la Constitución**, popularly known as 'La Consti' and surrounded by arcades. The numbers on the balconies date from the time when bullfights were held in the square and the balconies served as ringside seats. Although it has recently been given a much-needed facelift, La Consti can be somewhat on the seedy side and you may feel uncomfortable here late at night.

The walls surrounding the Parte Vieja were knocked down in 1863 as the city expanded on to the nearby marshland. The 19th-century extension, built on a grid system and beginning at Alameda del Boulevard, is now the business and commercial centre of Donostia-San Sebastián.

Accommodation

Niza € *Calle Zubieta 56; tel: 943 426663; fax: 943 441251; www.hotelniza.com*. This small, chic hotel right on the promenade is the best of the mid-range choices.

La Perla € *Calle Loiola 10; tel: 943 428123; www.pensionlaperla.com*. Clean, comfortable *pension* close to the cathedral, a few minutes on foot from the Parte Vieja and the beach. A good budget choice, though parking nearby will be a problem.

Monte Igueldo Mercure €€ *Paseo del Faro 134; tel: 943 210211; fax: 943 215028; email: reservas@monteigueldo.com; www.monteigueldo.com*.

Above
Plaza de la Constitución

Four-star hotel high above the town with views down over the bay. An added attraction here is the rooftop pool.

Parador de Hondarribia €€ *Plaza de Armas 14, Hondarribia; tel: 943 645500; fax: 943 642153; www.parador.es.* Many people prefer to stay in the border village of Hondarribia (*see page 75*), a short drive from Donostia-San Sebastián. This magnificent inn is situated inside a 10th-century fortress at the heart of the medieval walled village. The castle has been renovated to provide modern comforts and the peaceful inner courtyard makes a delightful place for a drink.

Abba de Londres y de Inglaterra €€€ *Calle Zubieta 2; tel: 943 440770; fax: 943 440491; email: reservas@hlondres.com; www.hlondres.com.* Hotel recalling the belle époque era, with a prime position on the seafront overlooking La Concha. The city's casino is located in the basement.

María Cristina €€€ *Paseo República Argentina 4; tel: 943 437600; fax: 943 437676; email: hmc@westin.com; www.westin.com.* If you want to relive the glory days of Donostia-San Sebastián, you should really spend a night at this hotel – thought by many to be the best in Spain. Opened in 1912, it combines period elegance with every modern luxury. Some of the rooms have balconies looking out over the River Urumea and the Victoria Eugenia theatre.

Food

For picnic food, stock up on bread, cheeses, cold meats, olives, salad and fruit at one of the city's two excellent markets – **La Bretxa**, on Alameda del Boulevard at the edge of the Parte Vieja, and **San Martín**, close to the cathedral on Calle Loiola.

Donostia-San Sebastián's reputation for gourmet cuisine extends throughout Spain and beyond – many French people regularly pop over the border for a meal. Despite the city's cosmopolitan nature, there are very few restaurants offering anything other than Basque cuisine, as though the locals are confident in the superiority of their own cooking and have no need to experiment with French, Italian or even Spanish styles. The city's passion for food is reflected in the dozens of male-only 'popular societies', whose members meet weekly for a communal meal, cooked by each of them in turn. Many of these societies are based in the Parte Vieja, particularly along Calle 31 de Agosto.

At the top end of the scale, Donostia-San Sebastián has more Michelin-starred restaurants than any other city of comparable size in Spain. At the other end, it is also known for its legendary backstreet *pintxos* bars. Throughout the Parte Vieja there are dozens of small bars where the *pintxos* are laid out along the counter during the vigorous early-evening *txikiteo* (*see page 72*). Among the regular offerings of cheese, ham and omelette, look out for treats such as monkfish kebabs, stuffed peppers and wild mushroom vol-au-vents.

Sidrería Petritegui €€ *Ctra San Sebastián-Hernani, Km 7, Astigarraga; tel: 943 47188.* Located just east of the city, this traditional cider house offers a menu of dishes that include the classic codfish omelette, beef chops and char-grilled steaks.

Urola €€ *Calle Fermín Cabeltón 20; tel: 943 423424; www.restauranteurola.com.* Chef Paxti Aizpuru creates unique and superior dishes in his Viejo restaurant. Specialities include both seafood and distinctive beef dishes.

Akelarre €€€ *Paseo del Padre Orcolaga 56, Monte Igueldo; tel: 943 311209; www.akelarre.net.* A Michelin-starred restaurant on the slopes of Monte Igueldo overlooking the sea. The specialities include roasted pigeon with *mole* and a gin-and-tonic ice cream.

Left
Santa María del Coro

Arzak €€€ *Avda Alcalde Elosegui 273, Alto de Miracruz; tel: 943 278465; www.arzak.es.* Juan Mari Arzak is the high priest of Basque cooking and this restaurant, with a maximum three Michelin stars, is the temple of the new Basque cuisine. It lies 2km east of the centre of town, on the road towards France.

Casa Nicolasa €€€ *Calle Aldamar 4; tel: 943 421762; www.casanicolasa.es.* Extreme attention to detail and pampering of customers make up for very high prices for the truly excellent cuisine prepared by chef José Juan Castillo.

Rekondo €€€ *Paseo de Igueldo 57; tel: 943 212907; www.rekondo.com.* Grilled meat and fish dishes in an old cider house on the road up to Monte Igueldo, with views from a pretty garden terrace in summer. The wine list is particularly impressive.

Entertainment, nightlife and festivals

After the *txikiteo* and dinner, many people head out once again and bar-hopping is a serious late-night pursuit. A youngish crowd gathers in Calle Reyes Católicos behind the cathedral, while the Parte Vieja

The *txikiteo*

Wander around the Parte Vieja during the early evening (1900–2100) and you will encounter numerous *cuadrillas* – groups of friends, mostly men, taking part in the ritual of the *txikiteo* or happy hour. Each group follows a pre-determined route as it moves from bar to bar, pausing in each one for a small snack and a *txikito*, a tiny glass of wine. Most people drink red wine from the Rioja Alavesa vineyards, but it is quite acceptable to order a *zurrito* of beer, or even a glass of *txakoli* or cider which will be poured into your glass from a great height. Joining a *txikiteo* can be great fun, but it is not supposed to be a substitute for supper – most of the members will be going home for a meal and the snacks are merely an aperitif.

Basque cider

The countryside around Donostia-San Sebastián is famous for its cider and there are several *sidrerías* ('cider houses') which open their doors between January and April to celebrate the new harvest. The atmosphere is rustic, and the meal on offer is always the traditional cider feast – salt cod omelette, charcoal-grilled steaks, cheese, walnuts and quince jelly, accompanied by cider from the barrel. Although it is not so authentic, a number of restaurants in the city advertise a *sidrería* menu – though unlike at the traditional cider houses, you are not expected to eat your meal while standing at a long wooden table.

The local football team, Real Sociedad, has a huge following among Basques. The team plays in the Spanish second division; matches are on Sunday afternoons between September and June at a stadium in the Anoeta sports complex south of the centre.

From June to September, horse-racing meetings take place at the Zubieta hippodrome, also on the outskirts of the city. This is the venue for the Copa de Oro, the Spanish Gold Cup, in August.

attracts all ages and types. Look out for live music, from Basque folk songs to heavy rock, in the streets around Plaza de la Constitución. Late-night bars and discos can also be found in the area behind Ondarreta beach, including the legendary Ku disco on Monte Igueldo.

Donostia-San Sebastián is firmly established on the European festival circuit. An international jazz festival, first held in 1966, takes place for several days at the end of July. The Victoria Eugenia theatre, which opened in 1912, is the venue for the city's Quincena Musical ('Musical Fortnight') in late August and the international film festival in September.

A more traditional festival takes place on 20 January for the city's feast day, **Fiesta de San Sebastián**. It starts in the Plaza de la Constitución at midnight and continues for 24 hours, as marching bands of drummers in Napoleonic costume parade through the street day and night. **Carnival**, the riotous pre-Lenten festival banned under Franco, is celebrated in Donostia-San Sebastián with gusto; the dates vary but it is usually in February. **Semana Grande** is a week-long Basque party beginning mid-August, with fireworks, regattas and traditional highland games. Regattas also take place on La Concha in front of an enormous crowd on the first two Sundays of September. The races, using specially built longboats with crews of 13 men, date back to a 19th-century contest between fishermen.

Right
Bar in the historic quarter

Suggested walk

Time: Allow around 3 hours, plus time for meals and drinks. The walk around the bay will add another 30 minutes in each direction.

Begin at the **tourist office** ❶ on Calle Reina Regente, opposite the Zurriola bridge. Follow the riverbank as it heads inland, passing the belle époque façades of the Victoria Eugenia theatre and the Hotel María Cristina. Continue along the riverside promenade to reach **Puente María Cristina** ❷, another reminder of the city's golden age, with its elegant pavilions, sculptures and lampposts.

Detour: A short diversion away from the river at this point leads to the neo-Gothic **Catedral Buen Pastor** ('Cathedral of the Good Shepherd'), built in 1897. The cathedral stands at the centre of a lively area of shops, bars and cafés at the heart of the modern city.

Cross the María Cristina bridge to reach the right bank of the river, with the railway station ahead of you. Now turn left to head back towards the sea along the riverside promenade. At the next bridge, **Puente Santa Catalina** ❸, turn right to plunge into **Gros**, a former working-class district with a distinctly bohemian atmosphere. The heart of the district is in **Plaza de Cataluña** ❹, but it is worth exploring the backstreets at random before making your way down to the beach, **Playa de la Zurriola** ❺. This is wilder and more windswept than La Concha, a mecca for surfers in summer. The beach runs out at the mouth of the river, dominated by a sparkling new auditorium designed by the Spanish architect Rafael Moneo.

Cross the Zurriola bridge to return to the left bank, and turn right on to Paseo de Salamanca. This is the start of **Paseo Nuevo**, a corniche promenade around the base of Monte Urgull. The *paseo* makes an attractive walk at any time, but is particularly dramatic at high tide as the waves lash the sea wall below and the spray shoots up on to the promenade. Near the end of the promenade, just before the **Aquarium**, a path leads up on to **MONTE URGULL** ❻. The gradual ascent to the summit is hard work in places, but worth it for the splendid views.

Return to the Aquarium and pass the **Museo Naval** ❼ on the way to the small harbour, lined with fishing boats, restaurants and souvenir shops. From the harbour, a narrow alley, Calle Virgen del Coro, leads into the **PARTE VIEJA**, arriving on Calle 31 de Agosto beside the church of **Santa María del Coro**. Continue along this street, then turn right to explore the warren of narrow lanes at the heart of the old city. Eventually you will emerge on to **Alameda del Boulevard** ❽, a modern shopping street close to where the walk began. This is the end of the main section of the route.

If you are feeling energetic, turn right and walk to the end of this street to reach the town hall, built in 1887 and used as a casino for many years. From here a miniature 'road train' makes a circuit of the city, continuing around the bay to the Monte Igueldo funicular. Save the train for another day and walk. Cross the gardens in front of the town hall to reach the Paseo de la Concha, then follow the promenade around La Concha to Ondarreta beach. Walk back after dark as the twinkling lights of the *paseo* are reflected in the bay.

Also worth exploring

The coastal area to the east of Donostia-San Sebastián makes a rewarding excursion from the city. **Pasaia** is the collective name for a group of small fishing ports, whose harbours and fishermen's cottages are rapidly being overtaken by urban sprawl. The prettiest of the three, Pasai Donibane, is connected by a motorboat launch to Pasai San Pedro. Beyond Pasaia, a narrow road offers spectacular views of the coast as it passes the foothills of Monte Jaizkibel and the 16th-century chapel of the Virgin of Guadalupe on its way to **Hondarribia**. This is a delightful border town on the Bidasoa estuary, with a well-preserved medieval ensemble at its centre and a quaint fishermen's quarter of gaily painted wooden houses with flower-decked balconies. From the long beach there are views across the estuary to the French port of Hendaye.

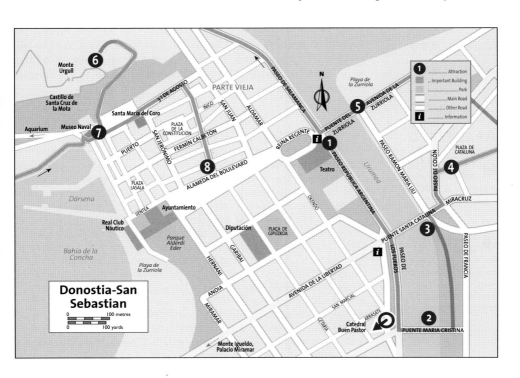

Gipuzkoa and the Basque highlands

Ratings

Basque culture	●●●●○
Mountains	●●●●○
Scenery	●●●●○
Towns/ villages	●●●●○
Beaches	●●●○○
Churches	●●●○○
Walking	●●●○○
Children	●●○○○

Between the coast and the Aizkorri mountains lies the smallest province in Spain, neatly divided into parallel valleys by the rivers that flow from the mountains to the sea. This is Gipuzkoa, the heartland of the Basque Country, where Euskara is most widely spoken and the traditional Basque festivals and highland games still dominate the calendar. Inland, a series of market and industrial towns, founded in the 13th century, are surrounded by lush green countryside, while fishing villages are spread out along the rugged coast. For centuries this mountainous region was largely cut off from the outside world, yet it has produced two men whose influence has spread far beyond its borders – Juan Sebastián Elcano, the first man to sail around the world, and St Ignatius of Loyola, founder of the Jesuit order of priests. The province is also home to the Basque Country's holiest shrine.

ARANTZAZU

Shrine *Open daily 0800–2000.* Mass is celebrated at 1200 on Sundays. *Free.*

Hospedería de Arantzazu €
Tel: 943 781313. If you feel like a night or two away from it all, the Franciscan friars run a simple but comfortable pilgrim hostel.

A **shrine** in the foothills of Monte Aizkorri is reached by a spectacular drive through the Arantzazu gorge. It was founded in 1469 after a local shepherd reported seeing a vision of the Virgin Mary and the villagers built a chapel on the spot. The tradition of pilgrimage was begun in 1522, when St Ignatius of Loyola, newly converted to Christianity after being wounded in a battle in Pamplona, spent a night here on his way to Montserrat. The present church was built in 1955 and is a showcase for modern Basque architecture, with doors by Eduardo Chillida and a façade by Jorge Oteiza. Inside, an image of the Virgin of Arantzazu, patron saint of Gipuzkoa, stands at the centre of a wooden altarpiece painted by Lucio Muñoz. The murals in the crypt, by Nestor Basterretxea, feature scenes from human history as well as the resurrected Christ. Although the brutalist concrete architecture comes as a shock to many, this church is a bold attempt to bring a historic place of pilgrimage into the present.

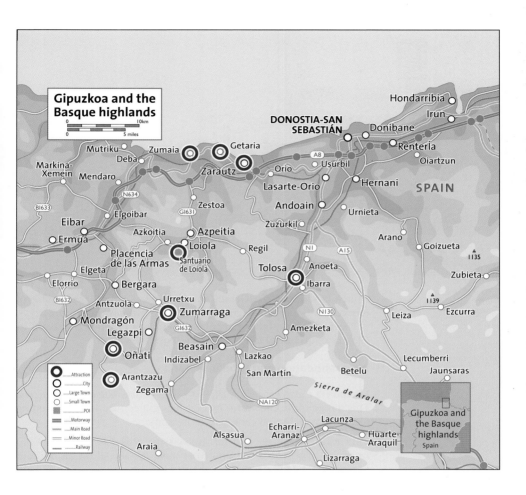

GETARIA

ℹ️ *Parque Aldamar 2; tel: 943 140957; email: udala@getaria.org; www.getaria.net. Open in summer only; in winter contact the Ayuntamiento, tel: 943 896024.*

🎉 Getaria's main festival, **San Salvador**, takes place on 6 August each year.

One of the prettiest of all Basque fishing villages is found on a narrow strip of land extending out to sea to the rocky islet known as *el ratón*, said to be shaped like a mouse. The islet shelters a natural harbour lined with fish restaurants. Getaria is best known for its most famous son, Juan Sebastián Elcano, who sailed with the Portuguese navigator Ferdinand Magellan on his ill-fated round-the-world trip and became the first man to circumnavigate the globe when he brought the ship home in 1522 after Magellan's death in the Philippines. Elcano is remembered with a statue outside the town walls and another overlooking the harbour, reached by a tunnel beneath the Gothic

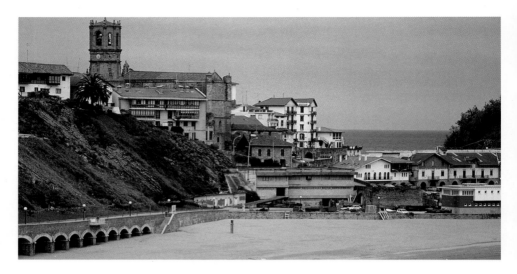

Above
Getaria

church of San Salvador. Getaria has a fine beach as well as a number of terraced vineyards where grapes for the best *txakoli* wine are grown.

The fashion designer Cristóbal Balenciaga (1895–1972) lived in Getaria and is buried in the cemetery above the village.

Accommodation and food in Getaria

Elkano €€€ *Calle Herrerieta 2; tel: 943 140024; www.restauranteelkano.com.* This restaurant is known for its excellent grilled fish dishes, including local turbot and squid cooked in its own ink.

Kaia Kaipe €€€ *Calle General Arnao 4; tel: 943 140500; www.kaia-kaipe.com.* Basque seafood and roast meat are served on an outdoor terrace overlooking the fishing port and the sea.

LOIOLA

ℹ️ *Basílica de Loiola;*
tel: 943 025000;
www.santuariodeloyola.org

The most famous Basque in history was born in a fortified farmhouse in the village of Loiola in 1491. Ignatius of Loyola was the youngest of 13 children; he trained as a soldier but was converted to Christianity when an image of the Virgin Mary appeared to him while he was recovering from serious wounds. Following a pilgrimage to the Holy Land, he moved to Paris where he wrote his *Spiritual Exercises* and founded the Society of Jesus, popularly known as the Jesuits. Later he returned to nearby Azpeitia where he lived in a pauper's hospital, preferring to identify himself with the poor rather than to return to his family home. He was canonised in 1622.

Santa Casa *1km from Azpeitia; tel: 943 025000. Open daily 1000–1300, 1500–1900. Free.*

Museo Mediambiental *Caserío Eguibar, Camino Viejo de Loiola; tel: 943 812448. Open Mon–Fri 1000–1300, 1500–1730, Sat 1000–1330, 1530–1730, Sun 1000–1330. Free.*

A short walk from the basilica along the River Urola leads to this interactive environment museum, with lots of hands-on activities for children. The museum is based in an old farmhouse.

Museo Vasco del Ferrocarril € *Calle Julián Elorza 8; tel: 943 150677. Open Tue–Fri 1000–1330 and 1530–1900, Sat 1030–1400 and 1600–1930, Sun 1000–1330. Times may vary throughout the year, see www.euskotren.es*

The old station in Azpeitia is now a railway museum with a fine collection of locomotives and machinery housed in an old engine shed.

Above right
The Santuario de Loiola

The tower house where he was born, **Santa Casa**, is now enclosed by a basilica, **Santuario de Loiola**, begun in 1689 in elaborate baroque style. A silver statue of St Ignatius, a gift from the Basques of Venezuela, sits in a niche above an altar inlaid with marble beneath an extravagant Churrigueresque (Spanish baroque) dome. The house itself is more simply adorned in an effort to re-create the atmosphere of St Ignatius' time. Displays tell the story of the saint's life as well as the history of the Jesuits, who now number more than 25,000 priests in 100 countries.

Accommodation and food in Loiola

Jai Alai €€ *Elosiaga Auzoa 393; tel: 943 812271.* Friendly, family-run restaurant dishing up superb local dishes accompanied by some of the best cider in town.

Kiruri €€ *Avda de Loiola 24; tel: 943 815608.* A large restaurant facing the basilica serving up traditional and modern Basque classics such as sea bass in *txakoli* wine.

OÑATI

ℹ️ *San Juan 14; tel: 943 783453; www.oinati.org*

⬇️ **Corpus Christi**, on the Thursday following Trinity Sunday, is marked in Oñati by a procession in which masked actors and dancers play the parts of Christ and his apostles. The festival, which dates back to the 15th century, usually takes place in late May or early June.

Oñati is an important centre of Basque nationalism and history. For centuries this small town was ruled by nobles as an independent seigneuralty and it only became part of Gipuzkoa in 1845; during the 19th-century Carlist wars, it was a stronghold of the pretender Don Carlos, brother of Fernando VII and uncle of the infant queen Isabel II. His supporters were traditionalists, in contrast to the liberal courtiers of Isabel. The First Carlist War (1833–9) was launched in support of the claim of Don Carlos to the throne following Fernando VII's death. The former university of Sancti Spíritus, founded in 1540, was for many years the only one in the Basque Country; its fine Plateresque façade can be seen on the left as you enter the town from Zumurraga. Other notable buildings are the Gothic church of San Miguel, and the 18th-century baroque town hall, seen facing one another across the main square.

Accommodation and food in Oñati

Bar Garoa € *Calle San Lorentzo Auzoa 29; tel: 943 781355*. A wonderful place for a traditional, laid-back meal overlooking terraced gardens. Don't be surprised to see locals' pets dining alongside the tables.

Soraluze Ostatua € *Barrio Uribarri, Ctra de Aranzazu km 1; tel: 943 716179*. This small modern hotel in a quiet setting on the road to Arantzazu has views over the Oñati valley and a restaurant featuring traditional Basque cuisine.

TOLOSA

⬇️ For a taste of the local pastries, seek out the delectable **Xaxu** at Plaza Zarra 7 near the parish church. The shop even has its own small confectionery museum.

Right
Tolosa

This solid Basque town, famous for its berets, its kidney beans and its sweet almond biscuits, was briefly the capital of Gipuzkoa in the 19th century. Although it is surrounded by modern paper mills, the old town, on the banks of the River Orio, retains a great deal of medieval charm. The town is entered across a stone bridge, looking across at the arcaded covered market, Tinglado, where on Saturdays farmers' wives still sell milk from the churn. Amid the baroque churches and Renaissance palaces, look out for Plaza Euskal Herria, whose handsome modern arches shelter an unexpected series of ceiling frescoes.

ZARAUTZ

ⓘ *Calle Nafarroa;*
tel: 943 830990;
email:
turismoa@zarautz.org;
www.turismozarautz.com

ⓜ **Photomuseo €**
Calle San Ignacio 11.
Open Tue–Sun 1000–1300,
1600–2000.

Although it has little of the style of its larger neighbour, Zarautz has long had pretensions to being a miniature San Sebastián. It, too, has a long seafront promenade backed with grand villas, and first rose to prominence in the 19th century when Isabel II made it her summer residence. The beach here is the longest in Gipuzkoa and a paradise for surfers. Another attraction is the **Photomuseo**, which traces the history of photography.

Accommodation and food in Zarautz

Karlos Arguiñano €€€ *Calle Mendilauta 13; tel: 943 130000; fax: 943 133450; email: kahotel@karlosnet.com; www.hotelka.com.* This elegant modern hotel, overlooking the sea, is owned by a well-known chef in the forefront of the new Basque cuisine. The creative menu features sophisticated seafood dishes as well as home-made pastries.

Above
Oñati's former university
of Sancti Spíritus

ZUMAIA

ℹ *Plaza Kantauri;*
tel: 943 143396;
www.zumaia.net. Open mid-Jun–mid-Sept only.

🏛 **Museo Zuloaga €**
Calle Santiago Etxea;
tel: 943 862341;
www.ignaciozuloaga.com.
Open Apr–Sept Wed–Sun
1600–2000.

The small summer resort and fishing port of Zumaia at the mouth of the Urola river has two beaches and a well-preserved old quarter of narrow, steep streets. The painter Ignacio Zuloaga (1870–1945) lived in the town and his studio beside Santiago beach has been turned into a **museum** of his work, including society portraits as well as rural and maritime scenes. The museum also contains Zuloaga's private art collection, featuring works by Goya, El Greco and Rodin.

ZUMARRAGA

🏛 **Santa María de**
la Antigua *Open*
May–Oct Tue–Sun
1130–1330, 1630–1930;
Nov–Apr Sat & Sun
1130–1330 and
1630–1800. Free.

This unremarkable industrial town surrounded by hills is worth a brief stop if only to see the 14th-century Gothic church of **Santa María de la Antigua**, reached by a winding road 2km above the town. The church has an unusual wooden roof truss and there are panoramic mountain views from the terrace.

Basque games

Rural sports, or *herri kirolak*, are a feature of all the major Basque festivals. Most of them are essentially feats of strength, such as wood-chopping and stone-lifting, with their origins in everyday farming tasks. Regattas take place in all of the fishing ports, and no Basque town or village is complete without its *frontón*, a squash-type court used for the game of *pelota* or *jai alai*, in which a ball is hurled against a wall at astonishing speed, using a long wicker glove or even the bare hand. As with all Basque sports, betting is an essential part of the game for spectators.

Suggested tour

Total distance: 141km. The detour to Oñati adds around 16km and the round trip to Arantzazu a further 18km.

Time: The main route will take around 3 hours to complete. Allow an extra hour for the trip to Oñati and Arantzazu.

Link: From Zumaia, a coast road leads west into the province of Vizcaya, where it joins up with the Vizcayan coast route (*see pages 58–65*) at Ondarroa.

Leave **Donostia-San Sebastián** **❶** (*see pages 66–75*) with La Concha beach to your right and follow signs for the N1 motorway to the Basque capital, Vitoria-Gasteiz. Continue on this busy motorway as far

Right
Zarautz

Euskal Herria

Unlike País Vasco (Basque Country), which refers to an autonomous region of Spain, Euskal Herria (Basque Homeland) is a political term used by those who believe in a wider Basque nation. Roughly corresponding to the former kingdom of Navarra, Euskal Herria encompasses the three Basque provinces of Alava, Bizkaia and Gipuzkoa, the modern-day province of Navarra, and the French provinces of Labourd, Basse-Navarra and Soule.

as **TOLOSA** ❷. After exploring this market town, rejoin the N1 and continue south. Shortly after bypassing Beasain, turn right on to the GI632. The road, wide at first, soon narrows and climbs steeply to reach **ZUMARRAGA** ❸.

Detour: From Zumarraga a minor road, the GI2630, leads through the grimy industrial outskirts of the town on its way towards Oñati. Passing **Legazpi**, a town noted for its iron foundries, the road rises and falls through steeply wooded valleys before entering **OÑATI** ❹. Just after passing the Renaissance university on your left, you have the opportunity of a further detour to **ARANTZAZU** ❺. This is a spectacular drive, climbing steeply through the Arantzazu gorge on its way to the hilltop sanctuary. Back in Oñati, rejoin the GI2630 as it crosses and re-crosses the Deba river on its way to **Mondragón**, where you turn right to return to the main route at Bergara.

Alternatively, continue on the GI632 from Zumarraga to **Bergara** ❻, climbing to the Puerto de Descarga pass on the way. Skirting Bergara, an industrial town with a well-preserved old quarter, follow signs to Elosua for a hair-raising drive over the **Puerto de Elosua** with its farmland and alpine views. The descent to **Azkoitia** involves numerous hairpin bends, so it is important to focus on the driving rather than the scenery. On arriving in Azkoitia, turn left through the town centre and bear right to reach the sanctuary at **LOIOLA** ❼.

Continue through **Azpeitia** and on to the GI631 which follows the pretty Urola valley through the spa town of **Zestoa** on its way to the coast at **ZUMAIA** ❽.

This is the start of a dramatic coastal corniche, with the road clinging to the sea wall and burrowing through the occasional tunnel on its way to **GETARIA** ❾ and **ZARAUTZ** ❿. Vineyards can be seen on the

Below
Getaria

hillsides to your right and the islet known as *el ratón* dominates the views on the seaward side.

Leaving Zarautz, the road rises and falls to **Orio**, another small fishing village with a good beach and the ever-present aroma of grilled fish from its open-air barbecues. From Orio the N634 follows a river valley to return quickly to San Sebastián.

Also worth exploring

The cross-country route from Tolosa to Azpeitia climbs steeply through a river valley, its hillsides dotted with sturdy Basque farmhouses, to reach the pass of Iturburu (550m) from where the hamlet of **Errezil** nestles in a picturesque green vale. This scenic road can be taken as a short cut from the main route, reducing the total distance to 103km.

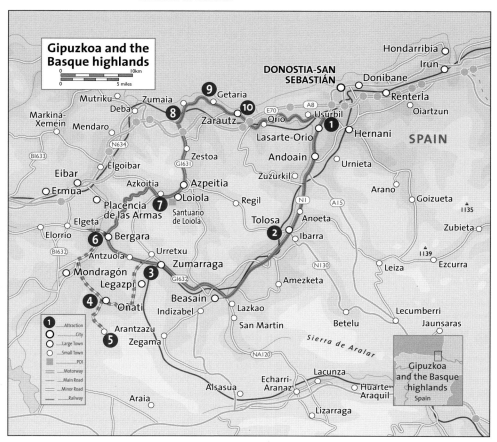

Rioja wine country

The word Rioja is synonymous with wine and this region produces some of Spain's best, aged in oak casks to create its distinctive appeal. Tucked between the Cantabrian mountains and the dry central *meseta*, the Ebro valley, with its half-Atlantic, half-Mediterranean climate, has the ideal conditions for growing grapes. The region is divided into three distinct areas. Rioja Baja ('Lower Rioja'), east of the provincial capital Logroño, produces young, fruity wines as well as the vegetables, particularly red peppers, for which the region is famous. Rioja Alta ('Upper Rioja'), around Haro, is known for its full-bodied red wines, as is Rioja Alavesa, situated inside the neighbouring Basque Country. Vineyards were introduced to Rioja by the Romans, the first of many invaders to have left their mark on this strategically important region, located between the historic kingdoms of Navarra and Castile on the medieval pilgrim road to Santiago.

HARO

ⓘ *Plaza Monseñor Florentino Rodríguez; tel: 941 303366; email: haro@lariojaturismo.com; www.haro.org*

ⓘ **Museo del Vino €** *Calle Bréton de los Herreros 4; tel: 941 310547. Open Mon–Fri 1000–1400, 1600–1900, Sat & Sun 1000–1900.*

The main wine town of Rioja Alta is as good a place as any to begin an exploration of the region. Although winemaking in Haro dates back to Roman times, the city really took off at the end of the 19th century when French viticulturalists, devastated by the *phylloxera* plague in Bordeaux, moved to Haro to experiment with the local grapes. Most of the wineries are situated in the area around the station; they can usually be visited, though it is best to book by telephone at least a week in advance. Of 17 *bodegas* in Haro, **López de Heredia** is the most old-fashioned and **Muga** the most geared up to receiving visitors. You can get a good overview of the wine production process at the **Museo del Vino**, attached to an oenological research centre.

The oldest part of town, with its palaces and seigneurial mansions, makes for some pleasant wandering. The focal point is Plaza de la Paz, a large square ringed by arcades with a bandstand at its centre.

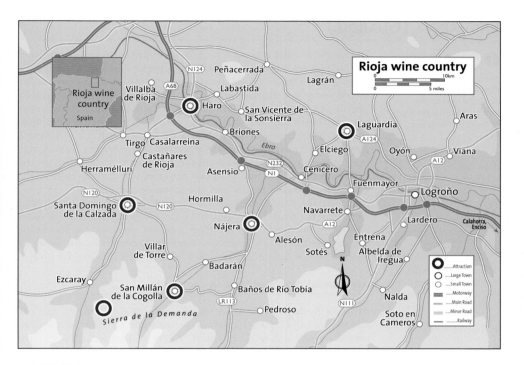

Rioja wine country

Map labels: Rioja wine country, Spain, Villalba de Rioja, Peñacerrada, Lagrán, Labastida, Haro, San Vicente de la Sonsierra, Aras, Laguardia, Briones, Tirgo, Casalarreina, Ebro, Elciego, Oyón, Viana, Castañares de Rioja, Herramélluri, Asensio, Cenicero, Fuenmayor, Logroño, Hormilla, Navarrete, Lardero, Calahorra, Enciso, Santa Domingo de la Calzada, Nájera, Alesón, Entrena, Villar de Torre, Sotés, Albelda de Iregua, Badarán, Ezcaray, San Millán de la Cogolla, Baños de Río Tobía, Nalda, Pedroso, Soto en Cameros, Sierra de la Demanda

Legend: Attraction, Large Town, Small Town, Motorway, Main Road, Minor Road, Railway

---

A narrow street from here leads to the parish church of Santo Tomás, with its Plateresque façade and baroque organ. From the terrace outside the church there are good views of the *bodegas* and the vineyards surrounding the town.

Accommodation and food in Haro

Los Agustinos €€ *Calle San Agustín 2; tel: 941 311308; fax: 941 303148; email: losagustinos@aranzazu-hoteles.com; www.hotellosagustinos.com.* A palatial hotel, in an old Augustinian convent, full of atmosphere. The lounge is hung with tapestries and the former cloisters have been turned into a shady courtyard, part of the excellent hotel restaurant Las Duelas.

Beethoven II €€ *Calle Santo Tomás 3; tel: 941 311181.* Restaurant specialising in high Riojan cuisine, such as peppers stuffed with lambs' feet, thistles with clams, breaded lambs' glands and oxtail in Rioja wine. The more informal **Beethoven I**, located across the street, is equally good.

Terete €€ *Calle Lucrecia Arana 17; tel: 941 310023.* This famous local restaurant has been going since 1877, serving succulent roast lamb from a wood-burning oven. Wines from the restaurant's own *bodega* are kept in the extensive cellar. Closed Mondays.

LAGUARDIA (GUARDIA)

ℹ *Plaza de San Juan; tel: 945 600845; email: turismo@laguardia-alava.com; www.laguardia-alava.com. Ask at the tourist office for the key to Santa María de los Reyes.*

The capital of Rioja Alavesa is a medieval walled town in a magnificent setting high on a hill, surrounded by vineyards and with the Sierra de Cantabria as a backdrop. Founded by Sancho Abarca of Navarra in the 10th century as a bulwark against the Moors, the town was originally known as La Guardia de Navarra. Inside the walls, the narrow streets are lined with fine old mansions, many dating back to the 16th century. The church of **Santa María de los Reyes** has a remarkable polychrome façade painted on to an earlier 14th-century Gothic portal; the vivid colours have been protected from the elements by the addition of an outer wall. The bell tower of the church, built in the 13th century, was originally part of a defensive fortress.

Beneath the streets and houses of Laguardia are numerous wine cellars belonging to small, family-run *bodegas*. A walkway around the outer walls gives fine views over the vineyards and the distant sierra. In the countryside around the town are several prehistoric sites, including **La Hoya**, a Bronze Age settlement with a museum of archaeological finds.

Sculpture

Don't miss the captivating sculpture in the small plaza by the church. It's a playful collection of boots and bags by well-known Vitoria sculptor Koko Rico.

Bodegas

The tourist office can supply a list of local wineries in Laguardia and Rioja Alavesa. One that can be visited without an appointment is **Palacio**, just outside Laguardia on the road to Elciego. Tel: 945 600057; www.bodegaspalacio.com. Tours Mon 1200, 1300, Tue–Thu 1200, 1300, 1630, Fri 1200, 1300, Sat 1100, 1200, 1300. Call ahead.

La Abacería, set into the medieval walls at Plaza Sancha Abarca 5, has a good selection of local wines for sale, as well as other Riojan products such as preserved red peppers.

Accommodation and food in Laguardia

Antigua Bodega de Don Cosme Palacio €€ *Ctra Elciego; tel: 945 621195; fax: 945 600210; email: antiguabodega@cosmepalacio.com; www.cosmepalacio.com*. The biggest winery in Laguardia has its own hotel, based in a *bodega* dating from 1894. It is situated just outside the medieval town.

El Bodegón €€ *Travesia de Santa Engracia; tel: 945 600793*. This back-street bar and restaurant serves Riojan classics such as roast lamb and potatoes with *chorizo* sausage, washed down with the local wine. Be careful what you order here as brains, cheeks, feet, tails and sweetbreads are all on the menu.

Castillo El Collado €€ *Paseo El Collado 1; tel: 945 621200; fax: 945 600878; www.euskalnet.net/hotelcollado*. This hotel, with a restaurant specialising in traditional Riojan cuisine, is situated inside a castle-like mansion at the start of the promenade around the town walls.

Marixa €€ *Plaza Sancho Abarca 8; tel: 945 600165; email: hotelmarixa@terra.es; www.hotel-marixa.com*. Small hotel facing the town walls making a very comfortable, economical choice. The restaurant serves creative Riojan-Basque cuisine and has magnificent views over vineyards and the Ebro valley.

Posada Mayor de Migueloa €€ *Calle Mayor 20; tel: 945 621175; fax: 945 621022; email: reservas@mayordemigueloa.com; www.mayordemigueloa.com*. This 17th-century town house inside the medieval walls has retained its original granite and wooden beams and is quite the most atmospheric place to stay. The restaurant features classic regional cuisine.

NÁJERA

Plaza de San Miguel *10; tel: 941 360041; email: najera@ lariojaturismo.com*

Monasterio de Santa María la Real
€ *Open Tue–Sat 1000–1300, 1600–1700, Sun 1000–1230, 1600–1730.*

This small town on the River Nájerilla was the capital of the kingdom of Navarra until Rioja was incorporated into Castile in 1076. The main attraction here is the **Monasterio de Santa María la Real**, a monastery church set into the cliffs and the burial caves on the edge of town. The church was founded by the king of Navarra in 1032 after he stumbled across a statue of the Virgin in a cave; the present polychrome statue dates from the 13th century. For many years this was the pantheon of the royal house of Navarra and among the many sarcophagi is the 12th-century tomb, with sumptuous carvings, of Doña Blanca de Navarra, the wife of Sancho III of Castile.

Accommodation and food in Nájera

San Fernando € *Paseo San Millán 1; tel: 941 363700; fax: 941 363399; email: sanfernando@sanmillan.com; www.sanmillan.com.* The best place to stay in town is in this modern three-star hotel overlooking the town and the river.

Los Parrales €€ *Calle Mayor 52; tel: 941 363730.* This busy bar in the old part of town has a good range of *pintxos* as well as a restaurant featuring fresh Riojan cuisine.

Above
Cloister, Nájera's Monasterio de Santa María la Real

SAN MILLÁN DE LA COGOLLA

ℹ The tourist office is situated in the courtyard of Yuso monastery. *Tel: 941 373259; email: sanmillan@ lariojaturismo.com; www.lariojaturismo.com*

🄷 Monasterio de Suso
€ *Tel: 941 373082. Open Oct–Easter Tue–Sun 0930–1330, 1530–1830; Easter–Oct Tue–Sun 1000–1325, 1600–1825.*

Monasterio de Yuso €
Tel: 941 373049; www.monasteriodeyuso.org. Open Tue–Sun 1000–1300 and 1600–1800 (extended summer hours).

Below
Monasterio de Suso

Born in the nearby village of Berceo in 473, San Millán 'of the cowl' was a shepherd who became a cave hermit and lived to the ripe old age of 101. Many miracles were attributed to him after his death, and his tomb soon became an important place of pilgrimage. A 10th-century church, **Monasterio de Suso**, with Visigothic and Mozarabic features, including some fine horseshoe arches, was hollowed out of the rock, and a second monastery, **Monasterio de Yuso**, was built further down in the valley. The story goes that the king of Navarra had decided to move the saint's tomb to Nájera, but the oxen pulling the cart from Suso refused to go further than the bottom of the hill – hence the building of the second church.

The monks at Yuso lead guided tours, pointing out San Millán's 11th-century reliquary, inlaid with intricate ivory carvings showing scenes from his life. The coffin was plundered by Napoleonic troops in 1813 but has been restored in a gilt silver casing. The present monastery buildings date from the 16th century; inside the church, look out for the *retablo* painting of San Millán Matamara (the Moor-slayer), purporting to show this modest local shepherd performing further miracles on the battlefield centuries after his death. The monastery also contains the first written example of the Castilian language, found in a manuscript written by a 10th-century monk who

lapsed into the vernacular in creating the footnotes to the Latin text that he was annotating.

Accommodation and food in San Millán de la Cogolla

Hostería del Monasterio de San Millán €€ *Monasterio de Yuso; tel: 941 373277; fax: 941 373266; email: hosteria@sanmillan.com; www. sanmillan.com.* This magnificent hotel is based in a wing of the Yuso monastery. The hotel's restaurant serves excellent local cuisine and there are several rustic bars nearby featuring roast lamb, vegetable dishes and other Riojan classics.

Santo Domingo de la Calzada

ⓘ *Calle Mayor 70; tel: 941 341230; email: santodomingo@ riojaturismo.org; www.lariojaturismo.com*

🏛 Catedral € *Tel: 941 340033. Open Mon–Sat 0930–1330, 1600–1830.* Although parts of the cathedral can be visited free of charge, the cloisters, museum and crypt are reached by a separate entrance on Calle del Cristo.

🍴 Vinos Castro *(Calle Mayor 66)* is a wonderfully old-fashioned wine shop with a fine collection of Riojas, including a number of vintages. **Mesón Los Arcos**, next door, has a good-value set lunch menu.

This charming town on the Río Oja (the river from which Rioja takes its name) is named after an 11th-century hermit who built a causeway (*calzada*) and a hospital for the many pilgrims who passed through the town on the road to Santiago de Compostela. King Alfonso VI of Castile responded with the gift of a church, which was consecrated three years before the saint's death in 1106 and is now the **Catedral**. The tomb of Santo Domingo is found in the crypt inside an extravagant Gothic temple. Opposite, a live cock and hen, permanently kept inside a henhouse in the south transept, are a reminder of an extraordinary miracle attributed to the saint. A German pilgrim, passing through the town, was falsely accused of theft by a local girl after he had rebuffed her advances. After he was hanged on the gallows, his parents went to pay their last respects before continuing on their journey to Santiago. Remarkably, their son was alive, and attributed his recovery to a miraculous intervention by the dead saint. When the parents went to see the local judge to plead for their son's release, the judge, who was sitting at a table, joked that their son was no more alive than the roast chickens on his plate – whereupon the roasted cock and the hen got up from his plate and crowed.

From the 16th-century cathedral ramparts there are views of the bell tower and the 14th-century town walls. The streets around the cathedral are perfect for gentle strolling, typical of the medieval pilgrim towns with their convents, hostelries and noble houses.

Accommodation and food in Santo Domingo de la Calzada

Parador de Santo Domingo €€ *Plaza del Santo 3; tel: 941 340300; fax: 941 340325; email: sto.domingo@parador.es; www.parador.es.* St Dominic's pilgrim hospital has been turned into a stylish hotel, accommodating today's pilgrims and tourists in comfort and luxury. The *parador* is situated beside the cathedral. The restaurant features classic regional dishes such as Riojan-style salt cod.

SIERRA DE LA DEMANDA

*Calle Sagastia 1,
Ezcaray;*
tel: 941 354679;
www.ezcaray.org

The mountain range in the southwest of La Rioja is covered in snow for much of the year and contains the region's only winter sports station at Ezcaray. For serious hikers, the sierra contains some challenging mountain walks, including an ancient pilgrim route from San Millán de la Cogolla to the **Monasterio de Valvanera**, Rioja's main Marian shrine, where a 12th-century wood carving of the Virgin is venerated.

Accommodation and food in Sierra de la Demanda

Hospedería Nuestra Señora de Valvanera € *Tel: 941 377044; fax: 941 377194; www.abadiavalvanera.com.* The monks operate a simple hostelry in a wing of the monastery. You eat with the pilgrims in the monks' refectory and there are several peaceful walks in the nearby hills.

Right
Monasterio de Valvanera

Right
Haro

Rioja wines

The system of *crianza* (ageing in oak casks) which gives Riojas their distinctive vanilla scent was begun in the 1860s when two local noblemen, Marqués de Murrieta and Marqués de Riscal, returned from Bordeaux keen to apply French wine-making techniques to their native Riojan wines. Most red wines are based on the Tempranillo grape with small quantities of Garnacha, Mazuelo and Graciano; the predominant white grape is Viura. *Cosechero* wines are from that year's harvest, designed to be drunk young; red *crianzas* are aged for a year in cask; *reservas* are aged for three years, at least one in oak; while *gran reservas*, the best of all, have spent at least two years in the cask and three in the bottle. These periods are all reduced in the case of white wines.

Riojan cuisine, with its emphasis on fresh, local ingredients, perfectly complements the local red wines. Classic dishes include slow-roasted lamb, lamb chops grilled over vine leaves, beans with *chorizo* sausage, potatoes with red peppers, and peaches in Rioja wine.

Suggested tour

Total distance: 104km. The detour adds around 25km.

Time: 2 hours. Allow an extra 45 minutes for the detour, plus time at the monasteries of Yuso and Suso.

Links: From Nájera, the N120 leads to the provincial capital Logroño, from where you can take the N111 into Navarra, linking with the Pamplona-Iruña and around route (*see pages 104–105*) at the medieval pilgrim town of Estella. The distance from Nájera to Estella is about 80km.

From the centre of **HARO ❶**, cross to the left bank of the river and head for the *bodega* district by the railway station. When you reach a roundabout with the Rioja Alta *bodega* on your left, go straight ahead towards **Labastida**, a fortified wine town at the entrance to the Rioja Alavesa vineyards. Reaching Labastida, turn right to skirt the town; as you leave the town, look for a turning on your left towards Peñacerrada. The road twists and turns as it climbs ever higher through the vineyards and on to the higher slopes, with views back down over the terraces and across to the distant sierra. After briefly returning to La Rioja province, you are back in the Basque Country as you reach **Peñacerrada**, a medieval fortress town on the border between Navarra and Castile.

Above
Nájera's Monasterio de Santa
María la Real

Turn right and then right again to join the A2124, which climbs gradually to the **Puerto de Herrera**. This mountain pass, 1,100m above sea level, is the historic entrance to La Rioja. It is marked by a monument beside the road, created out of wine barrels. The road now drops sharply to the **Balcón de La Rioja**, a mirador and picnic area from where the whole of the Ebro valley is spread out beneath you. Take time here to enjoy the views before you start out on the difficult descent.

At the next junction, turn left and drive through the vineyards towards Laguardia, with the great hulk of the Sierra de Cantabria looming to your left. After exploring **LAGUARDIA ②**, turn right beneath the village, passing more vineyards on the way to **Elciego**, home to one of the top Rioja Alavesa winemakers, Marqués de Riscal. At the end of the road, turn right to re-enter La Rioja proper at **Cenicero**. Drive through the village, then cross the N232 and follow the straight, flat road to **NÁJERA ③**, with dramatic views of the **SIERRA DE LA DEMANDA** ahead.

Detour: In Nájera, follow the complicated one-way system around the town, remembering not to cross the bridge, and look out for signs to Yuso and Suso monasteries. This will lead you on to the LR113. There are several routes to San Millán, but for the most scenic approach, continue on this road as far as **Bobadilla**, then turn right, climbing through the hamlet of **Villaverde** to reach a plateau with the peaks of the Sierra de la Demanda in the distance and the little town of San Andrés in a valley beneath you. Continue on this road to **SAN MILLÁN DE LA COGOLLA ④**. After visiting the two monasteries, follow signs from Suso to the village of **Bermeo**, crossing an undulating rural landscape on the way to Santo Domingo de la Calzada.

Otherwise, leave Nájera on the N120, retracing the medieval pilgrim route to **SANTO DOMINGO DE LA CALZADA ❺**. From Santo Domingo, an easy drive north across a flat fertile plain returns you quickly to Haro.

Also worth exploring

Logroño, the capital of La Rioja, is a modern industrial town with a handsome old quarter beside the River Ebro and a number of *bodegas* including the famous Marqués de Murrieta. From here, the Ebro crosses a fertile plain to reach the town of **Calahorra**, founded by the Romans. Parts of the original Roman wall survive, and there is a monument in the town to the Roman orator Quintilian, who was born here.

Southwest of Calahorra, near the remote village of **Enciso**, is Spain's answer to Jurassic Park, sometimes known as Parque Jurásico, where a number of dinosaur footprints can be seen in the rocks. There is a two-day waymarked walk in the area called La Ruta de los Dinosaurios.

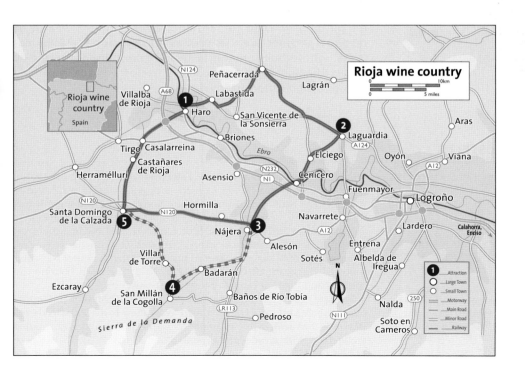

Rioja wine country

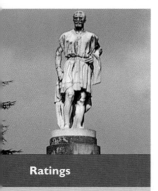

Pamplona-Iruña and around

Ratings

Historical sights	●●●●●
Churches	●●●●○
Festivals	●●●●○
Scenery	●●●●○
Food	●●●○○
Mountains	●●●○○
Wine	●●●○○
Children	●●○○○

Part Basque and part Spanish, the province of Navarra is all that remains of a powerful medieval kingdom which lasted until 1512. Even after Navarra was absorbed into Spain, it retained its own laws, parliament and taxes, as well as its ancient *fueros* or privileges, well into the 19th century. A stronghold of the reactionary, religious right, Navarra was the power base of the pretender Don Carlos during the First Carlist War (1833–9) and was strongly supportive of Franco during the Civil War. Franco, in turn, allowed Navarra a measure of independence, and until the return of democracy it was the only autonomous region in Spain. As a result of its central position on the pilgrim road to Santiago, Navarra has a wealth of medieval architecture – as well as a lively capital, Pamplona-Iruña, whose bull-running festival, immortalised in print by Ernest Hemingway, has become a rite of passage for many young foreign visitors to Spain.

ESTELLA

ℹ *Calle San Nicolás 1; tel/fax: 948 556301; email: oit.estella@cfnavarra.es; www.turismo.navarra.com*

P There is a small car park beside the river close to the Cárcel bridge, which makes a good starting point for exploring the town. You can reach it by turning left across a bridge as you enter the town from Pamplona-Iruña.

To pilgrims in the Middle Ages, Estella (also known by its Basque name of Lizarra) was Estella La Bella, a popular resting place astride the River Ega with a wealth of beautiful Romanesque buildings. It was Sancho Ramírez who put Estella on the map when he established it as a pilgrim town in 1076; by the 12th century it had become the royal seat of the kings of Navarra. Several centuries later, Estella once again occupied a central place in Spanish history; during the bitter wars that followed the death of Fernando VII in 1833, the town became the spiritual and political capital of the Carlist cause.

The size of the town makes it ideal for strolling. Start at the tourist office, where you can pick up a map. Next door is the **Palacio de los Reyes de Navarra**, a fine example of 12th-century civil Romanesque architecture with arcades and capitals along its façade. The palace now houses the **Museo Gustavo de Maeztu**, dedicated to the works of the

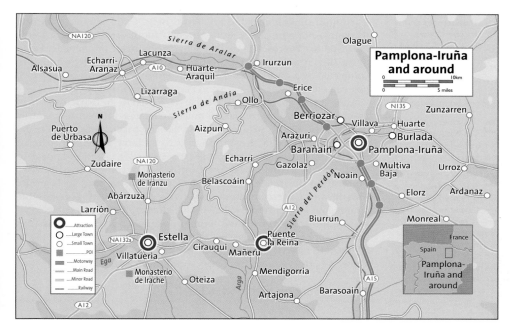

Pamplona-Iruña and around

Museo Gustavo de Maeztu *Calle San Nicolás 2; tel: 948 546037. Open Tue–Sat 1100–1300, 1700–1900, Sun 1100–1330. Free.*

Nuestra Señora del Puy
Calle Abárzuza 1; tel: 948 550 548. Open daily. Services held Mon–Sat at 1730. Sun services at 1300.

San Pedro de la Rúa
Calle San Nicolás s/n; tel: 948 550070; www.estella-lizarra.com. Guided tours available when services not in session. Services held weekdays at 1800 (1900 from Oct to 31 May), 2000 on Sat. Sun services at 0900, 1200 & 1300. Doors open half an hour prior to services.

Basque painter (1887–1947), son of a Cuban father and an English mother, who spent the last ten years of his life in Estella. The collection includes several expressive portraits and a number of female nudes. Even if you are not interested in art, it is worth going into the palace for the view down over Plaza San Martín, a delightful square with a fountain at its centre and the baroque law courts, once the town hall, on the far side.

Facing the royal palace across the square, and reached up a flight of steps, the church of **San Pedro de la Rúa** squats on the side of a cliff. The most notable features here are the richly sculpted 12th-century doorway, and the two remaining galleries of Romanesque cloisters – the other two galleries were destroyed when the nearby castle was blown up in the 16th century. The church is usually closed except for services, but the cloisters, reached by a separate entrance off Calle San Nicolás, are open throughout the day.

From Plaza San Martín, you can follow Calle Rúa, the main pilgrim route, along the right bank of the river. The street, lined with handsome palaces and mansions, leads to **Puente de la Cárcel**, a re-creation of an old Romanesque footbridge. Before crossing the bridge, it is worth continuing briefly as far as the church of **Santo Sepulcro**, with its beautifully carved Gothic portal. Above the church, the Gothic convent of Santo Domingo is now an old people's home.

The dominant building on the left bank of the river is **San Miguel**, whose restored north portal, showing St Michael slaying the dragon, is

Monasterio de Irache *Ctra de Logroño; tel: 948 554464.* Open Tue 0930–1330, Wed–Fri 0930–1330, 1700–1900, Sat & Sun 0830–1330, 1600–1900, shorter hours in winter. Free.

A market is held in the Plaza de los Fueros on Thursday mornings.

Estella's big festival, **San Andrés**, begins on the Friday before the first Sunday in August. As well as religious processions, it includes a whole week of bullfights and *encierros* ('running of the bulls'). Women take part in the bull-running here, unlike in Pamplona-Iruña, and the whole event makes a good alternative to the crowds and commercialism of Los Sanfermines (the bull-running festival).

Below
Estella

a triumph of Romanesque art. From here, Calle Mayor, a narrow medieval shopping street, leads through the heart of Estella towards **Plaza de los Fueros**, the market square. The main promenade, Paseo de la Imaculada, runs parallel to Calle Mayor; its two ends are connected by a pleasant riverside walk. From the east end of the *paseo*, you can cross a bridge to return to Plaza San Martín.

Above the town, the basilica of **Nuestra Señora del Puy**, inaugurated in 1951, contains a much-venerated 14th-century Gothic statue of the Virgin, patroness of Estella. The basilica was built on the spot where in 1085 the Virgin is said to have appeared to local shepherds, an incident which greatly increased Estella's appeal to medieval pilgrims. Another popular pilgrimage destination, **Monasterio de Irache**, is 3km out of town on the road to Logroño. This former Cistercian monastery has a 12th-century Romanesque church and a 16th-century Plateresque cloister, but most people come for the *fuente del vino* ('wine fountain') supplied by the monastery's *bodega*. For centuries it has been the tradition for pilgrims en route to Santiago to receive a free glass of wine here, and so long as you do not abuse the privilege, you can help yourself from a tap in the wall.

Accommodation and food in Estella

Hotel Yerri € *Avda de Yerri 35; tel: 948 546034, www.hotelyerri.es.* This is a comfortable, modern hotel near the centre with plain rooms, a downstairs bar-restaurant and good facilities, including Wi-Fi in the rooms.

Navarra €€€ *Calle Gustavo de Maeztu 16, Los Llanos; tel: 948 550040.* The top restaurant in town features traditional Navarrase cuisine in a medieval-style town house with lovely riverside gardens.

PAMPLONA-IRUÑA

ℹ *Calle Eslava 1;*
tel: 848 420420;
www.pamplona.net

🅿 There is limited
short-term parking
in the centre around Plaza
del Castillo, but for longer
visits the best bet is the
large car park near La
Ciudadela park.

🏛 **Catedral €€** *Plaza*
San José; tel: 948
222990. Open 15 Sept–
15 Jul Mon–Fri 1000–1400,
1600–1900, Sat 1000–
1400.

Museo de Navarra €
Calle Santo Domingo 47;
tel: 848 426492. Open
Tue–Sat 0930–1400,
1700–1900, Sun
1100–1400.

🍴 For cafés, bars and
snacks head for the
area around Plaza del
Castillo. On the square
itself, **Café Iruña** is a
stylish Art Nouveau coffee
shop and popular meeting
place. Calle Estafeta, the
main street on the bull-
running route, has many
tapas bars where the
pintxos are laid out on
plates – try **Bodegón
Sarria, Adoquin de La
Estafeta** and **Ostatu
Erretegia**. Across the
square, Calle San Nicolás
has numerous restaurants
and bars, most of them
specialising in roast and
grilled meat.

🛍 A popular souvenir is
a wineskin – ideal for
holding the excellent
Navarrase reds such as
Chivite and Señorío de
Sarría.

Founded by the Roman general Pompey on a bend in the Arga river, occupied by the Moors and sacked by Charlemagne, Pamplona-Iruña has played a central role in Navarrase history. These days it is a prosperous, modern university city of wide boulevards and spacious parks, best known for the riotous festival which takes place here each July.

It was the American author Ernest Hemingway (1899–1961) who brought Pamplona-Iruña to the world's attention with his first novel *Fiesta – The Sun Also Rises* in 1926. Hemingway was a great *aficionado* of the bullfight and his statue stands outside the city's bullring. From here, a stroll along the ramparts, looking down over the river, leads to the **Catedral**, its fine Gothic nave and cloister hidden behind a stern 18th-century neoclassical façade.

West of the cathedral, the narrow streets of the Navarrería (the old Basque artisan quarter) merge with the Judería ('Jewish quarter') to form an atmospheric pedestrian shopping district. Behind Santo Domingo market, the **Museo de Navarra**, housed in a 16th-century hospital, contains Roman mosaics, Gothic art and the capitals from the former Romanesque cathedral.

The nerve centre of Pamplona-Iruña is **Plaza del Castillo**, a porticoed square ringed with cafés and Hemingway's favourite hotel, La Perla. Jousts and bullfights were once held in this square but these days the entertainment mostly consists of families taking an evening stroll. On the edge of the square, the baroque **Palacio de Navarra** is the headquarters of the Navarrase government; its throne room contains a portrait of Fernando VII by Goya. From here a wide promenade, Paseo Sarasate, connects the old town to the 19th-century extension, squeezed between two of the city's finest parks – **La Ciudadela**, based around the remains of a 16th-century fortress, and **La Taconera**, a romantic park with a botanic garden.

Accommodation and food in Pamplona-Iruña

Otano € *Calle San Nicolás 5; tel: 948 227036.* This family-run restaurant, bar and hostel has a few simple rooms and a reputation for good Navarrase cuisine. Try the grilled meat or the lamb in *chilindrón* ('red pepper') sauce. Closed in July.

Sarasate € *Calle San Nicolás 19, 1st floor; tel: 948 225727.* In a street designed for carnivores, this is a revelation – a stylish vegetarian restaurant serving pasta and huge salads in the house where the violinist Pablo Sarasate was born.

La Chistera €€ *Calle San Nicolás 40; tel: 948 210512.* Roast meat, especially lamb, is the thing to order at this popular restaurant just off the Plaza del Castillo.

Eslava €€ *Plaza Virgen de la O 7; tel: 948 222270; fax: 948 225157; www.hotel-eslava.com; email: correo@hotel-eslava.com.* Small, quiet hotel close to the Taconera gardens, with views over the river and the city walls.

Europa €€ *Calle Espoz y Mina 11; tel: 948 221800; fax: 948 229235; email: europa@hreuropa.com; www.hreuropa.com.* This small, pretty hotel is in the thick of the action, a few steps away from Plaza del Castillo. The restaurant has gained a Michelin star for its innovative Basque-style cuisine.

Below
Pamplona-Iruña's Palacio
de Navarra

Iruña Palace Hotel Tres Reyes €€ *Jardines de la Taconera; tel: 948 226600; fax: 948 222930; email: reserv@hotel3reyes.com; www. hotel3reyes.com.* This large, modern hotel has all the facilities you could wish for, including a gym, sauna and heated pool. The balconies overlook the Taconera gardens and the old town is a short walk away.

Josetxo €€€ *Plaza Príncipe de Viana 1; tel: 948 222097; www.restaurantejosetxo.com.* Book well ahead if you want a table at this famous restaurant with its elegant belle époque dining rooms. The food and the service are both first class, and the specialities include venison in Merlot and steak with truffle sauce.

La Perla €€€ *Plaza del Castillo 1; tel: 948 223000; fax: 948 222324; www.granhotellaperla.com.* Hemingway's favourite haunt in Pamplona-Iruña continues to be the first choice for nostalgic visitors attracted by the elegant atmosphere. The balconies overlooking the *plaza* would make a great vantage spot during the fiesta. It was totally refurbished in 2007.

Los Sanfermines

Hemingway called it 'a damned fine show', though the visitors who end up gored by bulls might be inclined to disagree. For nine days each year, Pamplona-Iruña goes wild with fireworks, dances, Carnival processions and bullfights in honour of San Fermín, the city's first bishop. Hotel prices double, so does the population, and the streets are a riot of colour day and night. The highlight is the *encierro*, the running of the bulls, with its origins in the custom of walking the fighting bulls through the streets from corral to bullring each day. At 0800 each morning the bulls are released, to chase up Mercaderes and Estafeta streets accompanied by hundreds of runners in red berets and scarves. Every year people are hurt, often killed, and you have to be mad to take part. The whole thing is over in about three minutes; later that day the bulls are killed in the bullring. The festival starts at noon on 6 July, launched by a rocket known as *el chupinazo*; it ends at midnight on 14 July, with the mass singing of a lament, *pobre de mi*.

PUENTE LA REINA

ℹ️ *Calle Mayor; tel: 948 340845.*

This small town on the banks of the River Arga lies at the junction of the two main routes to Santiago and, even if you have not come here on pilgrimage, this is the best place to get a feel for the pilgrim experience. Just outside the town on the road to Pamplona-Iruña, a bronze statue of a pilgrim marks the point where the roads converge. You can park here and walk in along the ancient pilgrim road. The first notable building is the **Iglesia del Crucifijo**, built by the Knights Templar in the 12th century and containing a remarkable wooden crucifix, carved into a Y shape and featuring Christ with his arms upraised. It is thought to have been left by a 14th-century German pilgrim.

Left
Bridge over the River Arga at
Puente la Reina

The Camino de Santiago

The legend of St James arose in the 9th century when his relics were supposedly discovered by a shepherd in Galicia. Not long afterwards, the saint appeared on a white charger on a battlefield in Rioja, driving back the Moors and becoming forever Santiago Matamoros, St James the Moor-Slayer, patron of the Spanish Reconquest. By the 11th century his fame had spread abroad and his tomb at Santiago de Compostela had become one of the most visited shrines in Christendom, on a par with Jerusalem and Rome. Pilgrim towns sprang up along the route and the world's first known guidebook, written by a 12th-century French monk, described the conditions, sights and people along the way.

The two main routes through France converged at Puente la Reina. One, the *camino francés* from Paris, entered Navarra at Roncesvalles; the other, the *camino aragonés*, crossed the Pyrenees at the Somport pass before heading for Jaca in Aragón. Pilgrims would carry a staff, a gourd for water, and a scallop shell, the traditional sign of St James. After the Reformation, the pilgrimage gradually died out, but today the pilgrims have returned once more and in the weeks leading up to St James' Day on 25 July the scallop shell is again a common sight on the roads of northern Spain. These days, anybody can make the pilgrimage in a matter of days by car, but to qualify as a true pilgrim you need to walk at least 100km, or cycle or ride on horseback for 200km.

'A friendly crowd of locals awaking from their siestas gathered on their balconies and urged me on.'

Robin Hanbury-Tenison on Puente la Reina, *Spanish Pilgrimage*, 1990

You enter the oldest part of town through the Portal de Suso, the only surviving gateway from the medieval walls. This leads into Calle Mayor, the main street, where the shops sell scallop shells and rosaries for pilgrims as well as the local sausages and wine. On the right, **Iglesia del Santiago** is dedicated to St James, with a gilded wooden statue of the saint as pilgrim. The church, in a mixture of styles, has a Romanesque portal, a Gothic interior and a Baroque bell tower.

Eventually the street leads to the graceful humpback bridge from which Puente la Reina takes its name. The bridge was built in the 11th century by royal command of Sancho Ramírez, and probably named for his wife, Doña Mayor. As you stand on the bridge gazing out at the fields, you cannot but think of the generations of pilgrims who have stood on this spot, contemplating the final section of the long, arduous route to Santiago de Compostela.

Accommodation and food in Puente la Reina

El Peregrino €€€ *Ctra Pamplona-Logroño km 23; tel: 948 340075; fax: 948 341190; www.hotelelperegrino.com.* This stone-built inn at the junction of the pilgrim routes is now a luxury hotel and has a reputation for excellent Navarrase cuisine. An added attraction is the outdoor pool. Restaurant closed Sunday p.m. and Monday.

Suggested tour

Total distance: 125km. The longer route adds around 40km.

Time: 2½ hours. Because of the nature of the mountain roads, it is best to allow 4 hours for the longer route.

Links: From Estella the A12 and N111 continue to Logroño, from where you can take the N120 to join the Rioja wine route (*see pages 93–5*) at Nájera.

Leave **PAMPLONA-IRUÑA ❶** by taking the road between the Ciudadela and Taconera gardens, which soon becomes the A12 to Logroño. Crossing the ring road on the outskirts of the city, the road travels across flat grasslands with sweeping vistas before climbing towards the **Sierra del Perdón**, where 40 windmills, spread out along a ridge, make a strangely impressive sight. At the highest point of the road, Puerto del Perdón, a side lane, leads up on to the sierra from where there are views of the Pyrenees on a clear day.

Scallop shell signs beside the road remind you that this is an ancient pilgrim route. Descending from Perdón, the A12 continues quickly to Puente la Reina but most of the footsore pilgrims escape the traffic by turning left on to a quiet road through the village of **Uterga**. The road comes out at **Obanos**, where a short detour to the left leads to **Eunate**; its beautiful, octagonal Romanesque chapel is believed to have been used as a burial place for pilgrims unable to complete their journey. After visiting the chapel, return to Obanos along the final stages of the *camino aragonés* until it meets up with the *camino francés* at **PUENTE LA REINA ❷**.

As you leave Puente la Reina, be sure to glance to your right to admire the handsome pilgrim bridge. The road now bypasses **Cirauqui**, a medieval village of steep streets, whitewashed houses and a fine 13th-century church, on its way to **ESTELLA ❸**. Drive through the town centre and follow signs to San Sebastián on the NA120. This is a fantastic drive, with spectacular mountain views at every turn yet on a good, fast road. The road climbs gradually to a stony plateau where wild ponies graze on the moors. Eventually you reach **Puerto de Lizarraga** (1,090m) where you emerge from a tunnel to see the lush Ergoyena valley spread out in front of you between the sierras of Andia and Urbasa. From here the road twists sharply down the mountainside. When it reaches the A10, turn right to return to Pamplona-Iruña.

Detour: For a more scenic alternative, you can make a round trip through the Urbasa and Andia mountain ranges. From Estella, a winding road follows the Urederra river, travelling through a series of gorges on its way to the **Puerto de Urbasa**. Beyond the pass, the road drops steeply through a forest of oak and beech trees. Reaching the

A10, turn right towards Pamplona-Iruña, then after 8km turn right again to return to Estella via Puerto de Lizarraga. Shortly before Estella, a minor road to the left at Abárzuza leads through the peaceful Yerri valley before climbing to a mountain pass and dropping through the Etxauri valley. You pass **Etxauri**, with its medieval towered houses, and **Arazuri** with its Gothic church and castle, on the way back to Pamplona-Iruña.

Also worth exploring

If you have developed a taste for the pilgrim route, the N135 from Pamplona-Iruña leads northeast to **Roncesvalles**, the start of the Spanish section and an important pilgrim town. It was here in 778 that the rearguard of Charlemagne's army, led by Roland, was ambushed and massacred by Basque forces as they attempted to return safely to France – an event recorded in the French epic poem *La Chanson de Roland*. A 30-minute hike from Roncesvalles leads up to the Ibaneta pass, thought to be the scene of the battle. Once over the pass, the N135 continues into France and the town of **St-Jean-Pied-de-Port**, where several of the French pilgrim routes to Santiago converge.

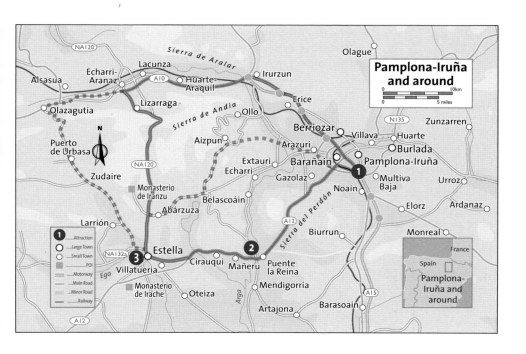

Zaragoza and around

Ratings

Architecture	●●●●○
Art	●●●●○
Historical sights	●●●●○
Wine	●●●●○
Food	●●●○○
Museums	●●●○○
Scenery	●●●○○
Children	●○○○○

Despite its size and historical importance, Aragón barely features on the Spanish tourist map. Stretching from the high Pyrenees to the dusty plains, and neatly bisected by the River Ebro, this sparsely populated region is surrounded by neighbours (France, Catalonia, Castile and Navarra), each of which has left its mark on Aragón's history and culture. The capital, Zaragoza, with its pilgrim church and fine *mudéjar* architecture, makes an obvious overnight stopping point on the motorway from Barcelona to Bilbao. South of the Ebro, the barren central plateau creates a harsh and unforgiving landscape, where life is hard, winters are long and cold and the summers searingly hot. This was the landscape that produced Francisco de Goya, one of the greatest of all Spanish painters. The hearty Aragonese cuisine, with its spicy stews, serious roasts and robust red wines, seems to reflect the harshness of the region.

BELCHITE

> 'When the republicans arrived, they fought from house to house, breaking in cellar doors to kill the nationalists like dogs.'
>
> Adam Hopkins in Belchite, *Spanish Journeys*, 1992

This part of Aragón saw some of the heaviest fighting of the Spanish Civil War, as Republicans and Nationalists battled for strategic control of the Ebro valley. In 1937, following a fierce battle, the small town of Belchite was left in ruins. After the war, it was abandoned and Franco decided that it should never be rebuilt. You can wander among the ruins of this ghostly town, the crumbling brick houses and hollow church bearing silent and eloquent witness to the awful realities of war.

FUENDETODOS

Fuendetodos, a solid, stone-built village of 180 people, attracts some 25,000 visitors a year because of its connections with the painter Francisco de Goya. He was born here in 1746, the son of a master

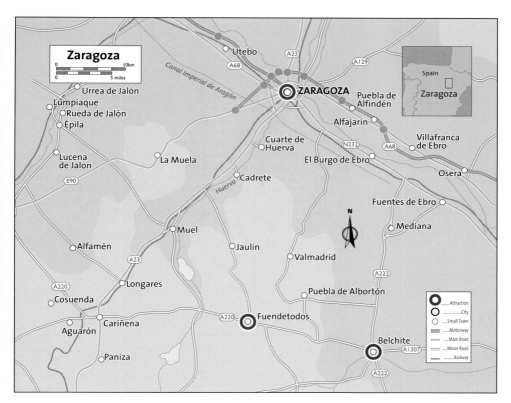

Zaragoza

Utebo
ZARAGOZA
Puebla de Alfindén
Alfajarin
Urrea de Jalón
Lumpiaque
Rueda de Jalón
Épila
Lucena de Jalon
La Muela
Cuarte de Huerva
El Burgo de Ebro
Villafranca de Ebro
Osera
Cadrete
Fuentes de Ebro
Mediana
Muel
Jaulín
Valmadrid
Alfamén
Longares
Cosuenda
Puebla de Albortón
Cariñena
Fuendetodos
Aguarón
Belchite
Paniza

Spain
Zaragoza

Canal Imperial de Aragón
Huerva

○ Attraction
○ City
○ Small Town
Motorway
Main Road
Minor Road
Railway

Fuendetodos
Calle Cortes de Aragón 7; tel: 976 143867; www.fuendetodos.org

Casa Natal de Goya € *Plaza de Goya; tel: 976 143830. Open Tue–Sun 1100–1400, 1600–1900.*
The museum, in Avda Zuloaga, is entered on the same ticket.

Follow the walking trail around the village for good views of the countryside. The trail takes around an hour and passes a ruined castle and the spring, *fuente de todos*, from which the village takes its name.

gilder who was working on a *retablo* in the parish church at the time. Although Goya's birthplace, **Casa Natal de Goya**, is a simple stone house, in 18th-century terms it is far from the humble dwelling which it is often claimed to be. The house was bought in 1916 by the Basque painter Ignacio Zuloaga; it was destroyed in the Civil War but subsequently restored, with exhibits and furniture relating to Goya's life and times. The nearby **Museo del Grabado de Goya** contains a collection of Goya's etchings, including the satirical set *Los Caprichos* (*see page 108*) and the apocalyptic *Los Desastres de la Guerra* ('The Disasters of War'). Also on display is *La Tauromaquia*, a series of etchings on the theme of bullfighting.

Accommodation and food in Fuendetodos

El Capricho de Goya € *Paseo Vista Alegre 2; tel: 976 143888*. If you fancy staying the night after the day-trippers have left, this small hotel on the edge of the village has seven double rooms. The restaurant serves reasonably priced Spanish meals, including a daily set lunch menu.

Goya

In many ways, Francisco de Goya (1746–1828) could be said to be the first Spanish Modernist, the central figure in a line that connects the Old Masters to Picasso, Miró and Dalí. He began conventionally enough, painting church frescoes, society portraits and tapestry cartoons, and in 1785 he was appointed official painter to the royal court – a position he used to produce some highly unflattering portraits of the royal family. Two subsequent events had a profound effect on him – an affair with the Duchess of Alba, and a life-threatening illness that left him deaf. In 1799 he produced *Los Caprichos*, a series of etchings that poked fun at society, using satirical imagery such as monsters, witches and humans that looked like donkeys. Politicised by the French Revolution and the Napoleonic invasion of Spain, in later life he produced several memorable and disturbing images focusing on the horrors of war. He died in exile in Bordeaux.

ZARAGOZA

ⓘ *Plaza del Pilar; tel: 976 393537; email: infoturismopilar @zaragoza.es; www.turismozaragoza.com.* There is also a provincial tourist office in Torreón de la Zuda, a *mudéjar* tower beside the Roman walls.

ⓗ **Aljafería €** *Calle Diputados; tel: 976 289683. Open 1 Apr–15 Oct daily 1000–1400, 1630–2000; 16 Oct–31 Mar Mon–Wed, Sat 1000–1400, 1600–1830, Fri 1600–1830, Sun 1000–1400. Closed Thur.*

The Roman town of *Caesaraugusta*, from which Zaragoza takes its name, was founded in the 1st century BC on the banks of the River Ebro. For 400 years a thriving Islamic city, it was captured by Alfonso I in 1118 and became the capital of the young kingdom of Aragón. These days it is a bustling, modern city, the fifth largest in Spain, with fine examples of *mudéjar* (Moorish-Gothic) architecture. In 2008 the city hosted the much-lauded Expo Zaragoza which celebrated the theme of water and sustainable development. Today the expo site, which flanks the river, features some exciting innovative architecture, such as an iconic 76m tall water tower.

The most impressive sight remains the historic **Aljafería**, which lies a short distance west of the city centre. This Islamic fortress-palace, begun in the 11th century, has been successively used by the Aragonese kings, the Spanish monarchs and now the regional assembly of Aragón. The original palace, based around a central courtyard with elaborate horseshoe arches, is the best preserved example of Moorish architecture in Spain outside Andalucía. Of special interest is the oratory inside the northern portico, with its *mihrab* (a prayer niche pointing towards Mecca) and finely decorated stuccowork. The tours of the palace also include the Gothic quarters added by Fernando and Isabel, with a stone stairway leading to a gallery and a throne room with an ornate, polychrome coffered ceiling.

Above
Zaragoza

Basílica del Pilar €
Plaza del Pilar; tel: 976 397497. Open daily Apr–Oct 0545–2130, Nov–Mar 0545–2030. There are guided tours departing daily from the tourist office on Plaza del Pilar. Times vary, so call ahead *(tel: 976 201200).*

The heart of the city, just south of the Ebro, is enclosed on two sides by the avenue of El Coso and to the west by Avenida César Augusto, where you can find the central market, as well as a surviving section of Roman wall and a 15th-century *mudéjar* tower. From here it is just a short walk to Plaza del Pilar, a huge open-air square where hawkers sell cheap jewellery and food for the pigeons which gather outside the church.

The church in question is **Basílica del Pilar**, whose domes and minaret-like towers dominate the city from the north bank of the river. The basilica owes its existence to the legend of the pillar, on which the Virgin is said to have appeared to St James in Zaragoza in the year AD 40, commanding him to use it as the foundation stone of a church. The site is now the leading Marian shrine in Spain and the

P There is an underground car park beneath Plaza del Pilar, but otherwise parking is difficult. It may be possible to find a space on Paseo de Echegaray, west of the old town. There is limited parking close to the Aljafería palace.

La Lonja *Plaza del Pilar; tel: 976 397239. Open for exhibitions only Tue–Sat 1000–1400, 1700–2100, Sun 1000–1400. Free.*

Museo del Foro de Caesaraugusta (Foro Romano) € *Plaza de la Seo; tel: 976 399752; www.ayto-zaragoza.es. Open Tue–Sat 1000–1400, 1700–2000, Sun 1000–1400.*

Museo del Teatro de Caesaraugusta € *Calle de San Jorge 12; tel: 976 205088. Open Tue–Sat 1000–2100, Sun 1000–1400.*

Below
Zaragoza's Aljafería

church is usually thronged with pilgrims queuing to touch a small section of exposed pillar behind the Santa Capilla chapel, where an image of the Virgin is venerated. The chapel, like much of the 17th-century Baroque church, is rather overblown but it is worth going in to see the frescoes by Goya decorating the cupolas and the fine Renaissance altarpiece by Damián Forment. Look out, too, for a pair of unexploded Civil War bombs; the church is said to have been spared from destruction by the intervention of Our Lady of the Pillar. A small museum off the nave contains preliminary sketches for the church by Goya and Francisco Bayeu.

Beyond the town hall, **La Lonja**, the former commodities exchange, is the best piece of civil Renaissance architecture in Zaragoza. It is used as an exhibition hall; go in if there is an exhibition on to admire the fine, florid vaulted ceiling. Outside in the square, a modern entrance leads down to the **Foro Romano**, the underground remains of the Roman city. Dating from the same period, a Roman theatre, excavated during building works, forms part of the fascinating **Museo del Teatro de Caesaraugusta**. A visit includes an audiovisual performance on the stage (evenings only). North of here is the cathedral, **La Seo**, built between the 12th and 18th centuries in a wide range of architectural styles. The façade is baroque; the nave, with its five aisles, largely Gothic. An exterior wall, seen on Calle del Sepulcro, is brilliantly decorated with brick and tiles in classic *mudéjar* style. A museum around the back of the cathedral, **Museo de Tapices**, contains medieval Flemish tapestries.

South of Plaza del Pilar and the cathedral, the oldest part of town is a familiar mix of atmospheric streets and squares with plenty of hidden delights. There are two museums here that are worth seeking out. The **Museo Camón Aznar**, in a 16th-century Renaissance palace, contains the collection of a local art historian, including several sets of engravings by Goya. The **Museo Pablo Gargallo** is situated inside one

utal

Museo de Tapices y Capitular de la Seo € *Plaza de la Seo; tel: 976 291238; www.cabildodezaragoza.org. Open 1 Apr–30 Sept Tue–Sat 1000–1400, 1500–1900, Sun 1000–1400; in winter evening hours 1600–1800.*

Museo Camón Aznar *Calle Espoz y Mina 23; tel: 976 397328. Open Tue–Fri 0900–1415, 1800–2100, Sat 1000–1400, 1800–2100, Sun 1100–1400. Free.*

Museo Pablo Gargallo *Plaza San Felipe 3; tel: 976 724922. Open Tue–Sat 1000–1400, 1700–2100, Sun 1000–1400. Free.*

Museo de Zaragoza *Plaza de los Sitios 6; tel: 976 222181. Open Tue–Sat 1000–1400, 1700–2000, Sun 1000–1400. Free.*

San Pablo *Calle San Pablo 42; tel: 976 446226. Open Mon–Sat 0900–1030, 1830–2030, Sun 0930–1300, 1830–2030.*

of Zaragoza's finest *mudéjar* palaces and is the perfect setting in which to display the sculptures of Gargallo, an early 20th-century sculptor and friend of Picasso.

El Coso, on the site of the old city walls, separates the old town from the modern city, where the main artery, Paseo de la Independencia, leads into Paseo Sagasta with its Modernist mansions. A few blocks away, in Plaza de los Sitios, a large Modernist memorial, erected in 1908, recalls the heroic defence of Zaragoza a century earlier under two long sieges by Napoleon's troops. Across the square, the **Museo de Zaragoza** has sections devoted to archaeology and fine arts; the substantial Goya collection includes portraits of Carlos IV and Fernando VII, as well as the Virgin of the Pillar in glory, surrounded by angels.

Zaragoza's finest *mudéjar* tower, dating from the 13th century, adorns the church of **San Pablo**, just outside the old town walls. The church also features a carved wooden *retablo* by Damián Forment.

Accommodation and food in Zaragoza

Posada de las Almas € *Calle San Pablo 22; tel: 976 439700; fax: 976 439143.* A simple hostelry in a town house built in 1705, set in a quiet backstreet just outside the town walls. The restaurant serves typical Aragonese cuisine, such as *migas* (fried breadcrumbs) and chicken in *chilindrón* sauce.

Gran Hotel €€ *Calle Joaquín Costa 5; tel: 976 221901; fax: 976 236713 email: nhgranhotel@nh-hotels.com; www.nh-hotels.com.* The grandest place in town was opened by Alfonso XIII in 1929 and the present king stayed there while studying at Zaragoza's military academy. The rooms and suites are luxurious and beautifully furnished.

La Matilde €€ *Calle Predicadores 7–9; tel: 976 433443; www.lamatilde.com.* A restaurant which prides itself on its originality, boasting 90 different ways to fold table napkins. The menu is varied and creative and there is a celebrated cellar of wines.

El Prior €€ *Plaza Santa Cruz 7; tel: 976 201148; www.elprior.es.* A fashionable Art Deco restaurant, set around the Renaissance patio of a former priory, serving an eclectic range of *tapas* plus roast meat, game and seafood specialities.

El Real €€ *Plaza del Pilar; tel: 976 298808.* Old-style coffee house in a 16th-century *bodega* with Art Deco stained-glass windows. The downstairs café is good for breakfast, while the restaurant upstairs features hearty Aragonese classics such as grilled lamb chops and T-bone steaks.

Tibur €€ *Plaza de la Seo 2–3; tel: 976 202000; fax: 976 202002; email: reservas@hoteltibur.com; www.hoteltibur.com.* This comfortable hotel is situated right in the heart of the old town, on a square facing the cathedral and the basilica.

Shopping in Zaragoza

For *tapas* bars, seek out the alleys of the old town between Plaza España and Plaza del Pilar. Voted one of the top 50 tapas bars in Spain by *El Mundo* newspaper, **Casa Pascualillo** on Calle de la Libertad has a fabulous and extensive range of *tapas*. **Bodeguilla de la Santa Cruz**, in Calle Santa Cruz, is a tiny, snug wine bar with lots of character.

Flaherty's is an authentic Irish Pub located next to El Pilar. *Calle Alfonso I; tel: 976 298094.*

For picnic food, visit the **Mercado Central** in an Art Nouveau hall on Avda César Augusto. *Open Mon–Fri 0900–1400, 1700–2000, Sat 0900–1400.*

If you want to buy wine, the best Aragonese wines come from the Cariñena and Somontano regions.

On Sunday mornings, a flea market takes place outside the bullring and artists sell their work in Plaza Santa Cruz.

The **Fiesta del Pilar** is celebrated for a week on and around 12 October each year. The festival involves religious processions, parades of giants, bullfights, concerts, folk dancing and flower displays.

The narrow streets of the old town, between Calle Alfonso I and Calle Don Jaime I, are full of small shops and souvenir stores specialising in religious kitsch. The smarter shops are situated along the boulevards of the new town, especially Paseo Sagasta with its avant-garde boutiques. There are two branches of **El Corte Inglés**; the one on Paseo Sagasta sells clothes, while that on Paseo de la Independencia has music and books. For serious shoppers, the **Grancasa** complex just north of the Ebro is one of the largest shopping centres in Spain, with hypermarkets and branches of **Zara**, **Mango** and **Benetton**.

Suggested tour

Total distance: 120km. The detour to Cariñena adds 20km.

Time: 2½–3 hours.

Links: Using the fast A23 from Zaragoza, it is 72km to Huesca.

Leave **ZARAGOZA ❶** on the N232, following signs for Alcañiz. Once you have driven through the dreary outskirts of the city, you find yourself crossing a flat valley with the Ebro hidden away behind the trees to your left. After 20km, turn right towards Belchite. This road is signposted 'Ruta de Goya'.

Almost at once you climb into a desolate, rocky landscape which can be beautiful or depressing according to your mood and whether the sun is shining. There are few trees, little fertile ground and barely so much as a mountain stream. The road ploughs on, curving around the single village of **Mediana** and then resuming its straight course. Eventually the unexpected sight of olive groves signals the approach of **BELCHITE ❷**.

Ignore signs for the modern town centre and continue to the next junction, where you turn right on the A220 towards Fuendetodos. The war-damaged shell of the old town of Belchite is clearly visible to your left; you can park your car beside the road and walk around. Now continue along this road, passing the 18th-century sanctuary of Nuestra Señora de la Pueyo, to reach **FUENDETODOS ❸**. If you feel like a break, this village is at the centre of a network of well-marked walking trails, including a simple one-hour circuit of the village.

The next part of the route is particularly scenic, as it drops down to the *meseta* with panoramic views of the reddish-brown soil. At **Villanueva del Huerva ❹**, a minor road to the right follows the course of the Huerva river to **Muel ❺**, whose small village chapel contains four frescoes by Goya inside its cupola. Beneath the church there is a children's playground and a shady park with fountains.

Guided walks

The tourist office organises guided walks on various themes, including Goya, Gothic art and Renaissance art, on Saturday and Sunday mornings. The walks start at 1100 and last two hours. There are also daily guided walks around the old town.

Detour: Instead of taking the road to Muel, you could continue along the A220 to **Cariñena** ❻, an important wine-producing town. The road travels through vineyards before reaching the town, where several *bodegas* offer tastings and sales of local wine. Take the N330 and A23 towards Zaragoza to rejoin the main route at Muel.

From Muel the N330 returns quickly to Zaragoza.

Also worth exploring

If you want to see more Goyas, the Carthusian monastery of **La Cartuja de Aula Dei**, 10km north of Zaragoza, has several Goya frescoes featuring scenes from the life of the Virgin Mary. Visits are by appointment on the last Saturday of each month (*tel: 976 714934* to arrange a visit).

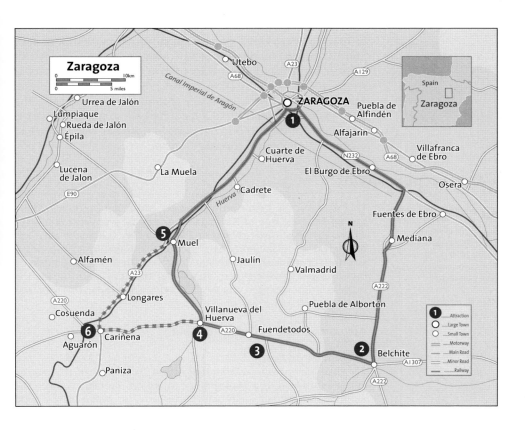

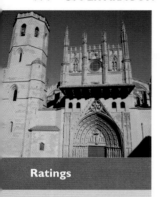

Upper Aragón

Ratings

Mountains	●●●●●
Scenery	●●●●●
Churches	●●●●○
Historical sights	●●●●○
Walking	●●●●○
Children	●●●○○
Food	●●●○○
Wildlife	●●●○○

The province of Huesca includes the Pyrenees' highest peaks as well as mountain villages, isolated valleys and two historic capitals of Aragón. For centuries this region, accessible from France by the Somport pass, was a crossroads of cultures and civilisations as crusaders, warring armies, priests, pilgrims and merchants all came and left their mark. It was here that Romanesque architecture crossed over the Pyrenees into Spain, producing remarkable churches such as the cathedral at Jaca and the nearby monastery of San Juan de la Peña. Today this region serves as a gateway to the Pyrenees, with their spectacular scenery of cliffs, gorges, rivers, waterfalls, glacial valleys and icy peaks – especially around the Ordesa valley, the centrepiece of Spain's first national park. In summer the park is a paradise for walkers and botanists in search of wild flowers; in winter it is completely covered in snow.

CASTILLO DE LOARRE

Castillo de Loarre
€ *Tel: 974 342166;*
www.castillodeloarre.com.
Open daily 1000–1400,
1600–2000 during summer,
and shorter, varied hours
during off-season.

This magnificent 11th-century fortress, built high upon a rock by Sancho Ramírez, king of Navarra and Aragón, is everyone's fantasy of what a medieval castle should be like. Children and adults alike can have great fun clambering over the ruins and getting lost among a labyrinth of stairways and ancient dungeons. The walls are flanked by round towers, giving superb views over the Ebro plain. Inside the castle is a Romanesque chapel and crypt, a reminder that this was once home to a religious community.

Accommodation in Castillo de Loarre

Hospedería de Loarre € *Plaza Mayor 7, Loarre; tel: 974 382706; fax: 974 382665; www.hospederiadeloarre.com.* The hotel in the nearby village is situated in a 16th-century palace on the main square. The rooms are simply but comfortably furnished. This would make a good base for exploring the area.

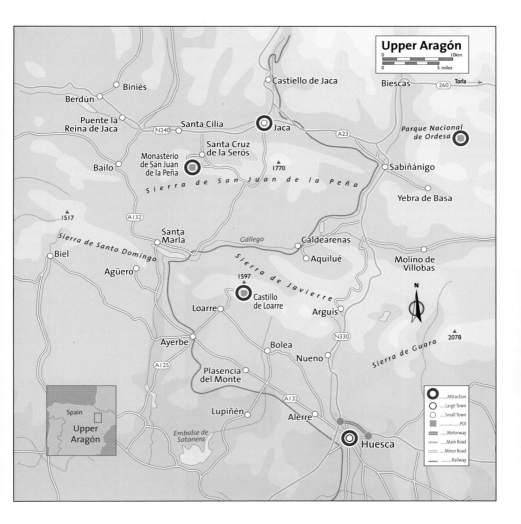

Upper Aragón

Biniés
Castiello de Jaca
Biescas
Torla
260
Berdún
Puente la
Reina de Jaca
Santa Cilia
N240
Jaca
A23
Parque Nacional
de Ordesa
Santa Cruz
de la Serós
Monasterio
de San Juan
de la Peña
Bailo
1770
Sabiñánigo
Sierra de San Juan de la Peña
Yebra de Basa
1517
A132
Santa
María
Gállego
Caldearenas
Molino de
Villobas
Sierra de Santo Domingo
Biel
Aquilué
Agüero
Sierra de Javierre
N
1597
Castillo
de Loarre
Loarre
Arguis
Ayerbe
2078
A125
Bolea
Sierra de Guara
Nueno
N330
Plasencia
del Monte
A132
Spain
Lupiñén
Alerre
Upper
Aragón
Embalse de
Sotonera
Huesca

Attraction
Large Town
Small Town
POI
Motorway
Main Road
Minor Road
Railway

HUESCA

ℹ *Plaza López Allué;*
tel: 974 292170; email:
turismo.aytohuesca@aragob.es;
www.huescaturismo.com

🏛 Catedral *Tel: 974*
220676. Open daily
1030–1330, 1630–1830.
Reduced hours in winter. Free.

The capital of a Roman province and later a Moorish stronghold, Huesca was captured by Pedro I of Aragón in 1096 and became the capital of the kingdom for 22 years. The old part of town, around the cathedral, has largely preserved its medieval layout. At the highest point of town is the **Catedral**, built on the site of a former mosque between the 13th and 16th centuries. The style is basically Gothic, but with a distinctive Aragonese touch in the carved wooden eaves above

Museo de Huesca
*Plaza de la Universidad
1; tel: 974 220586.
Open Tue–Sat 1000–1400,
1700–2000, Sun 1000–
1400. Free.*

San Pedro el Viejo €
*Calle Cuatro Reyes; tel: 974
222387. Open Mon–Sat
1000–1330, 1600–1930;
in summer open only in the
morning.*

The **Fiesta de San
Lorenzo**, from 9 to
15 August, has bullfights,
folklore festivals, dancers
and decorated floats.

the main portal (more of these eaves can be seen on the façade of the town hall across the square). Also of note is the Renaissance altarpiece by Damián Forment, with three large reliefs showing scenes from Christ's crucifixion.

A short walk from the cathedral, the excellent **Museo de Huesca** is situated inside the old university, which itself incorporates parts of the 12th-century royal palace. One of the chambers was the setting for the legendary 'Bell of Huesca' massacre, when Ramiro II is said to have summoned his nobles to witness the casting of a new bell which would be heard throughout the kingdom. As the courtiers arrived, the king had the most rebellious beheaded, thus ensuring that the Bell of Huesca did indeed reverberate across the land. The story is depicted in a painting which hangs inside the town hall. The museum itself has displays of archaeology and Gothic painting in galleries which lead off from a pleasant octagonal courtyard.

Ramiro II is one of two kings to be buried in the crypt of **San Pedro el Viejo**, Huesca's oldest church. The church was originally built in

Mozarabic style and has a splendid Romanesque cloister. It is situated a block back from the Coso, a busy promenade and shopping street on the site of the medieval walls which has become the nerve centre of the modern town.

Accommodation and food in Huesca

Lizana € *Plaza Lizana 6 & 8; tel: 974 220776; email: lizana2@ terra.es; www.hostal-lizana.com.* Two hostels offering a choice of double and single rooms with plenty of services, including 24-hour reception and Wi-Fi access.

Flor de Huesca €€ *Porches de Galicia 4; tel: 974 240402.* Lively, arty bistro found beneath the arches on a busy promenade. You can choose between the downstairs bar or an upstairs restaurant featuring duck, rabbit and salmon with *nueva cocina* flourishes.

Lillas Plastia €€ *Plaza Navarra 4; tel: 974 211691; email: rest-lillas@terra.es*. This elegant restaurant inside the old casino has been awarded a Michelin star. The best choice here is the sampling menu, with small portions of five different courses plus two desserts.

Pedro I de Aragón €€ *Avda del Parque 34; tel: 974 220300; fax: 974 220094; email: reserve@gargallo-hotels.com; www.gargallo-hotels.com*. This large, modern hotel overlooks a shady park, a short walk from the centre of town.

Sancho Abarca €€ *Plaza de Lizana 13; tel: 974 220650; fax: 974 225169; www.sanchoabarca.com*. Smart hotel centrally situated on a small square beneath the old part of town. The restaurant, **Puerta de Remian**, serves traditional cooking as well as dishes with a modern twist, such as carpaccio of ostrich or cod with roasted vegetables.

JACA

ⓘ *Plaza de San Pedro 11; tel: 974 360098; www.aytojaca.es*

ⓗ **Catedral** *Open daily 1130–1330, 1600–2000. Free.*

Museo Diocesano € *Tel: 974 356378. Closed for restoration works.*

ⓨ **Casa Fau** on the cathedral square is a lively bar with a great selection of *tapas*.

There are several good restaurants on or around Plaza del Marqués de la Cadena, a pretty square with a fountain and a tall stone tower. Try **Mesón Cobarcho** for rustic grills, **El Portón** for regional cuisine and **La Fontana** for pizzas.

For a small town of 14,000 souls, Jaca has a big-town feel, as befitting a former capital and a major Pyrenean resort. Its narrow streets are filled with restaurants and bars, popular with a young crowd who flock to the winter sports centres at Canfranc, Astún and Candanchú. In medieval times this was a staging post on the road to Santiago, where pilgrims would rest after their long trek over the Somport pass; these days the visitors are more likely to be French day-trippers using a less arduous form of transport.

The key date in Jaca's history is 795, when the town was captured from the Moors after a fierce battle in which local women played a prominent part. The event is recalled with mock all-female battles at Jaca's big festival each May. Later, in 1035, Ramiro I made Jaca the first capital of Aragón, a position it held for some 60 years before the centre of power gradually shifted southwards, first to Huesca and then to Zaragoza.

Pilgrims arriving from France brought ideas about art and architecture, and the **Catedral**, begun in 1040, was one of the first Romanesque churches in Spain. The cathedral saw the introduction of the classic three-aisled basilica, with a transept and three semicircular apses. It has been much embellished over the years, at times in dubious taste, but traces of the original church remain, especially in the carvings over the south portal. The **Museo Diocesano**, situated in the cloisters, has a fine collection of Romanesque and Gothic art, including a number of frescoes recovered from Pyrenean village churches.

The other sight in Jaca is the **Ciudadela**, a perfectly preserved 16th-century pentagonal fortress and moat. Inside the courtyard, which is framed by an impressive variety of arches, there is a small 17th-century Baroque church.

Left
Huesca's San Pedro el Viejo

Accommodation and food in Jaca

Conde Aznar € *Paseo de la Constitución 3; tel: 974 361050; fax: 974 360797; www.condeaznar.com.* On the edge of a pretty park square, this hotel makes a good choice in the centre of town.

La Cocina Aragonesa €€ *Calle Cervantes 5; tel: 974 361050; email: conde-aznar@condeaznar.com; www.condeaznar.com.* The restaurant of the Conde Aznar hotel, reached by a separate entrance, has developed an excellent reputation for its upmarket, modern regional cuisine.

La Fragua €€ *Calle Gil Berges 4; tel: 974 360618.* At this carnivores' paradise in the backstreets of town, you sit on low stools eating huge platefuls of meat, grilled over an open fire as you watch.

Oroel €€ *Avda de Francia 37; tel: 974 362411; fax: 974 363804; email: oroel@inturmark.es; www.inturmark.es.* This large, modern aparthotel to the north of town has apartments with balconies and facilities including a swimming pool.

The fiesta of **Las Tiendas**, commemorating the victory over the Moors, is held on the first Friday in May.

In odd-numbered years Jaca plays host to a Pyrenean folklore festival during the first week of August.

MONASTERIO DE SAN JUAN DE LA PEÑA

Monasterio de San Juan de la Peña €
Tel: 974 355119; www.monasteriosanjuan.com. Times vary throughout the year. Check the website.

Below
San Juan de la Peña

A twisting mountain road leads to this monastery church, spectacularly situated beneath an overhanging rock. During the Muslim era the church became a symbol of the continued existence of Christianity in the region, and it has since assumed a special significance as the spiritual home of the Aragonese Reconquest. Medieval pilgrims would stop off here, hoping for a glimpse of the Holy Grail, a Roman chalice said to have been hidden in the monastery and now on display in Valencia cathedral.

There are three distinct parts to the monastery. The lower church, later used as a crypt, was built in the 10th century in Mozarabic style, the style adopted by Christians living under Moorish rule. It features the horseshoe arches typical of the period, as well as a pair of aisles with apses hollowed out of the rock. A few traces of Romanesque wall painting are visible. The upper church, built in the 11th century, has a single aisle with the rock face acting as a roof. This was where the Latin Mass was first introduced to Spain by Cluniac monks in 1071. Alongside the church is the royal pantheon, containing the tombs of the early Aragonese kings. Most impressive of all are the 12th-century cloisters, or at least

those two galleries that remain, with richly carved capitals by the Maestro of San Juan de la Peña (the master stonemason who worked on the capitals and was subsequently given this epithet). The monastery was abandoned in 1837 and only recently restored.

PARQUE NACIONAL DE ORDESA

ℹ *Avda de Ordesa, Torla;*
tel: 974 486472;
www.ordesa.net. There is
also an information centre
just inside the park. The
park is open all year, but
conditions are best for
walking between April and
October. From October
to June it is possible to
take your car into the
park. Between July and
September, and in Holy
Week, a bus service
operates from Torla.

The Ordesa valley was declared a national park in 1918 and the park was expanded in 1982 to include Monte Perdido, the third highest peak in the Pyrenees. It now forms a continuous link with the Parc National des Pyrénées on the French side of the border, creating a sizeable area where Pyrenean flora and fauna are protected. Within the park you can find all the most dramatic elements of Aragón's mountain scenery, from pine and beech woods on the lower slopes to limestone cliffs, canyons and crystal streams. Bearded vultures and golden eagles can be seen flying above the cliffs, and you may spot chamois, red deer and the rare Pyrenean ibex.

The easiest approach is through **Torla**, a solid stone village with good tourist facilities. You can walk into the park from here in two to three hours, or take your car as far as the car park inside the park gates (*see information panel*). From the car park, there are several well-marked trails for walkers of all abilities. One of the best is the **Circo de Soaso**, passing waterfalls and gorges on a circuit of the valley, which should only be attempted by experienced walkers in proper boots. Take plenty of food and water and allow at least 6–7 hours. An easier walk is to follow the course of the River Arazas down to the valley floor.

The park can also be entered from near Nerín (off the Sarvise to Escalona road), with a walk along the steep-sided Añisclo gorge, or from Bielsa, following the Pineta valley to the foot of Monte Perdido.

Accommodation and food in Parque Nacional de Ordesa

Edelweiss € *Avda de Ordesa 1, Torla; tel: 974 486173; fax: 974 486372; email: hoteledelweiss@ordesa.com.* This traditional mountain refuge has been in the same family for generations. The restaurant serves hearty Pyrenean cuisine.

Ordesa €€ *Ctra de Ordesa; tel: 974 486125; fax: 974 486381; www.hotelordesa.com.* Swimming, tennis and mountain views are all on offer at this two-star hotel on the outskirts of Torla on the road towards the park.

Parador de Bielsa €€ *Valle de Pineta; tel: 974 501011; fax: 974 501188; www.parador.es.* Set in a wooded valley just outside the park boundary, this attractive modern *parador* features stunning views and excellent mountain cuisine.

Pyrenean wildlife

The Pyrenees provide a refuge for several species of mammals, including chamois, red deer, wild boar, marmots and otters. The Ordesa valley is the last remaining habitat of the endangered Pyrenean ibex, a species of wild goat which is rarely seen. Even rarer are the sightings of brown bear, a handful of which survive. Inside the national parks, bearded vultures and golden eagles fly overhead, the mountain streams are full of trout, and the cliffs are carpeted with orchids, gentian and edelweiss in summer.

Suggested tour

Total distance: 186km. The detour to San Juan de la Peña adds 30km.

Time: Allow 3–4 hours, plus at least an hour for the detour.

Links: From Sabiñánigo the trans-Pyrenean N260 winds its way across spectacular mountain scenery, eventually meeting up with the Catalan Pyrenees route (*see pages 139–41*) at Pont de Suert. This is a marvellous drive, but you need to allow at least a day to cover the 200km distance.

Leave **HUESCA ❶** on the A132, following signs for Ayerbe across an enormous plain. After 15km you reach **Esquedas**; turn right just beyond a petrol station to begin the climb into the mountains. It is worth a brief stop at **Bolea** to admire the 16th-century collegiate church, whose beautifully preserved altarpiece, by an unknown artist, is one of the gems of Spanish Renaissance art. Continue until you see the side turning to **CASTILLO DE LOARRE ❷**, reached by a tortuous climb.

Return from the castle to the main road and drive through the pretty village of **Loarre** before heading through the orchards to **AYERBE ❸**. Turn right here to rejoin the A132. Before long you get your first glimpse of the *mallos*, a series of tall, pink, sugarloaf crags which completely dwarf the village of **Riglos** on your right. For a close-up view, follow the signs to 'Mallos de Riglos', though the vistas are almost as spectacular from the main road. Another option is to take the side turn to your left, where a brief detour of 5km each way leads to **Agüero**, a dramatically sited hilltop village with a backdrop of *mallos*. Ask at the parish church for the key to the **Iglesia de Santiago**, a Romanesque chapel just outside the village.

The A132 now follows the River Gallego and crosses La Peña reservoir, then widens as it travels through the pine woods of the Sierra de la Peña before climbing to a high pass, Puerto de Santa Barbara, for your first views of the high Pyrenees. The road now drops to **Puente la Reina de Jaca**, a staging post on the pilgrim route to Santiago. The town is reached by a narrow bridge to the left; instead, turn right on the N240 and follow this flat road to **JACA ❹**.

Detour: Between Puente la Reina and Jaca, a side turn to the right leads to **Santa Cruz de la Serós**, with its 11th-century monastery church. The road now narrows as it curves up the mountainside towards **MONASTERIO DE SAN JUAN DE LA PEÑA ❺**. Higher up through the woods, you reach another monastery, built in the 17th century. This is a popular picnic spot, with several nearby trails. The road now drops gradually to **Bernués**, where you turn left to climb over the Oroel pass and return to the main route at Jaca.

From Jaca the A23 skirts the industrial town of **Sabiñánigo** before returning over the mountains to Huesca. This is a good, fast road but very scenic, with views over the Arguis reservoir and from the **Puerto de Monrepós** pass (1,260m).

Also by using this road, the **PARQUE NACIONAL DE ORDESA** ❻ can be reached by turning left off the N330 between Jaca and Sabiñánigo.

Also worth exploring

From Puente la Reina de Jaca you could make a round trip (about 80km in total) through the Ansó and Hecho valleys, remote areas which have preserved much of their traditional way of life. The houses are built of slate and stone, the economy is based on sheep and locals speak the ancient language of Aragonese. Just north of Hecho, the village of Siresa contains an 11th-century Romanesque monastery.

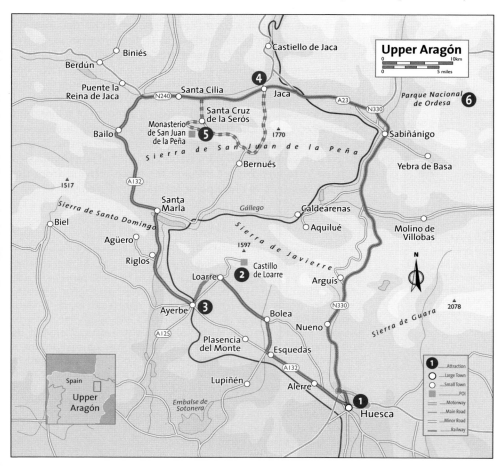

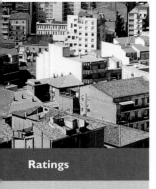

Lleida and the Serra del Montsec

Ratings

Scenery	●●●●○
Churches	●●●○○
Food	●●●○○
Historical sights	●●●○○
Mountains	●●●○○
Towns/ villages	●●●○○
Wine	●●●○○
Children	●●○○○

The largest and least populated of Catalonia's four provinces is also the least known to outsiders – perhaps because it is the only one without a coast. Yet Lleida, which borders Aragón in the west and stretches northwards to the Pyrenees, is central to an understanding of Catalan history. Carthaginians, Romans, Visigoths and Moors have all subdued the province, which has long been at the front line of resistance to invaders. Some would say that this historic role continues today. The south of the province, around the capital Lleida, is a region of plains, hills and market towns, cut through by three rivers which originate in the mountains and come together to form the Segre. Although it contains few unmissable sights, this region makes a pleasant introduction to Catalonia for those arriving from the west and serves as an entry point for the high Pyrenees.

BALAGUER

ℹ *Plaça Mercadal 1;*
tel: 973 446606;
www.balaguer.net; email:
lafira@balaguer.net

The capital of the Noguera county was founded in the 9th century under Muslim rule and later served as the seat of the Counts of Urgell, whose ruined castle still dominates the town. The town is neatly divided in two by the River Segre. On the right bank is the modern town centre, with most of the restaurants and shops but little of historical interest apart from the Gothic cloister of the **Convent de Sant Domènec**; on the left bank is the old town, centred around a huge arcaded market square. This square, the largest of its kind in Catalonia, is a direct result of the expulsion of the Jews from the town centre in 1333, clearing the way for a large open space. The cafés around the square make a good vantage point for observing the everyday activity of the town, especially on market day.

North of the square, a warren of narrow streets leads to Carrer de l'Escala, where you can climb the steps to reach the Gothic **Esglesia de Santa María**. This church, begun in the 14th century, has a single

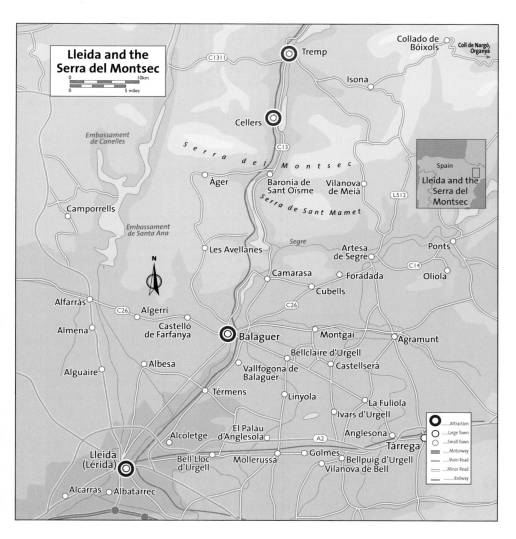

Lleida and the
Serra del Montsec

0   10km
0   5 miles

Tremp

Collado de
Bóixols

Coll de Nargó,
Organyà

Isona

Embassament
de Canelles

Cellers

Serra   del   Montsec

Spain

Lleida and the
Serra del
Montsec

Àger

Baronia de
Sant Oisme

Vilanova
de Meià

Serra de Sant Mamet

Camporrells

Embassament
de Santa Ana

Les Avellanes

Segre

Artesa
de Segre

Ponts

Camarasa

Foradada

Oliola

Cubells

Alfarràs

Algerri

Almena

Castelló
de Farfanya

Balaguer

Montgai

Agramunt

Albesa

Bellclaire d'Urgell

Vallfogona de
Balaguer

Castellserà

Alguaire

Térmens

Linyola

La Fuliola

Ivars d'Urgell

El Palau
d'Anglesola

Anglesona

Alcoletge

Tàrrega

Golmes

Lleida
(Lérida)

Bell'Lloc
d'Urgell

Mòllerussa

Bellpuig d'Urgell
Vilanova de Bell

Alcarràs   Albatarrec

○ ──Attraction
○ ──Large Town
○ ──Small Town
── ──Motorway
── ──Main Road
── ──Minor Road
── ──Railway

**Museo de la
Noguera** € *Plaça
dels Comptes d'Urgell 5.
Open Tue–Sat 1100–1400,
1830–2030, Sun
1100–1400.*

A market is held in
Plaça Mercadal on
Saturday mornings.

nave and a collection of Catalan religious art, including reproductions
of a number of famous statues of the Virgin Mary. From the church
terrace there are splendid views over the town, with the Pyrenees in
the distance. It is possible to walk down from here on to a section of
the medieval walls.

The **Museo de la Noguera**, just off the market square, tells the
history of Balaguer from its Islamic origins to the Catalan conquest.
Unfortunately the captions are in Catalan only.

Accommodation and food in Balaguer

Balaguer € *Carrer La Banqueta 7; tel: 973 445326*. This modest one-star hotel is marginally the best of the three establishments on both sides of the river. It is situated close to the market square.

La Barretina € *Estació 57; tel: 973 448405*. Good place to stop for a quick bite or afternoon meal.

Sapore € *Calle Pare Sanahuja 8; tel: 973 450508*. Prettily situated next to the river, this restaurant is famed for its rice dishes, particularly the *arroz con bogavente* (lobster with rice).

CELLERS

This tiny village overlooks a large man-made lake just north of the spectacular Terradets gorge, with the mountains of the Montsec range acting as a dramatic backdrop. A worthwhile excursion from here is to the nearby village of **Guardia de Noguera**, with its 10th-century castle and 11th-century collegiate church.

Accommodation and food in Cellers

Els Terradets €€ *Ctra C13; tel: 973 651120; fax: 973 651304; www.hotelterradets.com*. This lakeside hotel would make a good location for a relaxing break in the mountains. There is a swimming pool, tennis courts and the opportunity for mountain walks. The restaurant serves hearty Catalan cuisine, such as roast lamb and pigs' trotters in their own juice.

LLEIDA

ℹ *Carrer Major 31; tel: 902 250050; www.lleidatur.com*

🅿 The car park beneath Avda de Madrid is well placed for exploring the old town. If you don't fancy the climb, you can drive most of the way up to the Seu Vella, though parking is very limited.

Opposite
Lleida

Catalonia's second city, at the heart of the Segre plain, has been called the 'gateway to Aragón'. The city has been besieged at least nine times in its history. Pompey and Caesar fought a battle at Lleida, and it was here that the founder of Catalonia, Wilfred the Hairy, met his death at the hands of the Moors.

Like the province that takes its name, Lleida (Lérida in Castilian) has little immediate appeal, especially when compared with the more obvious attractions of Barcelona, Girona and Tarragona. The outskirts are sprawling and industrial, the shabby streets have a rough edge at times, but stay a while and you will find that Lleida has its rewards. The best place to start is **Catedral Vieja de Lleida**, built on high ground in the 13th century beside the 9th-century Arab citadel. Parts of the Moorish fortress still survive, though it has been severely damaged numerous times, most recently by Napoleon's troops in 1812

Catedral Vieja de Lleida € *Seu Vella; tel: 973 230653. Open Oct–May Tue–Sat 1000–1330, 1500–1730, Sun 1000–1330; Jun–Sept Tue–Sun 1000–1330, 1600–1930. Tue free.*

Museo Diocesano € *In the Church of Sant Martí and Palau Episcol, Carrer Sant Martí; tel: 973 273230. Closed for restoration works.*

Museu d'Art Jaume Morera € *Carrer Major 31. Open Tue–Sat 1100–1400, 1700–2000, Sun 1100–1400. Free.*

Museu de Lleida € *Carrer de Sant Crist 1. Open Tue–Sat 1000–2000, Sun 1000–1900.*

and again during the Civil War. The cathedral, too, is in a poor state of repair, having been used as a barracks, though restoration is slowly taking place. The highlight is the 14th-century Gothic cloister, whose south-facing gallery, with arches on both sides, offers sweeping views over the plain. You can climb the 238 steps of the bell tower for even better views. Make sure to walk around the outside of the church to admire the Romanesque carvings on the doorways.

Steps lead down to the 12th-century church of Sant Martí, where an annexe exhibits the treasures of the **Museo Diocesano**. From here it is a short walk to the Casc Antic, the oldest part of town, where tenement flats are crowded with migrant workers. Two interesting sights in this area are **Esglesia de Sant Llorenç**, a late Romanesque church with Gothic *retablos*, and the **Museu d'Art Jaume Morera**, which features 19th- and 20th-century Catalan art inside a former convent. At the foot of the old town is the **Seu Nova** or new cathedral, built in the 18th century in neoclassical style. Look out for the Modernista altarpiece by Gaudí's student Joan Bergós, and for the 'Virgin of the Bruise', so named after a master craftsman took a hammer to her head. Just south of here is the **Museu de Lleida**, a new archaeological and historical museum. It has a comprehensive, well-documented collection that dates from the Stone Age up to the 19th century.

A local speciality is *coca de recapte*, a kind of pizza base topped with tuna, salt cod or Catalan sausages. You can find it at festival time or throughout the year at many bakeries in the town.

Look out for **Raïmat** wine from the local vineyards. The Chardonnay-based *cava* from here is particularly good.

The central market is situated beside the river on Avda Tortosa. A flea market takes place on Rambla de Ferran on Sunday mornings.

Lleida's **Festa Major**, held on 11 May, features a parade of monsters and giants as well as a feast in which snails are roasted on embers and served up in the street.

From here, Carrer Major, once the city's main thoroughfare, leads past the 13th-century town hall and the only surviving medieval gateway to reach Plaça Sant Joan, a large modern square where escalators climb back up towards the hilltop citadel. Alternatively, you can head down to the river, where wide avenues and busy promenades give a clue to just how much Lleida has grown.

Accommodation and food in Lleida

Casa Lluis €€ *Plaça de Ramón Berenguer IV 9; tel: 973 240026.* House specialities include Catalan favourites like *fideua*, a noodle-based paella.

El Celler del Roser €€ *Carrer dels Cavallers 24; tel: 973 239070.* Snails and *bacalau* (cod) are the specialities at this popular restaurant which fills up with locals at weekends.

Condes de Urgel €€ *Avda Barcelona 17; tel: 973 202300; fax: 973 202404; email: reservas@hcondes.com; www.hcondes.com.* It may not have much character, but this modern high-rise hotel, located across the river on the road to Barcelona, makes a good, comfortable choice for a one-night stay.

Hotel Real €€ *Avinguda de Blondel 22; tel: 973 239405; www.hotelreallleida.com.* A comfortable, modern hotel with excellent facilities, including Wi-Fi in all rooms. There's also a good restaurant serving typical local cuisine.

Forn del Nastasi €€€ *Ctra Huesca km2.5; tel: 973 249222; fax: 973 247692.* A modern hotel and restaurant with a spa, massage and reflexology services. The restaurant serves gastronomic regional cuisine – try the chargrilled vegetables or the oven-baked snails. The same owners have developed a successful chain of local restaurants, trading on the Nastasi name and including everything from a 'tapas bus' to a large banqueting hall on the outskirts of the city.

El Petit Català €€€ *Cami Vell al Picat; tel: 973 736405; www.petitcatala.com.* Chef Salvador Alari opened this large, modern space as a vehicle for his inventive Catalan cuisine. Come here for the mahogany décor, attentive service and highly personal style of cooking.

TREMP

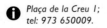
Plaça de la Creu 1; tel: 973 650009.

A market is held on Monday mornings.

The capital of the Pallars Jussà district, set in a huge basin, is primarily of interest as a gateway to the high Pyrenees. To many it is best known for its hydroelectric dam, whose celebrated Canadian engineer has been honoured with an attractive promenade, Rambla Dr Pearson. With its plane trees and outdoor cafés, this is definitely the best place to take an early-evening *paseo*. The old part of town has been well preserved, with three of the original defensive towers still standing.

Also of interest is the **Basílica de la Mare de Déu de Valldeflors**, where an image of the Virgin is venerated. The original church was destroyed in a fire and rebuilt in Baroque style in 1701; this in turn was badly damaged during the Civil War, and the present statue and altarpiece are copies. The eclectic range of styles continues with a Modernist iron sculpture over the portal. The organ was restored in the early 20th century by the aforementioned Dr Pearson.

Accommodation and food in Tremp

Alegret € *Plaça de la Creu 30; tel: 973 650100; fax: 973 651728.* If you don't mind not having a pool, this modern hotel makes a comfortable base right in the centre of town.

Segle XX € *Plaça de la Creu 8; tel: 973 650000; fax: 973 652612; www.hotelseglexx.info.* The best place in town for an overnight stop, with a swimming pool and a busy restaurant featuring Catalan mountain cuisine.

Right
Santa Eulalia church in Lleida

Suggested tour

Total distance: 140km. The detour adds around 8km.

Time: Allow at least 2½ hours, or 3 hours if taking the detour.

Links: From Tremp you could continue north for 15km on the C13 to join the Catalan Pyrenees route (*see pages 138–41*) at La Pobla de Segur.

Start at **BALAGUER** ❶ and follow signs for the C13 towards Tremp, travelling high above the Noguera Pallisera river with dramatic views over the river and its reservoirs.

Detour: For a slower, scenic diversion, leave Balaguer on the C12, passing between the Formós castle and the church of Sant Crist. You need to look carefully for this road, which begins beside a bridge at the end of the attractive riverside arcades. The road climbs slowly into the sierra, bypassing **Os de Balaguer** on its way to the huge abbey at **Bellpuig de les Avellanes**. Most of the monastery buildings are of recent origin but parts of the 12th-century cloister and an unfinished Gothic church remain. This is a peaceful spot with a shady picnic area and vineyards on the surrounding slopes. The road, which has been fast to this point, now deteriorates, climbing to the Àger pass from where the great bulk of the Serra del Montsec looms up like an impenetrable fortress. It then drops to the pretty village of **Àger** ❷, a popular hiking and climbing centre set in a peaceful valley and crowned by the ruins of an 11th-century church. After another 10km the road rejoins the C13 for the trip along the Noguera Pallisera.

The two routes come together near an 11th-century castle, **Baronia de Sant Oïsme**. Next comes the scenic highlight of the trip, as the road travels through the steep-sided **Pas dels Terradets** gorge on its way to **CELLERS** ❸. The road now follows the river as far as **TREMP** ❹, where you turn right at the roundabout to reach the village of **Isona** ❺, with Roman walls and a Romanesque church. Bear right out of the village as the road climbs through green fields high into the Montsec mountains, crossing a pass at 1,100m before dropping down to the plain at **Artesa del Segre** ❻, the commercial and industrial capital of the region and the centre of production for Costers del Segre wines. It is worth a brief stop here to wander around the old quarter, with its small, arcaded, triangular main 'square'. From Artesa del Segre the C26 crosses the fertile Segre plain, passing the villages of **Foradada** and **Cubells** on its way to Balaguer.

Also worth exploring

From Isona you could take the L511 over the **Collado de Bóixols**, a tremendously scenic road which looks down over a series of canyons from slopes covered in pine and holm oak. The road eventually reaches **Coll de Nargó**, a pretty mountain village with an 11th-century Romanesque church.

Just north of Coll de Nargó, in the village of **Organyà**, the oldest written text in Catalan (dating from the 12th century) is kept in a small building in the main square. The trip from Isona to Organyà is 48km each way, but you need to allow plenty of time.

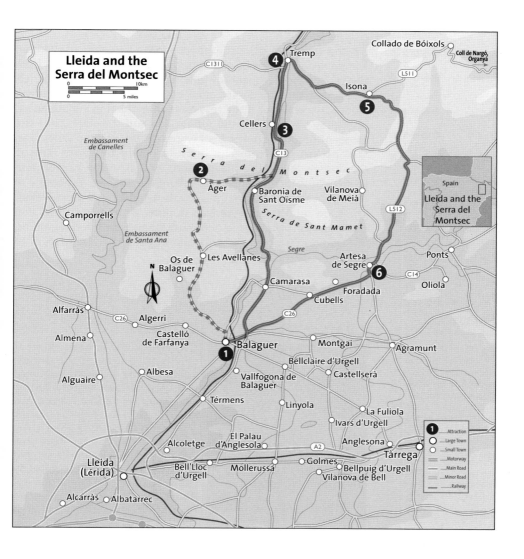

The Catalan Pyrenees

Ratings

Churches	●●●●●
Mountains	●●●●●
Outdoor activities	●●●●●
Scenery	●●●●●
Walking	●●●●●
Food	●●●●○
Nature	●●●●○
Children	●●●○○

In the far north of Lleida province, the Pyrenees rise like an impenetrable barrier, separating the Iberian peninsula from the rest of the European continent. Modern roads and tunnels mean that this region can now be reached in just four hours from Barcelona, but it still retains a sense of being a place apart. Men may have tamed the mountains and the rivers, but the forces of nature have the final word and the isolated valleys can still be cut off from the outside world by snow. This is Catalonia's adventure playground, with skiing in winter, and white-water rafting and fine walking in summer, especially in the Aigüestortes national park with its numerous alpine lakes. The food reflects the Pyrenean climate, with hearty stews and heavy use of trout, game and mushrooms from the mountains. This region also contains Catalonia's greatest concentration of Romanesque churches.

ESPOT

ⓘ There is a national park information office on the main street leading into the village. *Casa del Parc, Prat del Guarda 4; tel: 973 624036; email: info.aiguestortes@ oapn.mma.es*

⊙ Jeep taxis from Espot to Lake Sant Maurici are available daily 0900–1800 (0800–1900 in summer). *www.taxisespot.com*

Right
Espot

This picturesque farming village is chiefly of interest as the eastern gateway to the Aigüestortes national park. A river cascades through the village, passing under a Romanesque bridge and dividing Espot in two.

During the Civil War, the Nationalists lived on the right bank and the Republicans on the left, but these days the villagers are united by the success of outdoors tourism. Above the village, a narrow road leads to the downhill ski station at Super Espot.

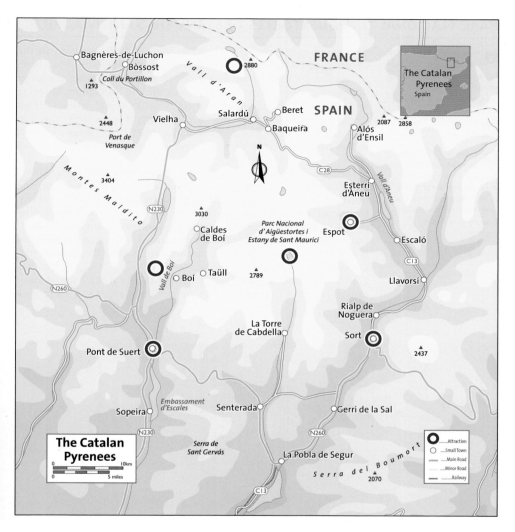

The Catalan Pyrenees

Accommodation and food in Espot

Ju Quim € *Plaça Sant Martí; tel: 973 624009.* For good-value Pyrenean cooking, it's hard to beat a wild boar casserole and a jug of red wine at this restaurant in the village square.

Saurat €€ *Plaça Sant Martí; tel: 973 624162; www.hotelsaurat.com.* This rustic mountain hotel has a wood-beamed dining room and log fires in the lounge in winter. The restaurant serves filling Pyrenean soups as well as river trout, civets of chamois and wild boar.

Parc Nacional d'Aigüestortes i Estany de Sant Maurici

ⓘ The park information offices are at Vall de Boí and Espot (*see separate entries*). From June to September, there are also information kiosks at Aigüestortes and Lake Sant Maurici.

Ⓟ From Boí and Espot, you can take a car to the park boundary. The walks from the car parks to Aigüestortes and Lake Sant Maurici take around 2 hours and 1 hour respectively.

Catalonia's only national park, established in 1955, contains all the elements of the most spectacular Pyrenean scenery. The peaks here, rising close to 3,000m, are forged out of granite and slate; the lower slopes are covered in beech, silver birch, fir and Scots pine. In spring and summer the meadows and river banks come alive with an abundance of wild flowers. Above all, though, it is the water that you notice. The Catalan name of the park, *aigües tortes*, means 'twisted waters' and everywhere there are rivers, streams, waterfalls, lakes and tarns.

The brown bears that once prowled these slopes have been hunted to extinction; some say that Franco created the park as his private hunting ground. Large numbers of Pyrenean chamois remain, frustratingly out of sight on the high slopes in summer but taking refuge on the lower ground in winter. Birds include golden eagles, capercaillie and a small population of bearded vultures, while the park is also home to the rare Pyrenean desman, a mole-like animal that lives in holes on the river banks.

There are two main approaches to the park, from the Boí and Espot valleys. In either case, private cars are forbidden and you need to walk

Jeep taxis leave the ranks at Boí and Espot 0900–1800 (0800–1900 in summer). The last taxi back is usually at 1900, but it is essential to check. The taxis only leave if they have a minimum number of passengers, which can be a problem for single travellers. *Tel: 973 624105.*

The nearest hotel and campsite accommodation is in Boí, Taüll and Espot. The national park maintains a network of basic shelters, with bunks and blankets available, which are staffed by wardens in summer.

Below
Parc Nacional d'Aigüestortes

or take a Jeep taxi from the nearest village, or park your car outside the park entrance. From Boí, the taxis stop at the spring of **Aigüestortes**, from where a popular walk is the gradual climb to Estany Llong, taking around 1½ hours each way.

From Espot, the jeep taxis will drop you at **Estany de Sant Maurici**, a magnificent glacial lake overlooked by the twin peaks of Els Encantats. According to local folklore, the peaks represent a pair of petrified hunters, turned into stone as a punishment for shooting chamois. Try to ignore the hydroelectric dam along one side of the lake, a project begun when the park was still under private ownership and completed after the national park was created.

A choice of paths fans out from around the lake. You can walk back down to Espot, a gentle descent of around 1½ hours along a river valley; you can climb up to a second lake at Ratera in an hour; or you can follow the signs to make a complete circuit of Sant Maurici. A tougher climb leads to the Agulles d'Amitges, the so-called 'needle' peaks. Serious climbers can also tackle Gran Encantat, the higher of the 'enchanted mountains'. If you have a couple of days to spare, it is possible to make a complete traverse of the park in summer, following a track across the pass of Portarró d'Espot. From Sant Maurici to Aigüestortes, the walk takes five to six hours; remember to allow enough time for your taxi, or you will have to walk down into Boí or Espot.

The park is open all year, but heavy snowfall often makes walking difficult and the lakes are frozen over in winter. Whenever you go, take warm clothes, food, water and sun protection. Weather conditions in the mountains can change rapidly; it is entirely possible that you will be sitting on a sunny café terrace in Espot while a blizzard is raging up in the hills.

PONT DE SUERT

ℹ️ *Calle Victoriano Muñoz 33; tel: 973 690640; www.elpontdesuert.com*

The capital of the Alta Ribagorça district lies on the Noguera Ribagorçana river at the junction of several valleys. The old quarter here is full of charm, with stone arches sheltering beneath Baroque palaces along the narrow Carrer Major. In stark contrast, the parish church, built in 1965, is a strikingly modern structure with a side chapel which from the outside resembles a giant egg.

Accommodation in Pont de Suert

Can Mestre € *Plaça Major 8; tel: 973 690306; fax: 973 690514; email: hotelmestre@terra.es.* This simple hotel is in a delightful setting, with flower-filled balconies overlooking the small main square.

SORT

ℹ️ *Cami de la Cabanera; tel: 973 621002; email: turisme@ pallarssobira.info*

🔘 A market is held on Tuesday mornings.

🔘 An international canoeing regatta takes place in Sort on the third weekend in July.

Although it contains the ruined 11th-century castle of the Counts of Pallars, this busy market town and dairy centre is better known these days as a base for adventure sports. Horse riding, hang-gliding and mountain biking are all available in the area, but the big attraction is canoeing and rafting on the River Noguera Pallaresa. During the rafting season, from April to August, several outfits in Sort and the nearby villages of Rialp and Llavorsí compete to offer the biggest adrenalin rush. River-rafting is incredibly thrilling, but potentially dangerous; if you decide to join in, it is essential to wear a buoyancy jacket and helmet and to follow the safety advice.

Accommodation in Sort

Condes del Pallars €€ *Avda Flora Cadena 2, Rialp; tel: 973 620350; fax: 973 621232; www.marvelhotels.com.* This huge riverside hotel in Rialp is firmly aimed at families on active holidays, with a heated pool, a sauna and gymnasium, tennis, mini-golf and activities for children.

Pessets II €€ *Diputació 3; tel: 973 620000; fax: 973 620819; email: info@hotelpessets.com; www.hotelpessets.com.* Overlooking the river, this large three-star hotel has a pool and tennis courts in its gardens.

VALL D'ARAN

ℹ *Carrer Sarriulera 10, Vielha;*
tel: 973 640110;
www.lavalldaran.com

ℹ **Museu de la Vall d'Aran** € *Carrer Major 26, Vielha; tel: 973 641815. Open Tue–Sat 1000–1300, 1700–2000, Sun 1000–1300.*

◔ A market takes place in Vielha on Thursdays.

◔ A walk of around 5km from Beret follows the headwaters of the Noguera Pallaresa to the abandoned village of Montgarri and the shrine of **Nuestra Senyora de Montgarri**. This is the scene of a mass *romería* ('pilgrimage') on 2 July each year.

Among the many traditional festivals which take place in the area, the biggest are on 3 May at Salardú, 24 June at Arties, 8–9 September at Vielha and 20 October at Bossòst.

The only north-facing valley in the Catalan Pyrenees is a historical and geographical anomaly; by any sense of logic it should really be in France. The fact that the Vall d'Aran is on the French side of the Pyrenean watershed accounts for both its Atlantic climate and its legendary greenness. This is a bucolic landscape, of lush, flower-filled meadows watered by the Garona (the French River Garonne, which rises here in Spain) and shady slopes hemmed in by towering mountain peaks.

Although the Vall d'Aran has belonged to Catalonia since the 12th century, until recently it remained largely cut off from the outside world. Access was only possible via the Bonaigua pass or the Coll de Portillón from France, and then only in summer. The boring of the Vielha tunnel in 1948 changed all that, opening up the area to tourist development and specifically the creation of ski resorts. The royal family now take their skiing holidays in **Baqueira Beret**, one of the few Spanish resorts with a reliable amount of snow.

In two generations, this area has gone from being one of the poorest parts of Catalonia to one of the richest. Despite the changes, Aran retains its distinctive culture, seen most notably in the language. The inhabitants speak Aranese, a dialect of Gascon which shares certain features with Catalan. In **Vielha**, the main town of the valley and the capital of Mijaran ('Middle Valley'), the **Museu de la Vall d'Aran** features local costumes and displays on the area's history, geology and language. Vielha is also a good place for picking up picnic provisions, with shops around the church square selling wild boar sausages, Pyrenean sheep's cheese and other local treats. Apart from this, Vielha serves mainly as a jumping-off point for wilder pastures. The parish church contains a 12th-century polychrome head and shoulders of Christ, rescued from a local monastery after it was destroyed during the Civil War, when Aran was a Republican stronghold.

Along the Garona in Nautaran ('Upper Valley') are several pretty villages with slate and granite cottages and fine Romanesque churches. It is worth stopping at **Salardú** to see the 13th-century church of Sant Andreu with its original carved wooden crucifix. Like most of the villages around here, Salardú has retained much of its charm but tourism is creating inevitable pressures. To see Aran as it was, you need to get off the main roads. One option is to head north from Vielha, following the Garona towards France and leaving the main road to climb to the sturdy stone villages of Aubert, Vila and Arròs. Beyond here you could continue to **Bossòst**, the capital of Baixaran ('Lower Valley'), with a 12th-century Romanesque church and a number of French-style restaurants designed to appeal to the day-trippers from across the border.

Accommodation and food in Vall d'Aran

Deth Pais € *Plaça de la Pica, Salardú; tel: 973 645836; fax: 973 644500.* Wake to the sound of sheep bells and magnificent mountain views from this charming two-star hotel at the top of an attractive village.

Parador de Arties €€ *Ctra Baqueira Beret, Arties; tel: 973 640801; fax: 973 641001; email: arties@parador.es; www.parador.es.* Built in local style with a grey slate roof, this comfortable *parador* is close to the ski resorts and has good facilities including a sauna and a heated pool.

Parador de Vielha €€ *Ctra del Túnel, Vielha; tel: 973 640100; fax: 973 641100; email: vielha@parador.es; www.parador.es.* This modern *parador* stands on a natural balcony offering unrivalled views over the valley from the circular lounge and the outdoor pool. The restaurant features hearty Pyrenean classics such as jugged wild boar and Aranese stew.

Casa Irene €€€ *Carrer Major 3, Arties; tel: 973 644364; fax: 973 642174; www.hotelcasairene.com.* When King Juan Carlos comes here to ski, he eats in this restaurant, famed for its elegant informality and Michelin-starred cuisine. The menu is heavy on treats such as *foie gras* and truffles, and the specialities include stuffed rabbit and an unusual green tea sorbet. If you don't want to stay in the village *parador*, there are cheaper rooms available in the restaurant's hotel.

The great outdoors

Summer and winter, on land and on water, the Catalan Pyrenees provide unlimited scope for adventure. Activities on offer include rock climbing, canoeing and paragliding as well as the popular local pursuits of hunting and fishing. The ski season lasts from December to April, with the best downhill skiing at Baqueira Beret in the Vall d'Aran; there are also ski stations at Boí-Taüll, Super Espot and Llessui near Sort, though the snow can be less reliable than in France. Cross-country skiing is possible in winter in the Aigüestortes national park. The Noguera Pallaresa is the top Pyrenean river for white-water rafting, and the stretch from Llavorsí to Sort one of the most challenging in Europe, with several terrifying grade 3–4 drops. More conventionally, the Pyrenees offer the finest mountain walking in Europe. The GR11 long-distance path crosses the entire range from Catalonia to the Basque Country, passing through the heart of the Aigüestortes national park.

Right
Pyrenean landscape

VALL DE BOÍ

ⓘ *Passeig de Sant Feliu 43, Barruera; tel: 973 694000; www.vallboi.com.* The tourist office for the entire valley is found on the main road through the village of Barruera.

National park information *Casa del Parc, Carrer de les Graieres 2, Boí. Tel: 973 696189.*

Ⓣ Taxis d'Espot run excursions in 4×4 vehicles into the national park. *www.taxisespot.com*

Ⓗ **Sant Climent de Taüll** *€ Tel: 973 694000. Open daily 1000–2000. The ticket also gives access to Santa María de Taüll.*

The valley which leads to the western end of the Aigüestortes park contains a wealth of Romanesque churches dating from the 12th century. These churches, the finest examples in Catalonia, are distinguished by their slate roofing, vivid frescoes and tall, slender bell towers. In all there are a dozen scattered around the valley, but the most impressive are in the villages of Erill la Vall and Taüll. Most people head straight for **Sant Climent** in Taüll, with its six-storey campanile silhouetted against the mountains. The original frescoes are now on display in the Museu Nacional d'Art de Catalunya in Barcelona (*see page 236*) but the church contains faithful reproductions, including the famous Pantocrator (Christ in Majesty) in the central apse. Other Romanesque paintings and altarpieces are stacked against the walls, creating the feel of an antiques warehouse. A short walk into the village along the cobbled main street leads to the church of **Santa María**, consecrated a day after Sant Climent in 1123. Again the original frescoes are missing, and the most notable feature is the leaning four-storey bell tower.

A footpath descends steeply in 2km from Taüll to **Boí**, the chief access point for the national park. There is another Romanesque church here, and a park information office in the square. Across the valley from Boí, climb up to Erill de Vall to see the church of **Santa**

Santa Eulàlia
The church in Erill la Vall is usually open daily 1000–1400 and 1600–1900.

A number of village houses in the area are part of the *casas de pagès* scheme, offering rooms and breakfast in local farmhouses and cottages. Some of these properties can also be rented by the week. Details are available from the tourist office in Barruera or in the annual guide published by the Catalan government (*Residències-Casa de Pagès*).

A traditional folk dance (the 'Ball Pla') festival takes place in Taüll on the third Sunday in June.

Eulàlia, with its arcaded portal and six-storey bell tower. Although it does not attract the same crowds as Taüll, many people consider this the most beautiful of all the Pyrenean churches.

Caldes de Boí, where the road runs out, is Catalonia's highest spa. Above the valley, and reached through Taüll, is the busy downhill ski resort of Boí-Taüll.

Accommodation and food in Vall de Boí

El Caliu € *Calle Pistes 11, Taüll; tel: 973 696212*. Enjoy Catalan specialities like lamb stew and Caliu cream while admiring views of the Boí Valley.

La Coma € *Avda les Feixes 11, Taüll; tel: 973 696147*. A sturdy, slate-roofed *pension*, open throughout the year, offering Pyrenean cuisine and tremendous mountain views. It is found at the entrance to the village, close to the church of Sant Climent.

Manantial €€ *Caldes de Boí; tel: 973 696210; fax: 973 696220; www.caldesdeboi.com*. This thermal spa resort has a choice of a modern four-star hotel or a simpler inn incorporating a medieval shrine. As well as the health and beauty treatments, the facilities include indoor and outdoor pools, tennis, badminton and volleyball. Open from late June to September.

Fire festivals

The custom of 'running the fires' has its origins in the pagan cult of sun worship. Around the time of the summer solstice, huge beacons are erected on the hillsides; the participants use these beacons to light their *falles* (pine torches), then run down the mountain forming a spectacular river of fire. The *falles* are run on St John's Eve (23 June) in Barruera, Boí and Pont de Suert, and in Erill la Vall and Taüll in July.

Suggested tour

Total distance: 188km. A trip into the Vall de Boí will add another 20km each way.

Time: Although the actual driving time is only around 4 hours, this is a long, testing drive which is best done over a couple of days.

Links: The start of the route at La Pobla de Segur is 15km north of Tremp on the Serra del Montsec route (*see pages 128–9*). From Sort, a switchback road over the Coll del Cantó leads in 52km to the Cerdanya route at La Seu d'Urgell (*see pages 150–51*).

Start in **La Pobla de Segur ❶**, the 'gateway to the Pyrenees'. Before setting off, make sure to check the overhead signs at the roundabout as you enter the town from Tremp to see whether the Bonaigua pass is open. (It is often closed in winter.) If it is open, turn left at the roundabout on to the N260, the trans-Pyrenean route. The road is in variable condition and you have to concentrate hard on the driving. After 25km you climb to the pass of **Perbes**, where cattle graze on the slopes and an isolated hamlet is surrounded by mountains. Continue on this road as it drops down to **PONT DE SUERT ❷**.

Just beyond Pont de Suert, a right turn leads into the **VALL DE BOÍ ❸**, an essential detour for lovers of Romanesque art. Once you have explored the valley, return to the main route and turn right on the N230 towards Vielha. The road crosses into Aragón and enters a dramatic mountain landscape as it passes beneath the Pyrenees' highest peaks, with Aneto, the highest peak of all, visible to your left. If you are expecting wilderness you will be disappointed. The views are spectacular and the peaks are usually covered in snow, but trucks trundle along the highway and pylons stand beside the road, a symbol of how the mountains have been tamed. Until the opening of the **Túnel de Vielha**, this region was inaccessible for much of the year; now you can simply drive through the 5km-long tunnel and emerge to see the **VALL D'ARAN** beneath you.

Below
Fire festival in Correfoc

Drive into **Vielha ❹**, the main town of the valley, and turn right to begin the climb to the Bonaigua pass. The road takes you through the heart of the Vall d'Aran, where a succession of slate-roofed hamlets is each clustered around a Romanesque church. After **Baqueira**, the serious climbing begins as the road twists its way above the tree line and up to Port de la Bonaigua (2,072m). Get out here to breathe the fresh mountain air and gaze over the landscape of snowcapped mountains and glacial cirques.

The drive back down the mountain is a testing succession of hairpin bends and you may decide to give your frayed nerves a rest at the bar-refuge halfway down. Eventually you drop to another beautiful green valley, **Vall d'Àneu**, whose capital is the small town of **Esterri d'Àneu ❺**. Turn right here to follow the course of the Noguera Pallaresa, your constant companion for the rest of the route. Just after the pretty lakeside hamlet of La Guingueta, a side turn leads to **ESPOT ❻**, the entry point

Right
Vall de Boí

Guided tours of the salt beds in Gerri de la Sal are available daily July–August 1100–1400, 1500–1900. The rest of the year, call ahead to arrange a visit (*tel: 973 662040*).

The monastery of Santa María is also open to visitors; call the tourist office (*tel: 973 662040*) for opening hours.

for the **Parc Nacional d'Aigüestortes** and a good place to break your journey for the night.

The main road continues south along the river. In many ways this is the most enjoyable section of the entire route; the road is good and flat, the scenery breathtaking and the driving a lot easier than up in the mountains. Drive through the rafting and canoeing centres of **Llavorsí** and **Rialp** to reach **SORT** ❼, then continue to **Gerri de la Sal**, where ancient salt beds, still in operation, are visible beside the road. It is worth a short stop here to admire the pointed Romanesque bridge. You can cross the bridge and walk along the riverbank to the 11th-century monastery of **Santa María**. Another waymarked walk leads to a sanctuary on the hillside in around 30 minutes.

If you are in La Pobla de Segur on the first Sunday in July, look out for the *raiers*, a river-rafting festival which re-creates the old times by using log rafts once used to carry timber downstream.

Beyond Gerri de la Sal, the river carves a dramatic gorge through tall limestone cliffs, though new road tunnels mean that you are denied the best of the scenery. To enjoy it at more leisure, pull into one of the car parks and picnic areas on either side of the Collegats gorge and take a walk along the old road, now only open to cyclists. The N260 now continues to La Pobla de Segur. Look out for the handsome collection of Modernist buildings, including the town hall and an olive oil mill, seen on your right as you enter the town. At the end of this street is a pleasant square with outdoor cafés – just the place to rest after your long mountain drive.

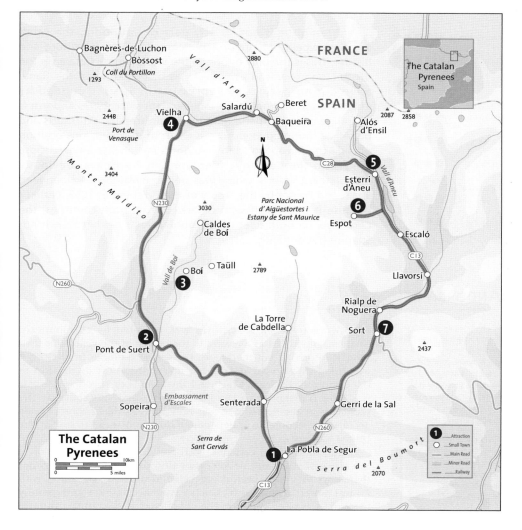

The Catalan Pyrenees

0 ___ 10km
0 ___ 5 miles

Attraction
Small Town
Main Road
Minor Road
Railway

Andorra and the Cerdanya

Although it is not strictly part of Catalonia, the small principality of Andorra is steeped in Catalan culture and history. This is the only nation in the world where Catalan is the official language and as such it has helped to keep the flame alive during periods of repression in Spain. Founded by Charlemagne and only fully independent since 1993, Andorra is a strange mixture of stunning mountain scenery, ski resorts and duty-free shopping emporia – a result of its anomalous position outside the European Union. Andorra has always enjoyed close links with the Cerdanya (Cerdagne in French), a previously independent county which was permanently divided between Spain and France by the Treaty of the Pyrenees in 1659. Perhaps because it finds itself semi-detached from both countries, the Cerdanya, on both sides of the border, feels neither French nor Spanish but defiantly Catalan.

ANDORRA

Entry regulations Make sure that you are carrying your passport and driving licence. Driving into Andorra is usually a formality but you may be subject to a customs check as you leave.

Currency Andorra has never had a currency of its own, but euros are accepted here, even though Andorra is not part of the European Union.

According to legend, Andorra was founded by the Emperor Charlemagne in 784 as a reward to the people of the valleys for their support in driving out the Moors. For several centuries from 1278, it was ruled as a feudal possession under the joint ownership of the Bishops of La Seu d'Urgell and the Counts of Foix – whose role was later transferred to the French kings and subsequently the presidents of the Republic. It was only in 1993 that Andorra finally decided to become an independent state and took its seat at the United Nations.

The portraits of the current French president and the Bishop of La Seu d'Urgell still hang in Andorra's tiny parliament chamber, but these days they have been downgraded to honorary co-princes with no real powers. The 28-seat chamber is housed inside a 16th-century mansion, **Casa de la Vall**, in the old quarter of the capital, **Andorra**

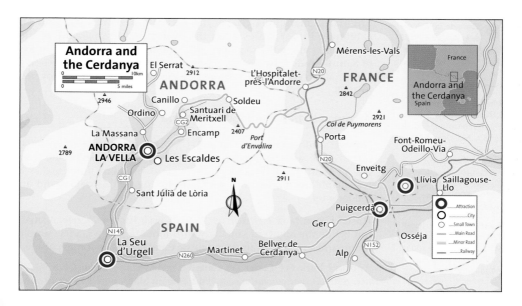

Andorra and the Cerdanya

Telephone When calling Andorra from Spain or elsewhere, all numbers should be preceded by 00 376; to call Spain from Andorra, use the prefix 00 34.

Driving The speed limit in Andorra is 70kph on main roads and 40kph in built-up areas. Petrol is around 25 to 30 per cent cheaper than in neighbouring countries.

P Parking The best bets are the Pyrénées department store on Avda Meritxell and the multistorey car park on Carrer Prat de la Creu.

i The main tourist office is at Plaça de la Rotonda, on the main road through Andorra la Vella (tel: 827117). There is also a tourist office at Carrer Dr Vilanova (tel: 891189); www.andorra.ad

la Vella. The building also contains the courts of justice and a working prison in the basement; book in advance for one of the excellent and informative guided tours. The nearby parish church of Sant Esteve has a lovely Romanesque apse, all that remains of the original structure. Beyond here, modern urban sprawl tells the story of Andorra's phenomenal growth, which has seen the population rise from 5,000 to 76,000 in 50 years (though only a quarter of these are Andorran citizens) and turned a sleepy Pyrenean village into a national capital.

A single main road runs across the country, linking Spain to France. During the skiing season and in summer, this road can get clogged with traffic as day-trippers visit Andorra for its duty-free shopping or pop across the border to fill up on cheap petrol. (This road must surely have the highest concentration of fuel stations anywhere.) If you want to get out into the mountains, you have to leave the main road and take a side trip to the far north or west. Staying on the through road, however, there are still one or two sights of interest. The **Museu Nacional de l'Automòbil**, in the town of Encamp, is a great place for children of all ages, with vintage Buicks, Bugattis and Morgans spread over five floors, along with bicycles, motorbikes and a fine collection of Matchbox and Dinky toys.

Another worthwhile stop is the **Santuari de Meritxell**, where an image of the patron saint of Andorra, the Virgin of Meritxell, is venerated. The sanctuary was built in 1976 by the Catalan architect Ricardo Bofill on the site of an earlier Romanesque shrine, destroyed by fire on the night of the saint's day pilgrimage four years earlier. The

Casa de la Vall *Carrer de la Vall; tel: 829129. Free guided tours. Mon–Sat 0930–1300, 1500–1800, Sun 1000–1400. Best to book in advance.*

Museu Nacional de L'Automòbil € *Avda Co Princep Episcol 64, Encamp; tel: 832266. Open Jul & Aug Tue–Sat 0900–2000, Sundays and holidays 1000–1400; Sept–Jun Tue–Sat 0930–1330, 1500–1800. Sundays, holidays 1000–1400.*

Santuari de Meritxell *Tel: 851253. Open Wed–Mon 0915–1300, 1500–1800; Jul & Aug 0900–2000 daily. Free.*

original Romanesque chapel has recently been restored and an exhibition in Catalan explores the history and iconography of the site. Further along the road, beyond Canillo, the 12th-century church of **Sant Joan de Caselles** has a Romanesque bell tower and frescoes, a Gothic altarpiece and the remains of a medieval necropolis, uncovered in 1988.

Accommodation and food in Andorra

Novotel Andorra € *Carrer Prat de la Creu, Andorra la Vella; tel: 873603; fax: 873653; www.novotel.com.* Conveniently situated beside the river on the main road through the town, this modern hotel makes a reasonable overnight stop, with car parking, tennis courts and an indoor pool.

Hostel L'Ermita €€ *Meritxell; tel: 751050; www.hotelermita.com.* A small inn beside the Meritxell sanctuary with mountain views, a few simple rooms and a restaurant featuring rustic Catalan and Andorran cuisine.

Andorra Park €€€ *Carrer Les Canals 24, Andorra la Vella; tel: 877777; fax: 820983; www.hotansa.com.* This elegant slate-roofed hotel is close

Caldea is a huge, modern thermal spa centre in Les Escaldes with whirlpools, Turkish baths, massage and hydrotherapy pools beneath a futuristic crystal dome. A three-hour entrance ticket gives access to most of the facilities. *Parc de la Mola 10; tel: 800999; www.caldea.com. Open daily 0900–2200 (until 2400 in Aug).*

The **Festa Major** in Andorra la Vella takes place over the first weekend in August. Andorra's national holiday is on 8 September, when there is a mass pilgrimage to Meritxell.

Below
La Massana, Andorra

to the centre of town but it has landscaped gardens, inspiring valley views and a swimming pool built into the mountainside. A lift gives access to the Pyrénées department store.

Borda Estevet €€€ *Ctra de La Comella 2, Andorra la Vella; tel: 864026; www.bordaestevet.com.* A *borda* is a barn-like restaurant offering traditional mountain cuisine, and this one on the outskirts of the capital features roasts, grills and dishes served *a la llosa* – on a hot stone plate for you to finish cooking at the table.

Shopping in Andorra

Although the entire country has been likened to a cut-price supermarket, the main shopping areas are Andorra la Vella, the neighbouring town of Les Escaldes and the ski resort of Pas de la Casa on the French border. In Andorra la Vella, most of the duty-free shops are strung out along a single road, which changes its name from Avda Príncep Benlloch to Avda Meritxell as it cuts across the old town. Most shops are open seven days a week, though many close on Sunday afternoons.

LLÍVIA

ℹ *Carrer Forns 11;*
tel: 972 896313;
www.llivia.org

🏛 **Museo de**
Farmacia de Llívia
€ *Calle Forns 10; tel: 972*
896011. Closed for
restoration works. The oldest
pharmacy in Europe, dating
back to the 15th century.

This small town would be quite unremarkable were it not for a historical anomaly which has left it as a little bit of Catalonia inside France. This situation came about as a result of the Treaty of the Pyrenees, negotiated at Llívia in 1659. Under the terms of the treaty, all 33 villages in the area were to be ceded to France – until the Spanish pointed out that Llívia was technically a town, not a village. Its status as an enclave (reached by a minor road from Puigcerdà) has certainly done Llívia no harm in establishing it on the tourist map. The **Museu Municipal** contains one of the oldest pharmacies in Europe, established in 1415. It has wonderful old phials and ceramic jars, and a Baroque '*retablo*' which served as a medicine cabinet.

Llívia is unique at present, but there is no guarantee that it will always be that way. In 1999, the mayor of the nearby village of Eyne announced that the 84 citizens of his village were tired of being ruled by France and suggested that they might apply to become part of Catalonia. It remained part of France, however.

Accommodation and food in Llívia

Can Ventura €€€ *Plaça Major 1; tel: 972 896178; www.canventura.com.* An elegant restaurant inside an 18th-century house serving sophisticated French, Catalan and Cerdanyan cuisine, from *magret de pato* (grilled duck breast) to civet of chamois. The starters include *trinxat*, the local equivalent of bubble-and-squeak, with potato, cabbage and bacon pressed into a cake.

Sant Guillem €€€ *Esport 2; tel: 972 146367; www.hotelstguillem.com.* Small, charming, luxury hotel in a picturesque location.

PUIGCERDÀ

ℹ *Carrer Querol 1;*
tel: 972 880542;
email: info@puigcerda.com;
www.puigcerda.cat

The capital of the Cerdanya is a pleasant summer resort, popular with French day-trippers who sit outside the cafés, *crêperies* and *churrerías* (doughnut stalls) of its twin main squares. In winter it takes on a different role as a centre for skiing holidays, with a dozen French, Catalan and Andorran resorts all within an hour's drive.

Built on a small hill at a height of 1,200m, the town offers unrivalled views along the green Cerdanya valley, especially from the bell tower, which is all that remains of the 17th-century church of Santa María. A short walk from the centre of town leads to a lake surrounded by villas built in the Modernist style. This makes a pleasant spot to while away a summer afternoon or relax after a testing drive over the Andorran mountains.

Right
Serra del Cadí in the Cerdanya

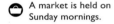 Most of the restaurants are situated around the twin squares of Plaça de Santa María and Plaça dels Herois. A popular choice in Plaça dels Herois is **Miamidos €€**, which has several French-style gastronomic menus with *cava*, wine and liqueurs included.

A market is held on Sunday mornings.

The nearby ski resort of **La Molina** is the largest in Catalonia, with some 22 downhill pistes and facilities for ski-jumping, slalom and cross-country skiing.

Accommodation and food in Puigcerdà

Chalet del Golf €€ *Devesa del Golf, Bolvir de Cerdanya; tel: 972 884320; www.hesperia.es.* A timber-framed hotel handily situated on the main road around the town. Each of the 16 rooms looks out over the local golf course and there are facilities for a wide range of sports.

Del Lago €€ *Avda Dr Piguillen 7; tel: 972 881000; fax: 972 141511; email: info@hotellago.com; www.hotellago.com.* Pretty hotel situated on the shores of the lake with a swimming pool in its shady garden.

Torre del Remei €€€ *Camí Reial, Bolvir; tel: 972 140182; fax: 972 140449; www.torredelremei.com.* This splendid hotel occupies a Modernist country palace near Puigcerdà. There are only 11 rooms, each individually decorated, with dark polished wood and contemporary art on the walls. One of the bathrooms is situated inside a turret. The restaurant is famous throughout Catalonia for bringing *nueva cocina* (new cuisine) touches to traditional Catalan cuisine; the chef cooked for the UK's Queen Elizabeth II on one of her visits to Spain. The same family owns a second restaurant, **Boix**, at Martinet on the road to La Seu d'Urgell.

LA SEU D'URGELL

Avda de les Valls d'Andorra 33;
tel: 973 351511;
www.turismeseu.com.
There is a smaller office in the Parc del Segre.

The chief town of the Catalan Pyrenees was ruled for many years by prince-bishops who also shared joint sovereignty over Andorra (*la seu* means 'cathedral'). This is a small town with a big history, and a delightful base from which to explore Andorra and the Cerdanya region. The main sight is the 12th-century **Catedral**, the only remaining Romanesque cathedral in Catalonia. Particularly notable

Above
Pyrenean landscape

Catedral € *Tel: 973 353242. Open Mon–Sat 1000–1300, 1600–1800, Sun 1000–1300.*

Museu Diocesà €
Tel: 973 353242; www.museudiocesaurgell.org. Open Mon–Sat 1000–1300, 1600–1800, Sun 1000–1300.

Parc Olimpic del Segre For information on rafting and canoeing activities; *tel: 973 351511; www.parcolimpic.com*

are the bell tower, with its Lombard Romanesque arches, the four apses set into the transept, and the statue of Santa María d'Urgell in the central apse. The irregular cloister, with carved granite capitals depicting human figures, is also appealing, but the piped monastic chanting, peaceful at first, soon grates. The cloister gives access to the beautiful Romanesque chapel of Sant Miquel. The **Museu Diocesà**, reached off the cloister, contains an illustrated 10th-century *Beatus*.

This is a town for strolling, around the well-preserved medieval quarter and especially along the dark, arcaded streets near the cathedral. Carrer Canonges and Carrer Major are full of old-fashioned shopfronts displaying cheeses, wine, pastries and defiantly unfashionable clothes. In Carrer Major, look out for a pair of stone grain measures; the earlier one dates from 1573. From the foot of this road, steps lead down to the **Parc del Segre**, with white-water rafting and canoeing courses designed for the 1992 Olympics. This is a good place for a walk on summer evenings, watching the canoeists and the canoodling lovers against a magnificent mountain backdrop. On the other side of town, **Parc del Valira** is the setting for an extraordinary modern 'cloister', designed by Lluís Racionero and sometimes used by the local youths as an impromptu football pitch. The cloister is an exact replica of that in the cathedral, except that the capitals show figures from 20th-century history. From here, a peaceful riverside walk leads to the old bridge to Castellciutat, at the confluence of the Segre and the Valira where the original city was built.

A market, first held in 1029, takes place on Tuesdays and Saturdays. The large Sant Ermengol fair, dating back to 1048, is held in late October or early November.

The **Festa Major** takes place on the last Sunday in August.

Right
La Seu d'Urgell

Accommodation and food in La Seu d'Urgell

Andria €€ *Passeig Joan Brudieu 24; tel: 973 350300; fax: 973 351425; email: info@hotelandria.com; www.hotelandria.com.* A small, old-style hotel on the *rambla* – which has been charmingly refurbished – and a restaurant serving hearty portions of Catalan highland cuisine.

Cal Pacho €€ *Carrer de la Font 11; tel: 973 352719.* A popular locals' bar offering traditional Catalan cooking, with an emphasis on grilled meat and sausages or combinations such as duck with pears.

Parador de la Seu d'Urgell €€ *Carrer Sant Domènec 6; tel: 973 352000; fax: 973 352309; email: seo@parador.es; www.parador.es.* From the outside it may look like a car park, but this modern *parador*, a stone's throw from the cathedral, has all the comfort and elegance you would expect. The most impressive feature is the courtyard, with hanging gardens set in an old Renaissance cloister. Another attraction is the heated indoor pool. The restaurant serves Catalan classics such as grilled snails, as well as steaks and fish dishes.

Hotel El Castell €€€ *Ctra N260, Castellciutat; tel: 973 350000; fax: 973 351574; email: elcastell@relaischateaux.com; www.hotelelcastell.com.* This luxury Relais hotel is situated next to the walls of a medieval castle, with wonderful views over the valley and the mountains. It offers a 'wellness' spa, a swimming pool in the garden, and a restaurant which serves gastronomic Catalan cuisine.

Suggested tour

Total distance: 140km.

Time: The actual driving time is between 3 and 4 hours, but mountain roads and heavy traffic in Andorra mean that it is best to allow a full day.

Links: There are various links to other routes in this book. From La Seu d'Urgell, a hair-raising drive over the Coll del Cantó leads to the Catalan Pyrenees route (*see pages 138–41*) at Sort. From Puigcerdà you can follow the trans-Pyrenean highway past the ski resort of La Molina to join the Garrotxa route (*see pages 160–61*) at Ripoll, or go through the Cadí tunnel to join the heart of Catalonia route (*see pages 220–21*) at Berga.

Start in **LA SEU D'URGELL** ❶. From the roundabout on the edge of town, follow signs to Andorra, travelling through the Valira valley between tall cliffs. After 10km you cross the border into **ANDORRA** ❷. Petrol stations beside the road, and a hypermarket with a car park full of Spanish-registered cars, are the first signs of Andorra's role as a cut-price shoppers' paradise.

The road across Andorra is a mixture of spectacular scenery and ugly commercialism. After **Andorra la Vella**, bear right across the river to continue towards **Encamp**. The road now passes beneath the shrine at **Meritxell** and continues through **Canillo**. If you want to get off the beaten track, a scenic byroad leads over the mountains to **Ordino**.

Beyond Canillo the serious climbing begins, with hairpin bends and breathtaking views all the way up to **Port d'Envalira**, at 2,400m the highest pass in the Pyrenees. The pass can sometimes be closed by heavy snows in winter, but the need to maintain access to Andorra's ski resorts means that it is usually quite reliable. It is worth pausing at the summit to fill up with petrol at Andorran prices. The road now drops down sharply to the ski resort of **Pas de la Casa**, where you have to pass through a border customs post.

Now you are in France. At the next junction, fork right over the **Col de Puymorens** ❸, another mountain pass which is snowbound for much of the year (if it is closed, follow the signs to the Puymorens tunnel instead). Reaching **Porte-Puymorens**, you follow the Carol valley into the heart of the Cerdagne, through **Latour-de-Carol**, the terminus for the 'little yellow train' (*see opposite*), and **Enveitg**, the 'balcony of the Cerdagne' with views out over the lush valley in the shadow of the Carlit massif. Arriving in the border village of Bourg-Madame, cross over the bridge to return to Spain at **PUIGCERDÀ ❹**.

From Puigcerdà the N260 goes through the villages of Bolvir and **Ger** on its way to **Bellver de Cerdanya ❺**, whose steep, cobbled old quarter culminates at the top of the town in a beautiful, arcaded church square. Beyond Bellver, a side road at **Martinet** climbs up to **Lles** for magnificent views of the Cadí mountain range. The main road continues along the pretty Segre valley, following the winding course of the river to return to La Seu d'Urgell.

Getting out of the car

Le Petit Train Jaune ('the little yellow train') is a narrow-gauge railway which chugs through the French Cerdagne between Latour-de-Carol, Bourg-Madame and the fortified village of Villefranche-de-Conflent. In summer some of the carriages are open-air, giving it the feel of a fairground ride. The journey passes through spectacular Pyrenean valleys surrounded by mountains and pine forests and climbs to **Font Romeu**, a popular winter sports resort that is the sunniest town in France. Several trains a day leave Latour-de-Carol in summer (fewer in winter), taking around two hours to reach Villefranche-de-Conflent, 50km away. *For information tel: (00 33) 468 048062.*

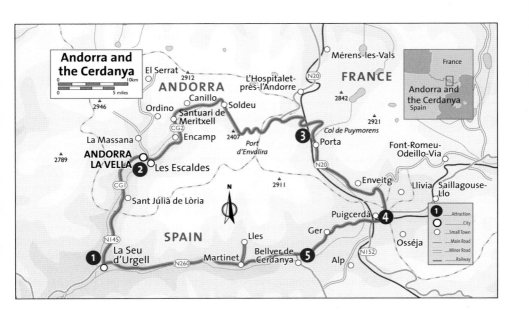

Ratings

Geology	●●●●●
Churches	●●●●○
Historical sights	●●●●○
Scenery	●●●●○
Children	●●●○○
Food	●●●○
Museums	●●●○○
Walking	●●●○○

The Garrotxa

The region of sleeping volcanoes between the Costa Brava and the Pyrenees is a result of geological activity that goes back hundreds of thousands of years. The green hills here shelter an astonishing variety of landscapes, from beech woods and oak forests to deep river valleys hidden beneath walls of stone. Even the human environment is shaped by natural forces – the towns are built out of volcanic rock and the dark landscapes of the Olot school of painters are rooted in the volcanic hills. This region has an important role in Catalan history. The first Count of Barcelona, Wilfred the Hairy, had his power base at Ripoll and it was from here that the Catalan Reconquest was launched. Of many Romanesque monuments surviving from this period, the most impressive are the monasteries founded by Wilfred at Ripoll and at Sant Joan de les Abadesses.

BANYOLES

 Passeig Indústria 25; tel: 972 575573;
email: turisme@ajbanyoles.org; www.banyolescultura.net. The tourist office organises guided walks and bicycle tours on summer evenings.

Museu Arqueològic €€ *Plaça de la Font 11; tel: 972 572361. Open Tue–Sat 1030–1330, 1600–1830 (Jul & Aug 1030–1330, 1630–1930), Sun 1030–1400.*

The capital of the Pla de l'Estany county is best known for its lake, which served as the venue for the 1992 Olympic rowing contests. The lake, 8km around its perimeter and fed by an underground spring, is both an important inland watersports location and a popular leisure resource – and not just for Olympic-standard rowers: many ordinary people come here at weekends to swim, fish and play about in rowing boats, or to picnic among the trees around the shore.

The town itself, a short walk away, is centred around its porticoed main square. The **Museu Arqueològic**, in the 14th-century Pia Almoina palace, contains the bones of ancient mastodons (elephant ancestors) found in the area, as well as a copy of the famous Banyoles Jaw, discovered in 1887 by local pharmacist Pere Alsius i Torrent. This human jawbone is believed to be more than 100,000 years old, which makes it one of the earliest known.

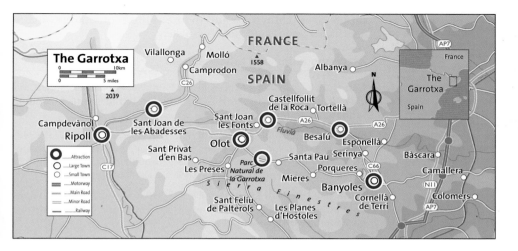

Accommodation and food in Banyoles

A market is held in Plaça Major on Wednesday mornings.

L'Ast € *Passeig Dalmau 63; tel/fax: 972 570414; www.hotelast.com.* This small hotel close to the lakeside has a swimming pool in its pleasant garden. There is no restaurant, but there are several places to eat on the nearby shore.

BESALÚ

Plaça Llibertat; tel: 972 591240; email: turisme@besalu.net; www.besalu.cat

If you don't mind looking like a typical tourist in summer, you can take a tour of the town on a miniature 'road train'.

Miqué € Open for guided tours. Ask at the Tourist Office.

A market is held on Tuesday mornings.

This small town on the banks of the River Fluvià has one of the most complete and best-preserved collections of Romanesque architecture in Catalonia. In summer it tends to get packed out with day-trippers from the Costa Brava, so unless you plan to stay for lunch it is best to arrive early or late in the day. Another good time is Tuesday mornings, when market stalls are set up beneath the arcades of the main square, Plaça Llibertat.

The best way to enter Besalú is to walk across its angled bridge, built in the 11th century and restored several times. In medieval times, visitors crossing the bridge paid a toll to enter the village. On the left as you enter is the **Miqué**, the only remaining Jewish bathhouse in Spain. Until their expulsion in 1492 there was a significant Jewish community in Besalú; these baths, with thermal springs and running water from the river, were used for ritual cleansing before prayer, marriage, childbirth and menstruation.

This is a town for strolling, for pottering along the ancient streets and looking up at the façades of churches, hospitals and mansions, with their hidden Romanesque and Gothic details. Of several Romanesque churches, the one to look out for is the 11th-century monastery church of **Sant Pere**, with a pair of stone lions adorning its

The **Festa dels Dolors** is a religious procession on the Friday before Palm Sunday. The procession, organised by a 17th-century fraternity, features Roman and Jewish soldiers, images of Christ and Mary, and people carrying lighted candles through the streets. It ends in Plaça Llibertat with the singing of hymns in Catalan and Latin.

façade. The church stands in the middle of a large square which once served as the town's cemetery.

Accommodation and food in Besalú

Can Quei € *Calle Sant Vicenç 4; tel: 972 590085*. Popular restaurant, on a quiet church square, with a good-value lunch menu as well as sandwiches and snacks.

Siques € *Avda Lluís Companys 6; tel: 972 590110; fax: 972 591243; email: siques@grupcalparent.com; www.grupcalparent.com*. This stone-built coaching inn on the main road through the town has simple rooms and a reputation for home-style Catalan cooking.

Curia Reial €€ *Plaça Llibertat 8; tel: 972 590263*. This restaurant serves Catalan classics in a former convent on the market square, with a pretty terrace overlooking the river.

Pont Vell €€ *Carrer Pont Vell 26; tel: 972 591027; email: info@restaurantpontvell.com*. Stylish modern Catalan cuisine on a riverside terrace beside the medieval bridge.

Els Fogons de Can Llaudes €€€ *Prat de Sant Pere 6; tel: 972 590858*. The top restaurant in Besalú is housed in an 11th-century chapel and a town house whose Romanesque courtyard contains the capitals from the Sant Pere cloisters. Come here for elegant Catalan meat dishes such as venison, wild boar and skewer-roasted lamb.

Below
Besalú

CASTELLFOLLIT DE LA ROCA

Museu d'Embotits
Ctra de Girona 10; tel:
972 294463. Open
Mon–Sat 0930–1330,
1600–2000, Sun 0930–
1400, 1630–2000. Free.

The best view of this remarkable village is the one from below, seen as you approach on the road from Besalú. From here you can see the entire village, perched precariously on a clifftop which is seemingly held together by columns of grey basalt. As you walk through the village you get a strong sense of how the inhabitants of the Garrotxa have always lived on the edge. Near the church at the end of town there is a splendid viewpoint, where you can gaze down over the precipice. Castellfollit is known for its almond biscuits, and its pork sausages, celebrated at one of Catalonia's more unusual museums – the **Museu d'Embotits** ('Sausage Museum'), owned by the Sala family, who have been making sausages here for more than 100 years.

OLOT

Carrer Hospici 8;
tel: 972 260141;
email: turisme@olot.org;
www.olot.org

Museu Comarcal
de la Garrotxa €
Carrer Hospici 8; tel: 972
271166. Open Tue–Fri
1000–1300, 1500–1800,
Sat 1100–1400, 1600–
1900, Sun 1100–1400
(summer Tue–Sat 1100–
1400, 1600–1900). The
ticket also gives entry to the
Museu dels Volcans.

Museu dels Volcans €
Avda de Santa Coloma;
tel: 972 266012. Museum
open Tue–Fri 1000–1400,
1500–1800, Sat
1000–1400, 1600–1900,
Sun 1000–1400 (summer
Tue–Sat 1000–1400).

A market is held on Monday mornings.

The largest town in the Garrotxa region is shaped by its environment, its buildings and promenades forged out of the local grey volcanic stone. Olot is a genuinely Catalan town that manages to be both traditional and forward-looking at the same time. Factories producing religious sculpture exist alongside avant-garde art galleries; there are restaurants serving hearty local stews and student cafés offering macrobiotic cuisine. The town is known for the richness of its festivals, especially the **Festa de la Tura** on 8 September, when a pair of giants created by the Modernist sculptor Miquel Blay dance through the streets accompanied by dwarves and hobby horses.

Blay was trained in the saint-making workshop of the brothers Marià and Joaquim Vayreda, of the Olot School of artists (*see page 156*). Much of their work can be seen in the **Museu Comarcal de la Garrotxa**, housed in an 18th-century neoclassical hospice. The museum also features paintings by the Catalan Modernists Ramon Casas and Santiago Rusiñol, sculptures by Blay and Josep Clarà, and displays on Olot's traditional industries, including textiles and bell-making. If you like Blay's sculptures, seek out his maidens on the façade of Casa Solà-Morales, a Modernist mansion on the *rambla*, Passeig Miquel Blay, which bears his name.

Of three dormant volcanoes surrounding the town, the easiest to climb is Montsacopa, reached by a 20-minute hike from the centre. Once at the top, you can walk around the rim of the crater or follow a path down to its floor. From the summit there are excellent views over Olot's rooftops and the surrounding volcanic landscape. A waymarked walk from here (signposted No 17) leads in about an hour to the **Museu dels Volcans**, a 19th-century Palladian villa inside the English-style botanical gardens at Parc Nou. On the ground floor is a museum exploring the geology and ecology of the area, while upstairs is an information centre for the natural park (*see page 156*).

Accommodation and food in Olot

La Deu €€ *Ctra La Deu; tel: 972 261004; email: email@ladeu.es; www.ladeu.es.* The famous stuffed potato dish known as *patatas de La Deu* ('God's own potatoes') was invented at this restaurant more than a century ago. The menu features this, plus classic 'volcanic' cuisine, including beans from the Garrotxa and pigs' trotters with black turnips.

Riu Olot €€ *Ctra de Santa Pau; tel: 972 269444; email: hotel.olot@riu.com; www.riu.com.* This four-star hotel is situated on the outskirts of town, close to some of the best Garrotxa walks. There is plenty of car parking here, but no restaurant.

The Olot School

The 19th-century Olot School of painters has been described as a branch of the Catalan Luminist movement and its members as early Impressionists. Whereas the Luminist painters of Sitges reflected the bright Mediterranean light, the landscapes of the Olot School were steeped in dark, volcanic colours. The key figures in the movement were Joaquim Vayreda, his brother Marià, and Josep Berga i Boix. A bust of Joaquim Vayreda stands on Carrer Vayreda, close to his family home and the saint-making workshop he founded. One of his descendants, Marian Vayreda, still has an art gallery in the town.

PARC NATURAL DE LA GARROTXA

ℹ️ *Centre d'Informatió Can Jordá; tel: 972 264666.* There are also natural park information offices at the Casal dels Volcans in Olot (*see page 155*) and at Can Serra (open only in summer). All can supply free maps showing various walking trails in the park.

🅿️ For the walk described, there is parking available at Can Serra and also at Santa Margarida, both between Olot and Santa Pau on the GI524.

The most significant region of volcanic activity in the Iberian peninsula was declared a natural park in 1982, the first such area to be created by the autonomous Catalan government. Although the most recent eruption was around 11,000 years ago, the volcanoes are still officially described as dormant rather than extinct. The green hills and craters left behind by the volcanic activity have produced an area of exceptional beauty, with a wide range of microclimates and several well-marked walking trails.

For day visitors, the easiest way into the park is from the Can Serra information centre between Olot and Santa Pau. A popular walk from here, signposted No 1, follows a 10km circuit through the beech woods known as Fageda d'en Jordà, to the Santa Margarida volcano (with a Romanesque chapel in its crater) and back past the Croscat volcano, where the scars caused by mining have produced the dramatic effect of exposing differently coloured layers of lava. The walk is not strenuous, but there are one or two steep climbs and you need to allow at least three hours.

The **Santa Margarida** bar, opposite the Lava campsite as you cross the GI524, is a good place to break your walk for a filling lunch or a plate of bread and ham.

The nearby village of **Santa Pau** is the holiday centre of the Garrotxa, with everything from horse-riding schools and carriage rides to flights over the volcanoes in a hot-air balloon. At the heart of the village is a fortified medieval centre, with a 14th-century castle, a Romanesque church and an attractive main square with porticoes and wooden balconies. The square was once used as a cattle market. From the nearby Portal del Mar, there are good views over the surrounding valleys and a distant view of the sea.

Accommodation and food in Parc Natural de la Garrotxa

Cal Sastre €€ *Placeta des Valls 6, Santa Pau; tel: 972 680421.* Hearty mountain cuisine, featuring local sausages, mushrooms and beans, is served beneath the arches of a delightful old town square. The same family owns a small hotel in a farmhouse outside the medieval walls.

Below
Els Hostalets d'en Bas near Olot

RIPOLL

ℹ *Plaça Abat Oliba;*
tel: 972 702351;
email: turisme@ajripoll.com;
www.ajripoll.com. Ask at the
tourist office for a leaflet
about the Modernist route
around the town.

**Monestir de Santa
María** € *Plaça Abat
Oliba; tel: 972 700243.
Church open daily
1000–1300, 1500–1900.*

Museu Etnogràfic €
*Plaça Abat Oliba;
tel: 972 703144;
www.museuderipoll.org.
Open Mon–Fri 1000–1300,
1600–1800.*

🛒 A market takes place
on Saturday mornings.

⛰ A traditional wool
festival, **Festa de La
Llana**, takes place in Ripoll
on the Sunday following 11
May. As part of the festival,
a 'rural wedding' is held,
followed by a public
reception in the main
square. Sometimes the
couple getting married,
dressed in period costume,
are a real bride and
groom; at other times the
wedding is simulated.

This county town in the Pyrenean foothills may not be terribly appealing at first, but it has one unmissable sight, an enjoyable museum and several interesting Modernist buildings. The main reason for coming here is to see the 12th-century Romanesque portal of the monastery of **Santa María**. Founded by Wilfred the Hairy in 880 on the site of an earlier Visigothic church, the monastery grew under Abbot Oliba into an important centre of power and learning. All that survives from those early days are the two-storey cloisters and the magnificent portal, whose vivid carvings record Bible stories, the seven deadly sins, the signs of the zodiac and the months of the year depicted through farming scenes. This is undoubtedly one of the great treasures of Catalan Romanesque art.

In the same square, the **Museu Etnogràfic** is a museum in the style museums used to be, with everything from matchboxes to birds' nests and pistols to Civil War posters gathered together by a local historian from objects in the archive of Sant Pere church. The main emphasis is on local industries, including farming, sheep-shearing, ironwork and guns. Ripoll is also home to a handful of striking Modernista buildings, including the whimsical church Sant Miquel de la Roqueta, which was designed by Joan Rubió, a contemporary of Antoni Gaudí.

Right
Ripoll's Santa María monastery

SANT JOAN DE LES ABADESSES

ℹ️ *Plaça de la Abadia 9;*
tel: 972 720599;
www.santjoandelesabadesses.
cat

🏛️ **Museu del Monestir**
€ Plaça de l'Abadia;
tel: 972 722353. Monastery
and museum open Jul & Aug,
Mon–Fri 1000–1900, Sat &
Sun 1000–1400,
1600–1800 (until 1900
May–Aug); Nov–Feb
1000–1400; Mar & Apr,
Sept & Oct 1000–1400,
1600–1800.

Below
The medieval bridge in Sant
Joan de les Abadesses

This small town was founded in 887 by Wilfred the Hairy as a gift for his daughter Emma, whom he appointed as the first abbess of the convent here. The current abbey church, in the form of a Latin cross, dates from the 12th century. Among the treasures inside it are a Gothic alabaster *retablo* and a carved Romanesque calvary, with seven polychrome wooden figures of almost human size. The attached museum contains more religious art, from a 12th-century cross with pagan sun and moon images to a 1987 homage by the avant-garde Catalan artist Antoni Tàpies.

As you leave Sant Joan de les Abadesses, look out for the pointed medieval bridge over the River Ter.

Accommodation and food in Sant Joan de les Abadesses

There are outdoor seats on the *rambla* at **Café La Rambla**, which serves snacks and set lunches. On Carrer Major, a narrow street connecting the *rambla* to the arcaded Plaça Major, you can find **La Forneria** for pasta and wood-fired pizzas and **Casa Rudes**, an old-fashioned delicatessen with a wine bar counter.

Suggested tour

Total distance: The main route is just 76km; the detour to Ripoll adds 60km.

Time: Allow 2 hours for the main route, 3 hours with the detour. With a visit to Besalú or Ripoll and a walk in the Parc natural de la Garrotxa, you need to allow a full day.

Below
Ripoll

Links: From Ripoll the N152 travels through a dramatic stretch of the high Pyrenees to join the Cerdanya route (*see pages 150–51*) at Puigcerdà in 64km.

Begin in **BANYOLES** ❶ and head north on the main road to Olot, keeping the lake to your left and the town centre to your right. After 4km this road merges with the C66 from Girona and almost immediately you see the high peaks of the Pyrenees up ahead. When you reach **BESALÚ** ❷, park on the left and walk across the bridge to explore the town. The road now becomes the A26 and follows the course of the River Fluvià; before long, **CASTELLFOLLIT DE LA ROCA** ❸ comes into view, perched along a ridge to your left. Drive through Castellfollit and continue on the A26 to Olot.

Detour: Shortly after leaving Castellfollit, turn right to **Sant Joan les Fonts**, signposted to Ripoll via a tunnel. You pass through the village of Sant Joan, with its Romanesque monastery, then turn right again on to a road which climbs sharply into the hills. Look in your mirror for magnificent views of the entire Garrotxa range. Where the road forks, keep left to go through a long tunnel, emerging on to the C26. Turn left to follow the Ter valley beneath the Pyrenean peaks, passing **SANT JOAN DE LES ABADESSES ❹** on the way to **RIPOLL ❺**. From Ripoll, the A26 snakes its way down to Olot, through a wooded valley and a succession of stunning views. This road is in a poor condition in places but it is being improved.

Once in **OLOT ❻**, follow signs to Santa Pau to reach the heart of the **PARC NATURAL DE LA GARROTXA**. If you have time, park at the Can Serra information centre and complete the circular walk (*see page 156*). The winding road now continues to **SANTA PAU ❼**, then drops slowly down to the plain with lovely views all the way. Just before you reach **Porqueres**, take the gravel track to your left to reach yet another Romanesque church. From here you can follow the shores of the lake to return to Banyoles.

Also worth exploring

The spa town of **Ribes de Freser** is 14km north of Ripoll. From here, one of Spain's only two rack railways, the *cremallera*, heads into the mountains to Catalonia's oldest ski resort at **Vall de Núria**. This is the only way into the valley, surrounded by the highest peaks of the eastern Pyrenees, and the journey offers magnificent views. At the top of the valley is a sanctuary where a 12th-century image of the Virgin of Núria, patron saint of Pyrenean shepherds, is venerated. The *cremallera* leaves Ribes de Freser several times daily in winter and more frequently in summer (closed November). *www.valldenuria.cat*

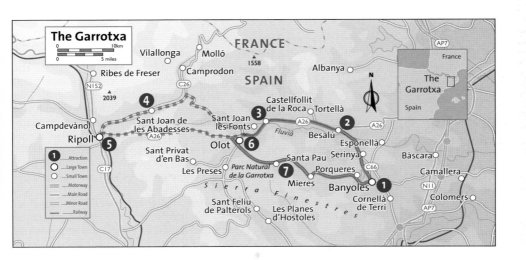

Dalíland

Ratings

Art	●●●●○
Geology	●●●●○
Scenery	●●●●○
Watersports	●●●●○
Beaches	●●●○○
Children	●●●○○
Historical sights	●●●○○
Museums	●●●○○

The wild northern stretch of the Costa Brava is closely associated with the Surrealist artist Salvador Dalí who was born in Figueres and lived for most of his life in Cadaqués. There are reminders of Dalí everywhere, including two key sights – the museum that he designed as his own epitaph, and his house, which is open to the public. Dalí was inspired both by the rugged beauty of this area, where the Pyrenees come down into the sea in what he described as 'a grandiose geological delirium', and by the intensity of the sunlight at this easternmost tip of mainland Spain. As you gaze out over the cliffs, carved into Surreal shapes by the wind and the sea, it is easy to believe that the artist and the landscape were made for one another. Not surprisingly, this area continues to attract artists today.

CADAQUÉS

🛈 *Carrer Cotxe 2; tel: 972 258315;* email: *turisme@cadaques.org; www.visitcadaques.org*

🅿 Cadaqués can get extremely crowded, especially in summer and at weekends, and it is best to leave your car in the large car park at the entrance to the village.

With its whitewashed houses and boats moored in a peaceful bay, this could be any Mediterranean fishing village – until you notice the statue of Dalí on the seafront, the art galleries in the back streets and the shops selling ethnic jewellery to fashionable French tourists. Dalí loved this place. As a child he spent his summer holidays here. It was also here that he produced his first paintings and where he eventually settled down, in a converted pair of fishermen's cottages in Port Lligat.

During the 1960s, Cadaqués was known as Spain's St-Tropez. Dalí's presence attracted numerous visitors, from guests such as Walt Disney and Mick Jagger to hippies and bohemians hoping to catch a glimpse of the master in a local bar.

Dalí's house and studio in Port Lligat, 1km north of Cadaqués, **Casa-Museu Dalí**, opened to the public in 1997, giving intriguing glimpses into the life of this tortured genius. A stuffed bear greets you in the entrance hall; a lamp is transformed into a snail; the patio is a

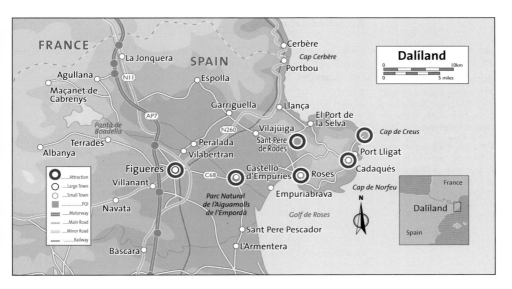

Casa-Museu Dalí
€€€ Port Lligat;
www.salvador-dali.org. Open
15 Mar–14 Jun, 16 Sept–6
Jan Tue–Sun 1030–1800;
15 Jun–15 Sept daily
0930–2100. Tickets must be
booked in advance; tel: 972
251015.

Museu de Cadaqués €€
Carrer Narcís Monturiol 15;
tel: 972 258877. Open
Mon–Sat 1000–1330,
1600–1900.

monument to 1960s kitsch, with Pirelli tyres, Michelin men, flowerpots in the shape of teacups and a fountain adorned with cheap Spanish tourist souvenirs. From the window of Dalí's studio there are magical views of the bay, enclosed by a small offshore island.

With the focus so heavily on Dalí, it is easy to forget that Cadaqués inspired artists before him and continues to do so to this day, as can be seen in the **Museu de Cadaqués** which houses works of contemporary Catalan art as well as works by Dalí. Other artists to have visited the town include Picasso, Miró, Duchamp and Man Ray. Since 1980, Cadaqués has hosted an annual international printmaking competition, some of the entries for which can be seen during the summer months in Taller Galeria Fort on Carrer Hort d'en Sanés (near Es Poal beach).

Right
Cadaqués

Accommodation and food in Cadaqués

A market is held on Monday mornings.

A procession of fishing boats is held in the harbour on 16 July for the festival of **Mare de Déu del Carme**.

L'Hostal is a popular jazz club on the waterfront where Salvador Dalí used to bring his friends. There is often live music here in summer. *Passeig del Mar 8. Open daily 2200–0500.*

Casa Anita €€ *Carrer Miquel Rosset 16; tel: 972 258471.* This backstreet restaurant was one of Dalí's favourite haunts. The cooking is rustic, the portions huge, and you eat at crowded wooden tables. The whitewashed walls are covered with photos of former clients and signed prints by Dalí.

Llané Petit €€ *Carrer Dr Bartomeus 37; tel: 972 251020; fax: 972 258778; email: info@llanepetit.com; www.llanepetit.com.* On the far side of the bay, this small hotel has a sunny breakfast terrace and rooms with balconies overlooking the sea. The ten-minute walk into the village passes Port Alguer, which looks much as it did when Dalí painted it in Cubist style in 1924.

Playa Sol €€ *Platja Pianc 5; tel: 972 258100; fax: 972 258054; email: playasol@playasol.com; www.playasol.com.* Harbourfront hotel, with a swimming pool and tennis courts in its gardens, facing a small shingle beach which is just right for the late afternoon sun.

CAP DE CREUS

The **Restaurant Cap de Creus** € beside the lighthouse serves an eclectic mix of Catalan cuisine, fresh fish dishes and Indian-style curries. *Tel: 972 199005.*

A spectacular drive from Cadaqués or a coastal footpath from Port Lligat leads to the lighthouse which marks the most easterly point on the Iberian peninsula. This is the first place to see the sun rise each day and the dawn of each new year is greeted with *sardana* dancing. The headland, designated a natural park in 1998, is carpeted with wild flowers and herbs and is also a haven for migrating birds. From the slate cliffs, battered by the *tramuntana* wind, you look down over a seascape of deep blue water and rocky coves.

CASTELLÓ D'EMPÚRIES

Plaça Jaume I; tel: 972 156233.

A market is held on Tuesday mornings.

A minstrel festival, **Terra de Trobadors**, with riders and dancers in medieval costume, takes place on or around 11 September each year.

This charming town of Gothic palaces and cobbled streets is set back just a short distance from the coast. The main attraction is the basilica of **Santa María**, sometimes referred to as the cathedral of the Costa Brava. This 14th-century Gothic church has retained some Romanesque elements, including the bell tower and the double font. The white marble portal is particularly attractive, with sculpted figures of the apostles and an Epiphany scene. The streets around the basilica make for some pleasant strolling. Most of them take their names from the former trades practised here such as Peixateries ('fishmongers'), Sabateries ('cobblers') and Bordel ('brothel'). Look out, too, for the *rentador*, the old public wash house, with a fountain at the centre and a view of the basilica through its porticoed gallery.

Accommodation and food in Castelló d'Empúries

Canet € *Plaça Joc de la Pilota 2; tel: 972 250340; fax: 972 250607; email: info@hotelcanet.com; www.hotelcanet.com.* This charming town-centre hotel is exceptional value, with a pool in its courtyard and a restaurant serving fresh local cuisine.

Empòrium € *Santa Clara 31; tel: 972 250593; www.emporium hotel.com.* Central yet beautiful locality offering all modern amenities, including Internet access in rooms. Breakfast and lunch served on site.

Salvador Dalí (1904–89)

The master of surrealism was born in Figueres in 1904, the son of a public notary. At the age of 15 he had his first exhibition of paintings in the town's opera house. In 1930 he moved to Port Lligat with his Russian lover Gala, whom he married in a secret ceremony in 1958. After Gala's death, Dalí moved into her castle at Púbol (*see page 175*), where he almost died in a fire in 1984. He lived out his final years in the tower of his theatre-museum in Figueres and is buried in the crypt beneath the stage. Always a controversial figure, Dalí enraged many with his political views (which veered from Communism to support for Franco) and with the sexual obsessions which characterised much of his work. After he was awarded the title of Marquis Dalí of Púbol by King Juan Carlos in 1982, he responded by leaving all of his works to the Spanish State – an act for which the Catalans have still not forgiven him.

Right
Statue of Dalí in Cadaqués

FIGUERES

ℹ️ *Plaça del Sol;*
tel: 972 503155;
email: fituris@ddgi.es;
www.figueresciutat.com

🅿️ Parking can be a problem, especially on market day, so use the large car park beneath Plaça de Catalunya, or try for free places on the road up to the Sant Ferran castle. From Barcelona, Girona and the Costa Brava resorts, it is best to arrive in Figueres by train or bus.

The county town of the Upper Empordà region has a fair sprinkling of attractions, but most visitors come here for just one thing – to see the museum Salvador Dalí created as his own memorial. The **Teatre-Museu Dalí** is built on the gutted ruins of the town's theatre, where Dalí had his first exhibition, but that is not the only reason for the name. Dalí did not want a conventional museum; he wanted the 'audience' to create their own Surrealist experience, without the distractions of catalogues and guided tours. From the moment that you set foot inside the building, its façade adorned with trademark Dalí symbols, you enter a fantasy world created by one man's fertile imagination.

The best way to explore is to do as Dalí wished, allowing your senses to guide you. In this museum, nothing is quite what it seems. A bright

Teatre-Museu Dalí
€€€ *Plaça Gala-Salvador Dalí; tel: 972 667500; www.salvador-dali.org. Open Jan–Jun & Oct–Dec Tue–Sun 1030–1745; Jul–Sept Tue–Sun 0900–1945.*

Museu de l'Empordà €
Rambla 2; tel: 972 502305; www.museuemporda.org. Open Tue–Sat 1100–1900, Sun 1100–1400.

Museu del Joguet €€
Carrer Sant Pere 1; tel: 972 504585; www.mjc.cat. Open Mon–Sat 1000–1300, 1600–1900, Sun 1100–1330.

Castell de Sant Ferran
€ *Carrer de Sant Ferran. Open daily 1030–1500 in winter, 1030–2000 in summer.*

Several markets are held each week in Figueres between 0900 and 1400 in the Passeig Nou, Calle Mestre Falla, Plaça del Gra, Plaça Catalunya and Plaça de l'Escorxador.

Dalícatessen is a trendy sandwich bar close to the Dalí museum on Carrer Sant Pere. The shops along this street sell arty gifts, including Dalí posters and T-shirts.

Left
Dalí museum's central patio

pink sofa reveals the lips of Mae West and a portrait of Gala, Dalí's wife, becomes Abraham Lincoln when seen from a different angle. In the courtyard, visitors feed coins into a meter to spray water over the inhabitants of a Cadillac, the centrepiece of a sculpture which also features a bronze statue of Queen Esther, the biblical Queen of Persia, a column of tractor tyres and Gala's fishing boat.

Among all the tricks and illusions are some remarkable paintings. Look out for *Self-Portrait with L'Humanité*, a statement of Dalí's Communist sympathies produced in 1923; *Soft Self-Portrait with Grilled Bacon*, in which his familiar obsessions are starting to emerge; *Galarina*, an enigmatic portrait of Gala; and *The Happy Horse*, a grim premonition of death painted in 1980. Other famous paintings include *The Spectre of Sex Appeal*, *The Apotheosis of the Dollar* and a bizarre portrait of Picasso.

At the top of the *rambla*, a monument recalls the town's other favourite son, Narcís Monturiol, the inventor of the submarine. The **Museu de l'Empordà** has a room devoted to Monturiol, as well as local archaeological finds and 19th- and 20th-century Catalan art. The nearby **Museu del Joguet** contains toys – everything from copies of terracotta animals discovered at the Roman site at Empúries to toy soldiers, skittles and a teddy bear which once belonged to Dalí's sister. The museum also has an impressive collection of *caganers*, little figurines of peasants that are a traditional part of the manger scene at Christmas. The figurines represent prosperity and luck for the coming year.

A short climb uphill from the Dalí museum leads to **Castell de Sant Ferran**, a star-shaped citadel which was the last bastion of Republican forces during the Spanish Civil War. A 3km footpath around the castle walls gives good views over the surrounding area.

Accommodation and food in Figueres

Durán €€ *Carrer Lasauca 5; tel: 972 501250; fax: 972 502609; email: duran@hotelduran.com; www.hotelduran.com.* The walls of this central hotel are adorned with Dalí memorabilia, a reminder of the days when it was one of his favourite haunts.

Empordà €€ *Avinguda Salvador Dalí 170; tel: 972 500562; fax: 972 500566; email: hotelemporda@hotelemporda.com; www.hotelemporda.com.* Smart hotel just north of Figueres, considered the birthplace of new Catalan cuisine. The restaurant still turns out imaginative creations, such as hare with beetroot sauce and stuffed squid with a hint of chocolate.

Mas Pau €€ *Avinyonet de Puigvenós; tel: 972 546154; www.maspau.com.* A charming hotel and restaurant housed in a 16th-century farmstead, 4km west of town. The menu is gourmet, while the rooms are washed in ochre and sumptuously furnished.

Roses

ℹ *Avda Rhode 101; tel: 902 103363; www.roses.cat*

🏛 **Ciutadella** *Avda Rhode. Open May–Sept daily 1000–2000; Oct–Apr daily 1000–1800. Free.*

🛒 Market day is Sunday. A fish auction is held beside the harbour on weekday afternoons.

🎉 A communal fish feast, **Suquet de Peix**, is held on 29 June to mark the festival of Sant Pere.

Processions of fishing boats take place on 16 July in honour of the Virgen del Carmen, the patron saint of fishermen.

The largest resort on the northern Costa Brava sits at the head of a sweeping sandy bay with superb beaches and facilities for all kinds of watersports. Founded by Greek settlers in the 8th century BC, Roses was named after the island of Rhodes. Later, it became an important Roman fishing port. The town still has a fishing fleet, though these days tourism is the biggest industry. The main sight is the 16th-century **Ciutadella** ('citadel') at the entrance to the town, built on the site of the Greek and Roman cities.

Beyond Roses are several small coves, each with its own sandy beach. A twisting drive high above the coast passes prehistoric dolmens on its way to the beautiful Cala Montjoi, where one of Spain's most famous restaurants (El Bulli; *see below*) can be found.

Accommodation and food in Roses

Almadraba Park €€ *Platja de Almadrava; tel: 972 256550; fax: 972 256750; www.almadrabapark.com.* This four-star hotel is situated on a clifftop overlooking a pretty cove 4km from the centre of the resort. There are marvellous views from the terraced gardens. Like most hotels in Roses, it is only open from April until October.

El Bulli €€€ *Cala Montjoi; tel: 972 150457; fax: 972 150717; email: bulli@elbulli.com; www.elbulli.com.* Celebrated restaurant in a perfect setting, looking down on an isolated cove where millionaires moor their yachts. You need to be rich to eat here, but you will never forget the experience. The chef, Ferràn Adrià, has gained three Michelin stars for his creative Catalan cuisine, which features signature dishes such as caviar with bone marrow. The restaurant is only open from April to September, and will close from 2012 to 2014 while Adrià travels and researches new dishes.

Sant Pere de Rodes

🏛 **Sant Pere de Rodes €** *Parc Natural Cap de Creus; tel: 972 387559. Open Oct–May Tue–Sun 1000–1700; Jun–Sept Tue–Sun 1000–2000.*

This former Benedictine monastery, begun in the 10th century, is one of the best examples of the transition to Romanesque art in Catalonia. The church has three naves, each crowned with vaulting and separated by tall columns with delicately carved capitals. Recent excavations have uncovered a lower cloister with traces of pre-Romanesque murals. For several centuries this was a place of pilgrimage and an important monastic power base with territory on both sides of the Pyrenees. Just as impressive as the church is the magnificent setting, high up in the mountains with views over the Cap de Creus and out to sea.

For a truly special experience, come up here at dawn to watch the sun rise out of the sea, or climb to the ruined castle above the monastery for 360-degree views.

Right
Dalí museum, Figueres

Suggested tour

Total distance: 83km. The detour to Espolla adds about 15km.

Time: 2–3 hours.

Links: From Figueres there are fast road links to Besalú on the Garrotxa route (*see pages 160–61*), to Girona (*see pages 194–203*) and to the Northern Costa Brava route at L'Escala (*see pages 182–3*).

Leave **FIGUERES ❶** by following signs for Roses, travelling through the drab industrial suburbs before reaching open countryside. The road bypasses **CASTELLÓ D'EMPÚRIES ❷** and crosses the Muga estuary towards **Empúriabrava**, a modern marina resort crisscrossed by a network of canals.

Reaching the outskirts of **ROSES ❸**, turn left at the hypermarket to begin the tortuous climb across the Cap de Creus headland, with breathtaking views of the Gulf of Roses to your right and the castle of Sant Salvador in the mountains to your left.

When the road forks, keep straight ahead to drop down to the coast at **CADAQUÉS ❹**. After exploring this town, and perhaps taking a detour to **CAP DE CREUS ❺**, retrace your route back up towards the fork. Now turn right and follow this road as it rises and falls towards **El Port de la Selva ❻**, a pretty beach resort with whitewashed cottages around a fishing harbour. Turn left along the beach; when the beach runs out, turn left again, then immediately right to begin the testing climb to the monastery of **SANT PERE DE RODES ❼**. As you climb, keep an eye on the views to your right, of El Port de la Selva nestling beneath the cape.

The views change once you have passed the monastery, with the Pyrenees now forming a backdrop to the Empordan plain. As you approach **Vilajuïga**, the ruined castle of Quermanço appears on a crag to your right. This was the castle that Salvador Dalí originally planned to buy for Gala, until he discovered Púbol (*see page 175*).

Turn right in Vilajuïga, past the wine co-operatives, then turn left at the next village of **Garriguella**, passing vineyards and old Civil War bunkers on the road to **Peralada**, an attractive medieval village with a casino inside the moated castle.

Detour: From Garriguella it is possible to make a short detour into the Albera mountain range. The main village here, **Espolla ❽**, is at the heart of the local wine industry. A number of footpaths from Espolla lead to prehistoric monuments, including burial chambers and rock carvings. Also near here is the 11th-century church of **Sant Quirze de Colera**, reached by car from the village of Vilamaniscle or on foot from Espolla. A minor road from Espolla returns to the main route at Peralada.

From Peralada the C252 returns you quickly to Figueres. On the way you pass the 11th-century monastery at **Vilabertran**, a fine example of Catalan Romanesque architecture with a Gothic abbots' palace.

Getting out of the car

The road south from Castelló d'Empúries to Sant Pere Pescador gives access to the **Parc Natural de l'Aiguamolls de l'Empordà**, a marshy nature reserve with well-marked walking trails. Herons, ducks and geese live on the ponds here and the marshes attract a large number of migrant birds.

Also worth exploring

The coast road north of El Port de la Selva continues to the French border, offering a series of unforgettable views between the mountains and the sea. **Llançà** has a pleasant old centre and several good fish restaurants by the harbour, while **Portbou**, with its day-trippers and duty-free shops, has all the feel of a border town. From here it is possible to drive into France, passing pretty **Banyuls-sur-Mer** and the artists' village of **Collioure** on the way to **Perpignan**.

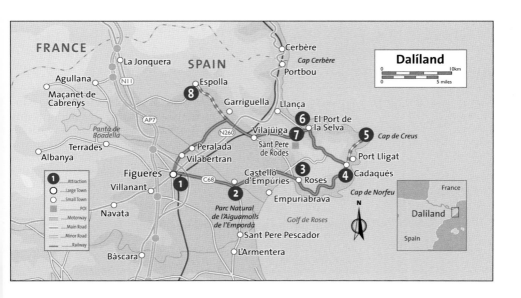

The northern Costa Brava

Ratings

Beaches	●●●●●
Archaeology	●●●●○
Diving	●●●●○
Scenery	●●●●○
Towns/villages	●●●●○
Children	●●●○○
Walking	●●●○○
Museums	●●○○○

Although the Costa Brava stretches for more than 200km from Blanes to the French border, the name really refers to the rocky section of coastline between Palamós and the Gulf of Roses. There are few long, flat beaches here, just a craggy shoreline of pine-scented creeks and coves, some of which have become decidedly upmarket resorts. It was the journalist Ferran Agulló who first labelled this the Costa Brava, which means 'wild and rugged coast', though the name could have hidden meanings, too. A sea which is *brava* is stormy and dangerous, like the Catalan coast when it is exposed to the fierce *tramuntana* wind; while people who are *brava* are brave and spirited, perhaps like the Catalans throughout their long history. Besides the coastal scenery, this area contains two fascinating archaeological sites, a perfectly restored medieval village and a pair of enchanting market towns.

AIGUABLAVA

For many people, this is the Costa Brava's most perfect spot, where the cliffs reach down into a turquoise bay backed by a beach of gently shelving sand. It was here in 1908 that Ferran Agulló, with an unwitting gift for marketing, first coined the term Costa Brava. Although Aiguablava (its name means 'blue water' in Catalan) has been 'discovered', and villas are creeping up the hillsides, this remains a good place to experience the Costa Brava as it was before mass tourism took over.

Accommodation and food in Aiguablava

Aigua Blava €€€ *Platja de Fornells; tel: 972 624562; fax: 972 622112; email: hotelaiguablava@aiguablava.com; www.aiguablava.com.* Four generations of the Sabater family have run this celebrated hotel,

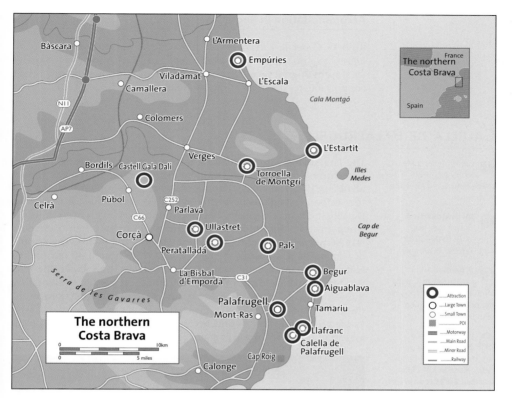

which tumbles down the hillside towards a tiny cove with views across the bay. This hotel combines luxury with conviviality.

Parador de Aiguablava €€€ *Platja d'Aiguablava; tel: 972 622162; fax: 972 622166; email: aiguablava@parador.es; www.parador.es.* This modern *parador* is situated high above the bay, with steps leading down to the beach through the pine groves. Unlike the hotel, which closes in winter, it is open all year.

BEGUR

ⓘ *Avda 11 de Septiembre 5; tel: 972 624520; email: turisme@begur.org; www.begur.org*

ⓐ A market is held on Wednesday mornings.

This hilltop town with a ruined castle at its summit is the access point for Aiguablava as well as the nearby coves at Aiguafreda, Sa Riera and Sa Tuna. It is worth climbing up to the defensive towers for views of the coastline, stretching north from the Medes islands to the Gulf of Roses.

Accommodation in Begur

Rosa €€ *Carrer Pi iRalló 19; tel: 972 623015; fax: 972 624320; email: info@hotel-rosa.com; www.hotel-rosa.com.* Although most people prefer to stay in Aiguablava, this small hotel in the town centre offers comfortable rooms in an attractive building.

CALELLA DE PALAFRUGELL

ⓘ *Carrer de les Voltes 4; tel: 972 614475.* The tourist office is only open in summer.

🏛 **Jardí Botànic €** *Castell Cap Roig. Open daily 0900–2000 (0900–1800 in summer).*

⊕ A number of operators in Calella offer scuba-diving trips to the nearby Formigues islands.

⛰ Calella's **Festa Major**, featuring folk dances and *sardanas*, takes place in July. The **Cantada d'Havaneres** is held on the first Saturday of July.

The **Costa Brava Jazz Festival** occurs each summer in the botanical gardens at Cap Roig. The concerts take place throughout July and August.

The largest of Palafrugell's beach resorts consists of a series of pretty coves strung out like pearls behind a fishing village with whitewashed arches on the promenade. Fishing boats are pulled up on the sand and the seafood restaurants beside the water are always busy at weekends. Development here has been low-rise and low-key, with everything on a human scale; this old-fashioned resort seems to have found a middle way between the excesses of mass tourism and the exclusivity of some of its smaller neighbours. A cliff path leads in around 30 minutes to Llafranc, making a delightful pre-dinner stroll. High above the bay, the **Jardí Botànic de Cap Roig** is a botanical garden designed by Russian émigré Nicolai Woevodsky and his English wife Dorothy in the 1920s. The gardens feature cypress, cedar and mimosa trees as well as Mediterranean flowers and herbs, plus a mock castle at the centre and stunning views of waves crashing against the cliffs.

Right
Enjoying the Festa Major

Calella is best known as the home of *havaneres* (*see below*), performed on the beach at a popular festival each summer. The singing of *havaneres* is usually accompanied by the drinking of *cremat*, a spicy Creole concoction of flaming coffee, rum and cinnamon with a twist of lemon.

Accommodation and food in Calella de Palafrugell

Sant Roc €€€ *Plaça Atlàntic 2; tel: 972 614250; fax: 972 614068; email: info@santroc.com; www.santroc.com.* Traditional seaside hotel standing on a cliff, with steps leading down from the gardens to the beach. All of the rooms have balconies, mostly with sea views. The hotel is open from April to October.

Havaneres

The revival of the *havaneres* is a heartening story of how tourism, often accused of destroying local culture, has helped to preserve it. These Caribbean-style sea shanties, brought back from Cuba by 19th-century Catalan fishermen, had been sung in the taverns of Calella de Palafrugell for more than 100 years. In the 1960s, as tourism replaced fishing as the main source of income, the tradition of *havaneres* began to die out – so the idea of an annual *cantada*, or song festival, was born. Designed as a tourist attraction, the festival caught on among locals and the leading singers soon became celebrities. Now *havaneres* are sung once more in the bars of Calella and the *cantada* each July attracts a wide mix of Catalans and foreign tourists.

CASTELL GALA DALÍ

Castell Gala Dalí €€
Plaça Gala Dalí, Púbol; tel: 972 488655; www.dali-estate.org. Open 15 Mar–14 Jun & 16 Sept–1 Nov Tue–Sun 1000–1800; 15 Jun–15 Sept daily 1000–2000.

Can Bosch €€
Tel: 972 488357.
Right beside the castle, the village restaurant serves no-nonsense Catalan cuisine in hearty portions and is very popular with locals at weekends. Lunch only on weekdays.

If you have enjoyed the sights of Dalíland (*see pages 162–71*), you should make the effort to visit this 14th-century castle in the small inland village of Púbol. Dalí bought it for his wife Gala in 1970 to fulfil a long-standing promise. This was to be her refuge, and Dalí boasted that he would never enter without a written invitation. He set about restoring it in typical Dalíesque style; his familiar obsessions and sense of mischief show in every room. There are some wicked *trompe-l'oeil* touches; for instance, Gala wanted the radiators covered up, so he created an alcove in the Piano Room and proceeded to paint it to look just like the radiator which it concealed. Cement elephants in the garden share space with classical sculptures, and a stuffed giraffe watches over Gala's body in the crypt. After Gala died in 1982, Dalí moved into her castle, where he almost died when he accidentally set fire to the bedroom in 1984. He was taken to hospital and never returned. The Cadillac in which he left Púbol for the last time can still be seen in the garage.

EMPÚRIES

Some time in the 6th century BC, the Greeks landed on this spot and established a trading post (*emporion*) on what was then an island. Three centuries later, the Romans docked at Empúries to begin their conquest of the Iberian peninsula. For a while the Greeks and Romans coexisted but the entire colony was abandoned in the 3rd century AD. The excavations of the last 100 years have taught us much about the early history of Catalonia and created one of Spain's most impressive archaeological sites.

Above
Reconstructed houses in Neápolis

ⓘ *Plaça de les Escoles 1, L'Escala;*
tel: 972 770603;
email: turisme@lescala.cat;
www.lescala.cat

🏛 **Empúries €** *Open Oct–May Tue–Sun 1000–1800; Jun–Sept daily 1000–2000.*

⚓ A procession of fishing boats takes place in L'Escala on 16 July for the feast of **Mare de Déu del Carme**, patron saint of fishermen.

The excavations continue, but there are two main areas that can be visited. The Greek city of Neápolis has been partly reconstructed, with houses, a marketplace and a statue of Asclepio, the god of healing. Higher up is the Roman city, standing like a balcony over the sea, with well-preserved mosaic floors inside some of the houses. Here you can appreciate the Roman contribution to Spanish town planning. The old Roman forum can be seen as the forerunner of today's main square, with shops beneath the porticoes and a temple at one end. From here, the main street runs to the city walls, decorated with potent Roman phallic symbols. Look carefully and you can still see the chariot ruts in the gateway.

There is a small museum on the site showing some of the finds, and an audiovisual show on the history of Greek and Roman colonisation. A short walk past the Greek jetty (where the 1992 Olympic flame came ashore) leads to the village of Sant Martí d'Empúries, the site of the earliest Greek settlement. There is a good beach here which rarely gets crowded. The nearby fishing town of **L'Escala** is now a major holiday resort, but it is best known for its anchovies, which have been salted here ever since the Greeks established a factory at Empúries.

Accommodation and food around Empúries

Mesón del Conde €€ *Plaça de l'Església 4, Sant Martí d'Empúries; tel: 972 770306.* For lunch after a visit to the ruins, this restaurant serves straightforward Catalan cooking on a pretty village square.

Nieves Mar €€ *Passeig Marítim 8, L'Escala; tel: 972 770300; fax: 972 773605; email: mail@nievesmar.com; www.nievesmar.com.* This comfortable hotel on the promenade in L'Escala has a swimming pool, tennis courts and great sea views.

L'ESTARTIT

ⓘ *Passeig Marítim;*
tel: 972 751910;
email: info@estartit.org;
www.estartit.org

Illes Medes

Boat trips to the islands operate every day in summer and at weekends in winter, but they are always dependent on the weather and may be cancelled at short notice.

L'Estartit is the classic Costa Brava summer resort, with a vast beach, a picturesque harbour and a long seafront promenade. With safe, shallow water and gently shelving sand, this is a particularly suitable resort for families with young children. The real reason for coming here, though, is to see the **Illes Medes**, a group of rocky islands that became Spain's first marine nature reserve in 1985. Several tour operators by the harbour compete to offer boat trips to the islands, sometimes with the opportunity for snorkelling or diving. Grouper, starfish and spiny lobster can be seen among the coral reefs and caves, and the islands also play host to a large population of seabirds.

Accommodation and food in L'Estartit

Panorama €€ *Avda de Grécia 5; tel: 972 751092; fax: 972 750119; www.hotelpanoramaestartit.com.* Open only in summer, this large seafront hotel makes a comfortable base, with gardens, an outdoor pool, a gymnasium and a sauna.

La Gaviota €€€ *Passeig Marítim 92; tel: 972 752019; email: gaviota26@tecnogrup.com.* The top restaurant in the resort has tables out on the street, looking across at the beach and the Medes islands. The emphasis is on seafood, such as fresh grilled lobster or turbot in *cava*.

Below
L'Estartit

LLAFRANC

ℹ️ **Llafranc** *Carrer de Roger de Llúria; tel: 972 305008 (just a kiosk).* Also **Tamariu** *Carrer del la Rieta; tel: 972 620193.* Both are only open in summer.

This small bay with a crescent beach is one of the gems of the Catalan coast. The people who stay here are second-home owners from Barcelona, or discerning foreigners who want to avoid the mass tourist resorts. A footpath leads around the coast to Calella de Palafrugell, or you can hike over the hills to **Tamariu**, another perfect cove with tamarisk trees leaning across the sand. From the lighthouse at Cap de Sant Sebastià, between Llafranc and Tamariu, there are wonderful views over the bay.

Festivals

Although they are smaller than the festival in Calella de Palafrugell, there are *cantadas d'havaneres* ('sea-shanty concerts') in Llafranc on the first Saturday in August and Tamariu on the first Saturday in September. On the first Sunday in September, a pilgrimage to the lighthouse at Cap de Sant Sebastià is followed by a communal *arrossada* ('rice feast').

Accommodation and food in Llafranc and vicinity

Chez Tomás €€ *Carrer de Lluís Marqués Carbó 2; tel: 972 306215.* Quality French restaurant serving innovative dishes that change according to what is fresh in the market that day.

Hostalillo €€ *Carrer Bellavista 22, Tamariu; tel: 972 620228; fax: 972 620184; www.hostalillo.com.* Open from April to October, this stylish hotel has wonderful views over Tamariu bay and steps leading down through the gardens to the beach.

La Txata €€ *Carrer Carudo 12; tel: 972 302878.* This arty Basque restaurant behind the promenade is run by a pair of sisters. Itziar does the cooking, *nouvelle cuisine* Basque style, while Yolanda does front of house. The restaurant is decorated with Yolanda's sculptures.

Llafranch €€€ *Passeig de Cípsela 16; tel: 972 300208; fax: 972 305259; email: info@hllafranch.com; www.hllafranch.com.* This smart hotel stands on the seafront overlooking the main square of the resort. The brothers who founded the Llafranch were friends of Salvador Dalí, and the bar is covered with photos of Dalí and Manolo, 'the gypsy of the Costa Brava'. The hotel is now run by Manolo's nephew Carlos.

PALAFRUGELL

ℹ️ *Hall de Theatre, Carrer Santa Margarida 1; tel: 972 300028; email: turisme@palafrugell.net; www.visitpalafrugell.cat.* You'll find another tourist office at *Calle Carrilet 2; tel: 972 300228; fax: 972 611261.*

The busy market town of Palafrugell has a strong Catalan atmosphere and a history as a centre of cork production. The **Museu del Suro** is devoted to the local cork industry and also has a display of cork sculptures. Palafrugell has been at the heart of attempts to promote an alternative image of the Costa Brava, using culture, festivals and gastronomy to attract a different kind of tourist outside the summer season. In December the restaurants serve *El Niu*, a local casserole featuring cod, hake, cuttlefish, egg and potatoes. Between January and March the speciality is sea urchins, which form the basis of a culinary festival known as *la garoinada*. Another unique Palafrugell event is the *Carroussel* Carnival parade on Whit Sunday, introduced in 1962 as a way round Franco's prohibition of the Shrovetide Carnival.

Museu del Suro €
*Carrer Tarongeta 31;
tel: 972 307825. Open
Tue–Sat 1700–2000, Sun
1030–1330; 15 Jun–
15 Sept daily 1000–1400,
1600–2100.*

A large market is
held in Palafrugell
on Sunday mornings.

The **Festa Major**,
with *sardana* dances
and other festivities, takes
place from 19 to 21 July.

Right
The Old Town, Pals

Food in Palafrugell

La Xicra €€€ *Carrer Sant Antoni 17; tel: 972 305630; www.
restaurantlaxicra.com.* This intimate restaurant is situated in a town
house close to the main square. The menu features classic Empordan
cooking, mixing flavours from the land and the sea in unusual
combinations such as octopus with ham.

PALS

*Plaça Major 7;
tel: 972 637380;
email: info@pals.es;
www.pals.cat*

A market is held on
Tuesday mornings.

The walled village of Pals was abandoned after the Civil War and then
slowly and lovingly restored by a local doctor. The restoration has
won many architectural awards, with the result that Pals has become
something of a showpiece and consequently a tourist trap. Come here
early or late in the day to appreciate the village, strolling along the
narrow lanes as you come across Gothic houses, medieval walls and a
Romanesque clock tower. Platja de Pals, 5km away on the coast, has a
glorious long sandy beach.

Accommodation and food around Pals

La Costa €€€ *Platja de Pals; tel: 972 667740; fax: 972 667736; www.resortlacosta.com.* The rooms of this modern four-star hotel, situated beside a championship golf course close to the beach at Platja de Pals, are set around a large pool area with pine trees.

Mas de Torrent €€€ *Torrent; tel: 902 550321; fax: 972 303293; email: info@mastorrent.com; www.mastorrent.com.* This five-star hotel, in an 18th-century *finca* ('farmhouse') just outside Pals, combines all the luxury you would expect with a relaxed, friendly atmosphere. There is swimming and tennis in the peaceful gardens, and a restaurant serving creative Catalan cuisine.

PERATALLADA

Can Bonay €€, on Plaça de les Voltes, serves traditional Catalan cooking and has a wine museum in its extensive cellar. *Tel: 972 634034.*

The name of this moated village means 'carved stone' and the cobbled streets are full of Gothic stone houses. At times the village is deathly quiet; at others it is thronged with day-trippers, who crowd the antique shops, art galleries and excellent Catalan restaurants around the arcaded main square.

Right
Local flora

Accommodation and food in Peratallada

La Riera €€ *Plaça de les Voltes 3; tel: 972 634142; www.lariera.es.* This rustic hotel and restaurant serves Catalan meat dishes in a medieval house on the main square.

TORROELLA DE MONTGRÍ

ⓘ **Can Quintana**
Centre Cultural de la Mediterrània, Carrer d'Ullà 31; tel: 972 755180; email: canquintana@torroella.org; www.torroella.org

ⓘ **Museu de la Mediterrània** *Carrer d'Ullà 31; tel: 972 755180; www.museudelamediterrania. org. Open Mon–Sat 1000–1400, 1700–2000. Free.*

Sheltering beneath the Montgrí massif at the mouth of the River Ter, Torroella is a market town of Gothic palaces, Renaissance courtyards and narrow lanes fanning out from a porticoed main square. On Monday mornings the square and the surrounding streets are taken over by one of Catalonia's most colourful small-town markets. The town museum, **Museu de la Mediterrània**, has sections on local history, culture and music, including the marine environment of Illes Medes. A climb of about an hour from the town centre leads to the **Castell del Montgrí**, a restored 13th-century castle offering panoramic views of the coast, the Empordan plain and the distant Pyrenees. Beneath the castle, the hermitage of Santa Caterina is the scene of a mass pilgrimage each November.

ULLASTRET

ⓘ **Museu Arqueològic de Ullastret** € *Puig de Sant Andreu, 2km from the village of Ullastret; tel: 972 179058. Open Jun–Sept Tue–Sun 1000–2000; Oct–May Tue–Sun 1000–1400, 1500–1800. Access to the site is free during these times.*

Hidden among the almond and olive groves of the Empordan plain is the most significant known settlement of the Iberian civilisation, which flourished in Catalonia between the 6th and 2nd centuries BC. The Iberian culture, which probably came about as a result of contact with Greek settlers, is believed to have been the first indigenous culture of modern Spain, with a written language, a system of money and the development of agriculture, pottery and metalwork. Most of what we know about the Iberians is a result of excavations on this site, and as you poke around among the ruins and visit the on-site museum you can feel the ancient world coming to life. Parts of the original walls and defensive towers remain, together with cisterns, grain stores and temples dating from the 3rd century BC.

Left
Pals

Suggested tour

Total distance: 98km.

Time: 2 hours. It is best to allow at least half a day, longer if you want to visit the archaeological sites at Empúries and Ullastret.

Links: This route passes within 2km of the southern Costa Brava route (*see pages 192–3*) at La Bisbal.

Start at **PALAFRUGELL** ❶, with a choice of routes down to the coast. A fast dual carriageway leads directly to Llafranc, but the more scenic approach is on the old road to **CALELLA DE PALAFRUGELL** ❷, passing pine woods, fields and farmhouses turned into discos. Reaching Calella, turn left, then right at the roundabout to drop down to **LLAFRANC** ❸.

Drive along the seafront, then turn left in the main square, halfway along the beach. At the top of this road, bear right to Tamariu. The road climbs to the headland of Sant Sebastià, with wonderful views over Llafranc. Ignore all temptations to take a side turn to your right and keep to this road until it joins the road from Palafrugell. Now turn right to descend through the pine woods to **Tamariu**, arriving beside the beach. Keep straight ahead towards Begur. The signposts are confusing, variously indicating Aiguaxelida, Aiguablava and Begur, but they take you through a modern villa development and then on to the cliffs around **AIGUABLAVA** ❹.

At the bottom of this road, turn right for Aiguablava beach or left to continue your journey to **BEGUR** ❺. As you approach the town, 200m above sea level, the castle is perched on a rock up ahead and the coast is spread out beneath you. Turn left and follow signs for **PALS** ❻. Unless you are stopping here, take the ring road around the village towards **TORROELLA DE MONTGRÍ** ❼. The town is already visible, its hilltop castle dominating the surrounding plain. Arriving in Torroella, you have the option of a side trip to **L'ESTARTIT** ❽ or you can continue around the town on the road to Girona. Passing through **Ullà**, turn right towards **L'Escala** on a straight, flat road across the plain.

In L'Escala, turn left to reach the ruins at **EMPÚRIES** ❾. Leaving the ruins, follow signs for Girona. After a few kilometres, leave this road on a slip road to the village of **Viladamat**. Now drive south across the plain, passing through **Verges** ❿ on the way to **Parlavà**, after which you turn left towards **ULLASTRET** ⓫. Take the next right at **Serra de Daró** and follow this road to reach the Iberian village. The road then continues through Ullastret, passing close to **PERATALLADA** ⓬ before reaching the outskirts of **La Bisbal d'Empordà** (*see page 185*). Turn left here to return to Palafrugell.

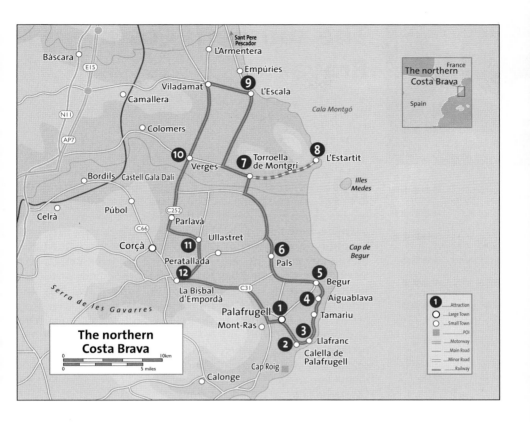

Getting out of the car

The GR92 footpath runs along this coastline and is particularly scenic between Aiguablava and Calella de Palafrugell. The easiest section is the 30-minute stroll around the cliffs between Calella and Llafranc. The entire route is waymarked with red and white stripes.

Also worth exploring

A minor road from Empúries leads north around the Gulf of Roses to the village of **Sant Pere Pescador**. This is a wild and lonely shore, with campsites among the sand dunes and sweeping views of the bay. The long beach is protected from tourist development by its status as part of the Aiguamolls de l'Empordà nature reserve. From Sant Pere Pescador, a short drive inland leads to the village of **Sant Miquel de Fluvià**, with its 11th-century Romanesque church.

The southern Costa Brava

Ratings

Beaches	●●●●●
Children	●●●●●
Nightlife	●●●●●
Restaurants	●●●●○
Scenery	●●●●○
Watersports	●●●●○
Towns/villages	●●●○○
Historical sights	●●○○○

More than anywhere else on the Spanish mainland, the southern stretch of the Costa Brava epitomises the growth of mass tourism. Until the 1950s, the towns along this coastline were little more than fishing villages; now they have been turned into some of Europe's busiest resorts, with visitors far outnumbering the local population in summer. Resorts such as Lloret de Mar and Platja d'Aro attract thousands of tourists with their mixture of cheap hotels, superb beaches and legendary nightlife. Yet despite the appearance of large-scale hotels, there are still places where you can find that quiet cove, and working fishing ports which revert to their original occupation in winter when the tourists have all gone home. The coastal scenery is some of the most spectacular anywhere, while inland lies a region of cork and oak forests, punctuated by solid Catalan villages and market towns.

LA BISBAL D'EMPORDÀ

● The pottery shops are situated on Carrer l'Aigüeta, on the road out of La Bisbal towards Girona. Most sell a similar range of goods, but among the more unusual are **Vila Clara** at No 56, **Rogenca d'Ullastret** at No 112, **Diaz Acosta** at No 136 and **Artfi** at No 278.

Most people come to La Bisbal for just one thing – to buy some of the pottery for which the town is famous. There are dozens of pottery shops strung out along the main road, selling everything from mass-produced factory pieces to wacky local designs. Much of it is piled up on the pavement, making an impressive sight as you drive through the town. One of the best buys, which you can get anywhere, is a simple glazed earthenware cooking pot (*greixoneras*) – cheap, practical, long-lasting and very Catalan.

In medieval times this was the seat of the bishops of Girona, and the Romanesque episcopal palace still stands on the old town square. This is the scene of a lively market which takes over the alleyways of the old town each Friday.

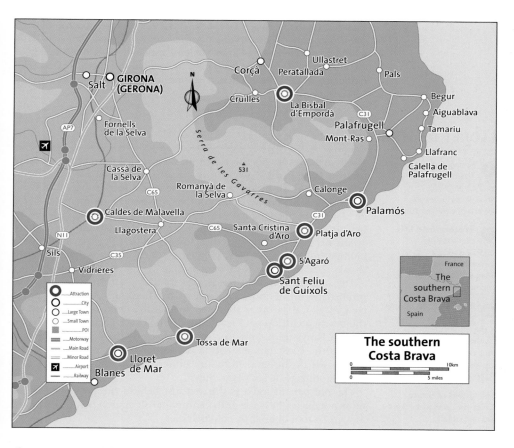

CALDES DE MALAVELLA

Spa water

Many people find that Vichy Catalán water has a salty, mineral taste and they prefer the cleaner taste of Fontdor from the spa town of Sant Hilari Sacalm.

This small town surrounded by pine forests is known throughout Spain as the home of Vichy Catalán, a popular brand of mineral water which is bottled here. There have been hot springs here since Roman times and there are still two spa hotels, offering a range of health and beauty treatments.

Accommodation and food in Caldes de Malavella

Balneari Prats €€€ *Plaça de Sant Esteve 7; tel: 972 470051; fax: 972 472233; email: info@balneariprats.com; www.balneariprats.com.* A neoclassical spa hotel dating back to the 19th century, when it was the fashion to visit Caldes in order to 'take the waters'.

Vichy Catalán €€€ *Passeig Dr Furest 32; tel: 972 470000; fax: 972 472299; email: balneari@vichycatalan.es; www.balnearivichycatalan.com.* This splendid spa hotel, designed in Modernist style in 1898, offers therapies including massage, reflexology, mud treatments and thermal pools. The restaurant serves typical Catalan cuisine with an emphasis on seafood. Full board only.

LLORET DE MAR

ⓘ *Passeig Camprodoni i Arrieta 1–2;* tel: 972 364735; email: lloret-turisme@ llorret.org; www.lloret.org

🅗 Waterworld €€€ *Ctra Vidreres;* tel: 972 368613; www.waterworld.es. Open 1000–1900 daily in summer.

☯ If you want to sample the nightlife, **Tropics** is the most famous disco on the Costa Brava, while tour operators sell tickets for the extravagant **Gran Palace** flamenco show.

The festival of **Santa Cristina** takes place from the end of July.

Below Lloret de Mar

The biggest resort on the Costa Brava is a classic example of mass tourism gone berserk; what little remains of the old town has been swamped beneath a tide of hotels, discos and foreign bars. With the introduction of walking trails and *sardanas* on the promenade, Lloret de Mar has been trying hard to change its image, but most visitors still have their sights firmly set on sun, sea and sex. When they want some Spanish culture, they visit the town's bullring, little aware that bullfighting has never been popular in Catalonia and that it is only thanks to tourism that it survives at all.

The main attraction is the beach, stretching all the way along the promenade to the mock castle at its northern end, where the rocky cove of Sa Caleta offers sheltered swimming. From the other end of the beach, a clifftop path leads around the coast, passing the tiny bay of Cala Banys on its way to a second beach, Platja de Fenals. Further around the coast, Santa Cristina is another pretty cove, where steps lead down to the sand from an 18th-century hermitage, scene of a mass pilgrimage by boat every July.

The old part of town is situated just behind the promenade. The most notable sight is the 16th-century parish church, with its striking Modernist roof of brightly coloured tiles.

For children, **Waterworld**, just outside Lloret de Mar, is a large waterpark with numerous pools and rides, including a wet roller coaster.

Between June and September, *sardana* dances take place from 2230 every Saturday evening in front of the town hall on Plaça de la Vila.

Accommodation and food in Lloret de Mar

Les Petxines €€ *Passeig Verdaguer 16; tel: 972 364137; email: reservas@excelsiorlloret.com.* In a place where it is sometimes easier to get a curry than a Spanish meal, this Catalan restaurant comes as a pleasant surprise, offering creative fresh market cuisine and a gastronomic menu. It is situated on the promenade.

Planiol €€ *Domènech Carles; tel: 972 369342.* Paella and other seafood dishes are served on a seaside terrace at the quiet end of Fenals beach.

Santa Marta €€€ *Platja de Santa Cristina; tel: 972 364904; fax: 972 369280; email: info@hotelsantamarta.net; www.hotelsantamarta.net.* Rather than stay in the resort, it is far better to escape to this elegant hotel, set amid pine woods behind the Santa Cristina cove.

PALAMÓS

Pere Joan 44; tel: 972 600550; email: turisme@palamos.cat; www.palamos.cat

A market is held in Palamós on Tuesday mornings. The fish auction takes place by the harbour at around 1700 on weekdays.

This busy fishing port stands on a headland overlooking the harbour, scene of a lively fish auction every weekday afternoon. Although the modern town has gradually extended along the waterfront, its old quarter remains largely unaffected by tourism. In the 19th century, Palamós was the main export harbour for Catalonia's cork industry, and several shops in the centre continue to sell cork artefacts. From the harbour, a palm-lined promenade leads around a long, sandy beach, a popular centre for watersports. In 1992 this was chosen as the venue for the Olympic sailing competition.

Accommodation and food in Palamós

Trías €€ *Passeig del Mar; tel: 972 601800; fax: 972 601819; email: infotrias@hoteltrias.com; www.hoteltrias.com.* A long-established beach hotel, directly facing the sea, with facilities including car parking and a heated pool.

La Gamba €€€ *Plaça Sant Pere 1; tel: 972 314633; email: restaurant@lagambapalamos.com.* This top-quality seafood restaurant, with a terrace overlooking the harbour, knows how to make the most of the local ingredients. Specialities are prawns, oven-baked fish and seafood casserole, all simply but beautifully prepared.

María de Cadaqués €€€ *Carrer Taula i Servià 6; tel: 972 314009.* Another top seafood restaurant with a charcoal grill and a good line in local-style casseroles.

Festivals

There is a large **Carnival** parade in the streets of Palamós on the last Saturday before Lent, which usually falls in February. Another traditional festival, **Mare de Déu del Carme**, takes place on 16 July, with a procession of fishing boats in honour of the protector of fisherfolk.

PLATJA D'ARO

ℹ️ *Carrer Jacint Verdaguer 4; tel: 972 817179; email: turisme@platjadaro. com; www.platjadaro.com.* Guided tours of Castell d'Aro take place between June and September at 1730, 1830 & 1930 daily. At other times they can be arranged through the tourist office.

🎢 **Aquadiver €€€**, on the edge of the resort, is a waterpark with plenty of thrills and spills for younger and older children. Other family attractions include **Magic Park**, an adventure play area, and the **Museu de la Nina**, a doll museum in Castell d'Aro.

🎭 The **Carnival** parade takes place on the last Saturday before Lent, which usually falls in February.

In 1950 this was merely the fishing harbour for the nearby village of Castell d'Aro; now it has grown into the Costa Brava's second resort, completely dwarfing the town from which it takes its name. The beach is glorious, the discos are loud, but otherwise it has little to recommend it – unless you come in winter, when the locals reclaim their town for one of the biggest pre-Lenten Carnival parades in Spain. The original village survives inland, dominated by a medieval castle. In summer the tourist office organises walking tours of the village, in a largely futile effort to persuade tourists to look beyond the beach.

Accommodation and food in Platja d'Aro

Big Rock €€€ *Barri de Fanals 5; tel: 972 818012; fax: 972 818971.* Rather unexpectedly, Platja d'Aro has one of the very best restaurants on the Catalan coast. Owned by chef Carles Camós, it is based in an old manor house above the town. The cuisine is inventive, using fresh local ingredients in unexpected ways. If you want to stay, there are five luxury suites upstairs; book well ahead.

Candlelight (Hostal de la Gavina) €€€ *Plaza de la Rosaleda s/n; tel: 972 321100; www.lagavina.com.* Service and cuisine are unparalleled here, with creative specialities from both sea and land.

Joan Piqué €€€ *Barri de Crota 3, Platja d'Aro; tel: 972 817925.* Hidden away in a 14th-century farmhouse, this modern Catalan restaurant offers highly personal creations, such as turbot with pigs' trotters in oyster sauce.

Tourism on the Costa Brava

In the late 1950s, in an effort to improve Spain's standard of living, the Franco government decided to market the Spanish *costas* as an alternative to the French and Italian rivieras. Tourist offices were set up all over Europe, promoting Spain as a sun-and-sea destination, with paella and flamenco adding a dash of local colour. Catalonia and the Balearic islands were used as test cases, with very little control over the early growth of tourism. The British author Norman Lewis, who spent three years in a Costa Brava fishing village, has described in his memoir *Voices of the Old Sea* how he watched the old way of life being destroyed by the desire for a quick buck.

By the 1990s, more than five million foreign tourists were visiting the Costa Brava every year and the autonomous Catalan government had become aware of the limitations and destructive effects of mass tourism. Efforts are under way to rebrand the Costa Brava as an upmarket, cultural destination; even the name Costa Brava, with its *viva España* connotations, is gradually giving way to the more neutral 'Catalan coast'.

Right
Lloret Castle overlooking Sa Caleta beach, Lloret de Mar

S'AGARÓ

P Only residents are allowed to take their cars into the resort; everyone else has to park outside the barrier by Platja Sant Pol.

To some this is an example of tasteful tourist development; to others it represents vulgar ostentation and exclusivity. Designed by the Catalan architect Rafael Masó on a headland in 1924, the small resort is a mixture of Italianate villas, landscaped gardens and a coastal promenade which connects two fine beaches around a series of rocky creeks.

Accommodation and food in S'Agaró

Barcarola €€ *Platja Sant Pol, Sant Feliu de Guíxols; tel: 972 326932.* One of a row of restaurants offering fresh fish and seafood.

Hostal de la Gavina €€€ *Plaça de la Rosaleda; tel: 972 321100; fax: 972 321573; email: reservas@lagavina.com; www.lagavina.com.* Film stars and politicians have long flocked to this elegant retreat, designed by Rafael Masó in the style of a Gothic villa. Everything is perfect, from the tapestries and antique furniture to the fine Catalan cuisine and the gardens overlooking the sea.

SANT FELIU DE GUÍXOLS

ℹ *Plaça del Mercat 6; tel: 972 327000; email: turisme@guixols.net; www.guixols.cat*

Porta Ferrada

The Porta Ferrada can be seen at all times, but the monastery church is generally open for services only, at 2000 on weekdays and on Sunday morning.

Museu d'Història € *Carrer Abadia; tel: 972 821575. Open Tue–Sat 1000–1300, 1700–2000, Sun 1000–1300.*

A big **Carnival** parade takes place in Sant Feliu on the Saturday before Lent. There is also a procession of fishing boats on 16 July for the festival of **Mare de Déu del Carme**.

An international music festival is held in the parish church in July and August.

This working fishing port was the Costa Brava's biggest resort until the high-rise boom which created Platja d'Aro and Lloret de Mar. The beach, an arc of fine sand, leads around to the fishing harbour at its north end. The seafront promenade is lined with handsome Modernist mansions, a reminder of the town's earlier wealth as a result of the cork trade. Behind the promenade, a well-preserved old quarter of narrow streets and squares leads to **Porta Ferrada**, a 10th-century gateway with horseshoe arches. This is all that remains of a pre-Romanesque monastery, though the church has since been developed in Romanesque, Gothic and Baroque style. The complex of buildings includes the **Museu d'Història de la Ciutat**, with local archaeological finds and displays on the cork and fishing industries.

Accommodation and food in Sant Feliu de Guíxols

Bahía €€ *Passeig del Mar 18; tel: 972 320219.* One of the best of the many seafood restaurants along the promenade. You can start with a *pica-pica*, a selection of fish titbits.

Eldorado Mar €€ *Rambla Vidal 23; tel: 972 321818.* The top restaurant in the resort serves exquisite Catalan-French cuisine, with a grill-bar offering simpler and cheaper options next door.

Edén Roc €€€ *Port Salvi; tel: 972 320100; fax: 972 821705; www.edenrochotel.com.* This large hotel is situated beside a cove on the southern edge of the resort. A road from here climbs to the chapel of Sant Elm for panoramic views of the coast.

TOSSA DE MAR

Avda Pelegrí 25;
tel: 972 340108;
email: oftossa@ddgi.es;
www.infotossa.com

Museu Municipal €
Plaça Roig i Soler;
tel: 972 340709. Open
Oct–May Tue–Sat
1000–1400, 1600–1800,
Sun 1000–1400; Jun–Sept
Tue–Sat 1000–2000, Sun &
Mon 1000–1400,
1600–2000.

The Vila Nova, behind
the beach, is the best
place for shopping,
especially at the boutiques
along Carrer Portal.
Tossa's weekly market
takes place on Thursday
mornings.

Although it is one of the Costa Brava's busiest summer resorts, Tossa de Mar retains a good deal of its charm – largely because of the survival of its fortified old town, **Vila Vella**, founded on a headland by the Abbot of Ripoll in 1186. The sight of Tossa's medieval walls rising above the beach is one of the most enduring images of the Catalan coast. Within the walls is a warren of narrow streets, reached by a fairly easy climb. At the heart of the old town, the **Museu Municipal**, in the former Abbot's palace, displays archaeological finds and modern art, including a painting by Marc Chagall, who stayed here in 1934. There is a small sheltered beach directly below the museum but most people stick to the main beach, Platja Gran, or follow the promenade to its northern end to reach Platja Mar Menuda.

Accommodation and food in Tossa de Mar

Bahía €€ *Passeig del Mar 29; tel: 972 340322.* Fresh fish dishes on a seafront terrace, with specialities including squid and *cim i tomba*, a fish, potato and garlic stew.

Diana €€€ *Plaça d'Espanya 6; tel: 972 341886; fax: 972 341103; email: info@diana-hotel.com; www.hotelesdante.com.* This Modernist villa with stained-glass windows stands out on the seafront. The balconies have marvellous views over the beach.

Mar Menuda €€€ *Platja Mar Menuda; tel: 972 341000; fax: 972 340087; email: hotel@marmenuda.com; www.hotelmarmenuda.com.* A hotel belonging to the Best Western chain with direct access to Mar Menuda beach, making a good escape from the bustle of the town. There are peaceful gardens and an outdoor pool.

Above
Medieval walls at Tossa

Tursia €€ *Carrer Barcelona 3; tel: 972 341500; www.tursia.com.* French and Catalan cuisine on a quiet backstreet, with a few tables outside. Specialities include grilled duck breast with tarragon. Closed mid-October to mid-April.

Suggested tour

Total distance: 114km.

Time: 2½–3 hours.

Links: From Platja d'Aro, the coast road continues north to the start of the northern Costa Brava route (*see pages 182–3*) at Palafrugell. The two routes also intersect at La Bisbal. From Tossa de Mar, a short drive south through Lloret de Mar leads to the start of the Montseny mountain route (*see pages 210–13*) at Blanes.

Start in **TOSSA DE MAR** ❶ and head north along the coastal corniche, a dizzying drive around a seemingly endless series of bends. There are pine woods to your left, and cliffs plunging sheer into the sea on your right. Driving in this direction, you feel very close to the sea and there are several opportunities to pull in at miradors and look down over the rocky coves. Take your time along this first stretch of road; it is the classic Costa Brava drive.

After a long 23km you reach **SANT FELIU DE GUÍXOLS** ❷. Turn right to pass along the seafront and then left at the end of the beach to continue on the coast road. Shortly after passing **S'AGARÓ** ❸, keep straight on at the roundabout to drive through the main street of **LA PLATJA D'ARO** ❹, perhaps saying a quiet prayer of thanks that not all the Costa Brava is like this. Reaching the small resort of **Sant Antoni de Calonge**, you finally leave the coast road, turning left through the village of **Calonge** ❺ and climbing steadily through wild olive groves on a beautiful, shady, traffic-free road to **LA BISBAL D'EMPORDÀ** ❻, where you turn left to reach the town centre.

As soon as you have crossed the bridge on to the Girona road – the pottery shops are just starting to appear – look for a minor road on your left, signposted to **Cruïlles**. This tiny hamlet has a delightful medieval centre, dominated by an 11th-century monastery church. The road now climbs gently towards the hilltop chapel of Santa Pellaia, with occasional glimpses through the trees of the Montseny mountain range in the distance and the bay of Roses far behind you. Soon after the chapel, the road drops down to the village of **Cassà de la Selva**.

Keep straight ahead at the junction for the spa town of **CALDES DE MALAVELLA** ❼, then turn left to reach **Llagostera**, which once had a significant cork industry. Keep right in Llagostera and follow a minor road, crossing the C35 and twisting down the beautiful Tossa valley to return to Tossa de Mar.

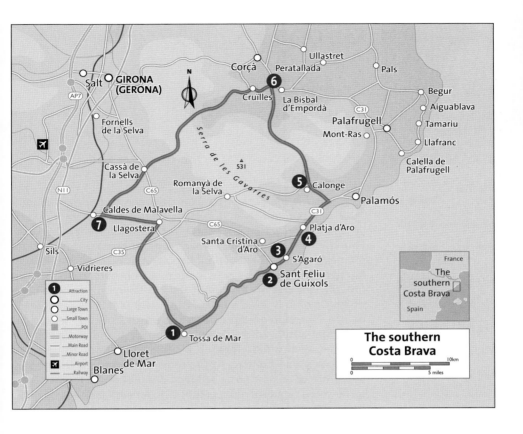

Getting out of the car

A good way to get a feel for this rocky coastline is to take one of the boat trips that depart regularly in summer from all the main resorts. One of the best is the short trip from Tossa de Mar to Lloret de Mar, passing several small coves and beaches that are best viewed from the sea.

Also worth exploring

The minor road from Calonge to Llagostera travels through cork and oak woods in the foothills of the Serra de les Gavarres. On the way you pass **Romanyà de la Selva**, where a 4,000-year-old burial chamber, Cova d'en Daina, is surrounded by a megalithic stone circle. This is the most spectacular of all Catalonia's ancient monuments, and it is reached by a short walk, signposted from the road.

Girona

Ratings

Historical sights	●●●●●
Architecture	●●●●○
Museums	●●●●○
Parks/ gardens	●●●●○
Restaurants	●●●○○
Shopping	●●●○○
Walking	●●●○○
Children	●●○○○

G irona is the perfect Catalan city, blending ancient dignity with modern style. It is small enough to explore in a day, yet infinitely rewarding for those prepared to give it more time. Founded by the Romans, sacked by the Moors, captured by Charlemagne and besieged by Napoleon, it is sometimes known as 'the city of a thousand sieges'. Girona wears its history proudly, and the restoration of the old town on the right bank of the Onyar has given many of its ancient buildings a new lease of life. The narrow lanes of the Jewish quarter, where an important school of mysticism was founded, and the streets of the medieval guilds, named after their former trades, are particularly atmospheric. At the same time, this is a thoroughly modern city with a large student population, a thriving arts scene and a reputation for radical Catalan nationalism.

Getting there

ℹ️ *Rambla de la Llibertat 1; tel: 972 226575; email: turisme@ ajgirona.org; www.ajuntament.gi. The tourist office is a useful source of information on Girona and the rest of Catalonia. The office also sells combined tickets to all of Girona's museums, which are good value if you intend visiting several.*

If you are staying in one of the Costa Brava resorts, there should be regular buses to Girona in summer. The bus station is situated in the modern Eixample district, about a 15-minute walk from the old town. The railway station is in the same area, with frequent connections to Barcelona and Figueres.

Parking

Arriving by car from Barcelona or Figueres, you will come to Passeig de la Devesa, on the south side of the Devesa gardens. Except on market days (Tuesday and Saturday) it is usually possible to find free parking here. Alternatively, you could try your luck around Plaça de Catalunya, where there are limited spaces, or in the underground car park beneath Plaça de la Constitució.

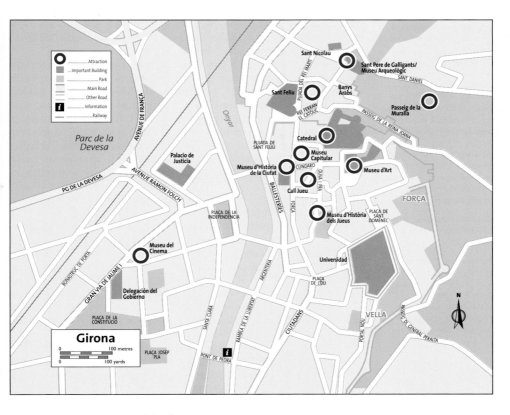

Sights

Banys Àrabs €
Carrer Ferran el Catòlic;
tel: 972 213262;
www.banysarabs.org.
Open Apr–Sept Mon–Sat
1000–1900, Sun
1000–1400; Oct–Mar
1000–1400 daily.

Banys Àrabs

The so-called Arab baths were actually built in the 13th century, 500 years after Girona was liberated from Arab rule. Designed to resemble a Roman bathhouse, they remain one of the best-preserved examples in Spain. The most appealing feature is the *apodyterium* or changing-room, with an octagonal pool beneath a domed skylight through which natural light floods in. From here you can walk through the cold, warm and hot chambers to reach a rooftop gallery for good views of the city's skyline.

Call Jueu

The earliest records of a Jewish community in Girona date back to 890, when around 20 families settled close to today's cathedral. Over the next six centuries, the Jewish population expanded to become one of the largest in Spain, numbering up to a thousand people. The heart of the community was on Carrer de la Força, the old Roman Vía

Museu d'Història dels Jueus € *Carrer Força 8; tel: 972 216761. Open Jun–Oct Mon–Sat 1000–2000, Sun 1000–1500; Nov–May Mon–Sat 1000–1800, Sun 1000–1500.* Ask to see the video (available in several languages) which tells the history of Catalonia's Jews, including the 15th-century expulsion and the recent renaissance – in which this small centre is playing a significant part.

Catedral *Open winter daily 1000–1900; summer daily 1000–2000.*

Museu Capitular € *Tel: 972 214426; www.catedraldegirona.org. Open Apr–Oct Mon–Sat 1000–2000, Sun 1000–1400; Nov–Mar Tue–Sat 1000–1900.*

Augusta, where at one time there was a synagogue, a Jewish school, a ritual bathhouse and a Jewish butcher. The Jews were expelled from Girona, as elsewhere in Spain, in 1492.

The dark, humid, steep streets of the Jewish ghetto have recently been opened up, and they provide one of the most atmospheric corners of the city. By day, sunlight throws shadows on the golden stone; by night, old-fashioned streetlamps create an eerie glow. The last synagogue in Girona is now the **Museu d'Història dels Jueus**, a museum and cultural centre devoted to Catalonia's Jewish history. It was here in Girona that Rabbi Nahmánides founded the Cabbalist school of Judaism, a secret system of mysticism, metaphysics and mathematics that continues to influence Jewish thought to this day.

Catedral

The narrow streets of the Jewish quarter come to an end at Plaça de la Catedral, a large, open square with a Baroque style stairway leading up to Girona's splendid cathedral. This is definitely the best way to approach the cathedral, giving yourself time to admire the exquisite stone carvings on its façade. Inside, the most impressive feature is the immense Gothic nave, at 23m the widest in Europe. The original plan was for the church to have three naves, but in 1417 the bold decision was taken to experiment with a single aisle. Also of note, beneath a silver canopy, is an embossed silver altarpiece dating from the 14th century and featuring scenes from the life of Christ.

Among the treasures in the **Museu Capitular** is a 10th-century *Beatus*, an illustrated manuscript of St John's Commentary on the Apocalypse, with brightly coloured miniature drawings produced by a nun. The highlight, though, is the 11th- and 12th-century *Tapestry of the Creation*, a unique piece of embroidery whose vivid colours show scenes from everyday farming life as well as the sun and the moon, the sea and the sky, Adam and Eve, angels, and Christ in majesty at

Below
Girona's River Onyar

ⓝ Museu Arqueològic
€ *Carrer de Santa Llúcia; tel: 972 202632; www.mac.es. Open Oct–May Tue–Sat 1000–1400, 1600–1800, Sun 1000–1400; Jun–Sept Tue–Sat 1030–1330, 1600–1900.*

Museu d'Art € *Pujada de la Catedral 12; tel: 972 203834; www.museuart.com. Open Tue–Sat 1000–1800 (Mar–Sept 1000–1900), Sun 1000–1400.*

Museu del Cinema €
Carrer Sèquia 1; tel: 972 412777; www.museudelcinema.org. Open Oct–Apr Tue–Fri 1000–1800, Sat 1000–2000, Sun 1100–1500; May–Sept Tue–Sun 1000–2000.

Museu d'Història de la Ciutat € *Carrer de la Força 27; tel: 972 222229; www.ajuntament.gi/ museuciutat. Open Tue–Sat 1000–1400, 1700–1900, Sun 1000–1400.*

the centre. The museum also gives access to the 12th-century cloisters, part of the original Romanesque cathedral on this site.

Museu Arqueològic

Girona's archaeological museum, in the Romanesque monastery of **Sant Pere de Galligants**, contains artefacts from prehistoric to medieval times. Among the oldest exhibits are a 4th-century Roman sepulchre and three milestones indicating the distance to Gerunda, the Roman name for the city. The 12th-century cloister, with its beautifully sculpted capitals, contains a number of Jewish tombstones. There are peaceful gardens around the back, and a riverside walk leading to another Romanesque monastery, Sant Daniel. On the way back, climb to the John Lennon gardens for views of the cathedral and the medieval walls.

Museu d'Art

The art museum is located in the former episcopal palace, built between the 12th and the 14th centuries. It houses a representative collection of Catalan art from the Romanesque period to the present day. Among the highlights are a 10th-century portable altar from the monastery of Sant Pere de Rodes, a polychrome crossbeam from the church at Cruïlles, a Gothic altarpiece from Púbol by Bernat Martorell, and Ramón Martí's painting of the 1809 siege of Girona. There are also scenes of 20th-century Girona by the Catalan Modernist artist Santiago Rusiñol, who spent long periods in the city.

Museu del Cinema

Girona's newest museum, on the left bank of the Onyar river, is devoted to the early history of the cinema. It is based on a collection of more than 30,000 objects acquired by Tomàs Mallol and bought by the city of Girona in 1994. Among the exhibits are cinema projectors, optic boxes and magic lanterns from the beginning of the 20th century.

Museu d'Història de la Ciutat

The city history museum is housed in an 18th-century Capuchin monastery, built over Roman ruins which date from the 2nd century AD. One of the first things you notice as you enter is the monastery's cemetery, where mummified corpses were placed in niches on the walls. The rest of the museum gives an overview of Girona's history, beginning with the earliest Bronze Age inhabitants. There is a gallery devoted to the history of the *sardana* dance, and an interesting section on 20th-century industrial history, featuring printing presses, computers and an old petrol pump.

Passeig de la Muralla

Girona's medieval ramparts have been painstakingly restored and it is possible to walk along certain sections of the old walls. From the southern edge of the old town near Plaça de Catalunya, a stairway

For bar-hopping, head for the area around Plaça del Vi, or join local students and expatriates at the **Excalibur** ale house on Plaça de l'Oli. There are also several outdoor cafés on the Rambla; **L'Arcada**, at No 38, has good *tapas*, an upstairs restaurant and occasional live music. After dark, the late-night club scene shifts to Carrer Pedret, north of the centre beside the River Ter.

leads up on to the walls for great views over the city. When the walkway runs out, a second path outside the walls continues to the Jardins d'Alemanys ('German Gardens'), where you can clamber up to an old watchtower, Torre Gironella. From here, various paths follow the ramparts towards the **Passeig Arqueològic**, a series of landscaped gardens leading down to the River Galligants, with excellent views of the cathedral as you descend. This walk ends very close to both the Arab baths and the archaeological museum and can be easily combined with a visit to either.

Accommodation and food

Bellmirall € *Carrer Bellmirall 3; tel: 972 204009.* A medieval mansion in the heart of the old town has been turned into a charming hostel with simple but comfortable rooms overlooking the cathedral.

Costabella € *Avda de França 61; tel: 972 202524; fax: 972 202203; www.hotelcostabella.com.* A modern hotel with a pool, located just outside Girona on the road to Figueres, yet close enough to make a convenient base for exploring the city.

Crêperie Brotona € *Carrer Cort Reial 14; tel: 972 218120.* Authentic French pancakes and cider from Brittany are the specialities at this playful bistro in the old town.

Peninsular € *Avinguda San Françesc 6; tel: 972 203800; fax: 972 210492; email: peninsular@novarahotels.com; www.novarahotels.com.* What this hotel lacks in character it makes up for in location, just across the river from the old town on a pedestrian shopping street. Overnight parking could be a problem around here.

Boira €€ *Plaça Independència 17; tel: 972 211132.* A choice of a *tapas* bar or a more formal Catalan restaurant, with window tables overlooking the river. The daily set menu is always good value here.

Cal Ros €€ *Carrer Cort Reial 9; tel: 972 219176.* The emphasis here is on Catalan meat dishes, including pigs' trotters and snails.

Mimolet €€ *Carrer del Pou Rodó 12; tel: 972 202124.* An upbeat contemporary restaurant in the old town with an innovative menu which includes plenty of light eats and vegetarian dishes. There are also more substantial set menus.

Mozart €€ *Plaça Independència 2; tel: 972 207542.* Simple, well-prepared Italian cuisine, from salads and grilled meat dishes to pizzas from a wood-fired oven.

El Pou del Call €€ *Carrer de la Força 14; tel: 972 223774.* Traditional Catalan cooking on the main street of the Jewish quarter, close to the cathedral. The set menu is the best value here and the restaurant also serves kosher wine.

Right
Church towers of Girona

Albereda €€€ *Carrer Albereda 7; tel: 972 226002; www.restaurantalbereda.com.* Widely considered Girona's top restaurant, the Albereda serves modern Catalan cuisine in a quiet backstreet just off the Plaça de Catalunya.

Carlemany €€€ *Plaça Miquel Santaló 1; tel: 972 211212; fax: 972 214994; email: carlemany@carlemany.es; www.carlemany.es.* This large, modern designer hotel is situated between the station and the old town. There is no pool but there is a car park, a useful facility in Girona. It holds exhibitions of contemporary art. The restaurant, El Pati Verd, is known for its Catalan specialities, such as rabbit with snails.

Mar Plaça €€€ *Plaça de la Independència 3; tel: 972 205962.* This elegant restaurant specialises in fish and seafood in numerous guises – in soups, stews, casseroles and rice dishes, as well as simply grilled.

Right
Defenders of Girona monument,
Plaça de la Independència

Shopping

Above
The Rambla

The streets of the old town, between the Rambla and the Jewish quarter, are full of small, specialist boutiques selling everything from candles to masks. This is a great area for strolling, especially during the early-evening *paseo*, when window-shopping and people-watching are all part of the fun. Wander around this area between 1800 and 2000 and you are bound to find a shop which appeals, whether your taste is for ethnic art, books stacked floor to ceiling or the latest fashions.

The best arts and crafts shops are on Carrer Ballesteries – try **Anna Casals** for jewellery and **Ramón Boix** for artistic objects made from metal. **Tíbur** has good reproductions of ancient art at nearby Pujada de Sant Domenec. Also on Carrer Ballesteries, **Eco-Opció** features alternative and eco-friendly gifts, and **Ulyssus** has a wide range of travel books, mostly in Spanish and Catalan.

Girona's indoor market, just south of Plaça del Lleó, is a good place for stocking up on picnic food. Markets also take place twice a week, on Tuesday and Saturday mornings, on Passeig de la Devesa, though the emphasis is on clothes and household goods rather than fresh produce. A flower market is set up on the Rambla on Saturdays.

For clothes shopping, head across the river to Carrer Santa Clara and Carrer Nou.

Other streets worth exploring are Carrer Mercaders for arts, books and antiques, and Carrer Argenteria for upmarket leather and jewellery shops. This street also contains two of Girona's most tempting food shops – **Gluki**, makers of chocolate since 1880, and **Candela**, whose speciality is nougat. For cheeses, cured meats and wine, check out **Joan Puig**, a wood-panelled grocer's shop on the Rambla, and **Colmado Moriscot** on Carrer dels Ciutadans. The nearby **Celler d'en Pere**, on Plaça de l'Oli, sells wine straight from the barrel.

Girona's festivals

Good Friday (Mar/Apr): Girona's Good Friday procession re-enacts Christ's death, with his body carried through the streets by actors dressed as Roman soldiers.

Sant Jordi (23 Apr): St George's Day is marked all over Catalonia by the giving of roses to women and books to men. Flower and book markets are set up on the Rambla.

Sant Narcís (end Oct–beginning Nov): Girona goes wild for a week of festivities in honour of its patron saint, with street parties, bullfights, bonfires and parades of giants.

Suggested walk

Time: The walk can be completed in 1–1½ hours, but it is best to allow plenty of time. This is a lovely walk to do during the early evening *paseo*, when the cafés on the Rambla are full of people enjoying a drink or a snack.

Start at the **Pont de Pedra ❶**, the stone bridge over the Onyar, taking your time to appreciate the best-known image of Girona – the tenement houses with their backs to the river, painted in bright ochre and orange colours. The cathedral tower and the broken spire of Sant Feliu dominate the skyline. Now cross to the old town, and the arcaded square of Plaça del Vi, the old wine market. Each of the streets in this quarter takes its name from one of the medieval guilds that practised here – merchants in Carrer Mercaders, blacksmiths in Carrer Ferreries Velles, fishmongers in Carrer Peixateries Velles. You can plunge into these narrow lanes, or follow Carrer dels Ciutadans, once Girona's main street, to reach **Plaça de l'Oli ❷**, where oil was traded.

Turn right in Plaça de l'Oli to climb the steps towards the Jesuit church of Sant Martí. Halfway up, pass beneath the archway of the Gothic Agullana palace to your left. Keep climbing and eventually you will reach **Plaça de Sant Domènec ❸**, with a 14th-century convent and the recently restored university buildings. You could stop for a coffee at one of the student cafés lining the square.

Turn left across the square to reach Carrer dels Alemanys, with a glimpse of the medieval ramparts to your right. Turn left again along this street, then right into Carrer Bellmirall ('good view'). You now cross a small square, passing the **MUSEU D'ART ❹** to reach the side entrance of the **CATEDRAL ❺**. After visiting the cathedral, walk down the long staircase, admiring Pia Almoina, a fine 14th-century almshouse, on your left. The staircase ends in the cathedral square.

Detour: At this point you could turn right to pass beneath the **Portal de Sobreportes**, built on the site of the Roman gateway to the city. Look up at the statue of the Virgin of Good Death, in a niche above the arch – a reminder that prisoners were led through this gate on their way to execution. Almost immediately, turn left to reach the church of **Sant Feliu**, where several Roman sarcophagi are built into the sanctuary walls. Outside the church, steps lead down to a bridge across the Onyar. Crossing to the left bank, turn left to reach Plaça de la Independència, where a monument recalls the siege of Girona by Napoleon's troops in 1809. This pleasant square is surrounded by cafés and restaurants. On the far side of the square, take Carrer Santa Clara and cross **Pont de Ferro**, cutting straight through the houses to rejoin the main route on the Rambla. This charming iron bridge was designed by the French firm Eiffel and Company, creators of the famous tower in Paris.

Turn left at the foot of the cathedral steps to enter Carrer de la Força, the main street of the **CALL JUEU** ❻. Here you are on the ancient Roman Vía Augusta. Reaching a small square, descend the steps to your right to **Carrer Argenteria** ❼, a smart shopping street. This eventually leads into the **Rambla**, the city's main promenade.

Also worth exploring

The **Eixample** district, on the left bank of the Onyar, was built in the early 20th century. Several of the buildings were designed in the Modernist style of the time. Two outstanding examples, both by local architect Rafael Masó, are Casa Battle on Carrer Nou, with yellow ceramic owls adorning its façade, and Casa Teixidor on Carrer Santa Eugènia near the station, with its distinctive green ceramic spire.

Also on this side of the river, **Parc de la Devesa** is the city's largest outdoor space. The avenues of plane trees are planted so close together that they have grown to heights of more than 50m. It was plane trees from La Devesa that were used to line the Ramblas in Barcelona.

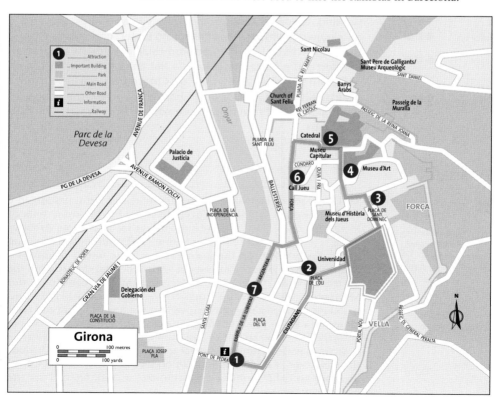

The Serra de Montseny

Scenery	●●●●●
Beaches	●●●●○
Mountains	●●●●○
Nature	●●●●○
Walking	●●●●○
Children	●●●○○
Villages	●●●○○
Historical sights	●●○○○

The region straddling the borders of Girona and Barcelona provinces is a microcosm of Catalonia, with mountains, forests, long sandy beaches, crowded resorts, fishing villages and solid inland towns. At the heart of this region is the Montseny massif, whose green hills, covered in beech, oak and pine, harbour an abundance of plant and animal life. For the people of Barcelona this is the great outdoors, a place to go walking, cycling or mushroom-hunting at weekends. The area is also known for the purity of its spring water, particularly around the spa towns of Viladrau and Sant Hilari Sacalm. At the foot of the sierra, the Costa Maresme is a flat coastal strip with several excellent beaches and some of Catalonia's earliest tourist resorts. Although mass tourism has now arrived, the appeal of the region is that it remains more popular among Catalans than foreigners.

ARBÚCIES

 Carrer Major 6; tel: 972 162477.

🏛 **Museu Etnòlogic del Montseny**
Carrer Major 6. Open Tue–Sat 1100–1400, 1700–2000, Sun 1100–1400, also open Sun pm in Jul & Aug. Free (admission charge for audiovisual show).

Seen from above, this village makes an impressive sight, nestling in a valley between tall hills and overlooked by the imposing bulk of Montsoriu castle. Like most of the villages in this region, Arbúcies makes a pleasant place to break a journey and while away a couple of hours. Pastry shops on the main street sell the town's delicacies – fennel sponge and honey macaroons – while beyond the arches of the porticoed town square is the excellent **Museu Etnòlogic del Montseny**. The museum brings to life the human history and traditions of the region, with displays on farming, hunting and local industries such as coach-building, as well as a reproduction of an old tavern. There is also an audiovisual show entitled *Legends of Montseny*.

Arbúcies is the setting for several traditional festivals. They include the Enramades, a display of floral art on the week after Corpus Christi in June, and the Trobada de Flabiolers, a flute festival on the penultimate weekend of October.

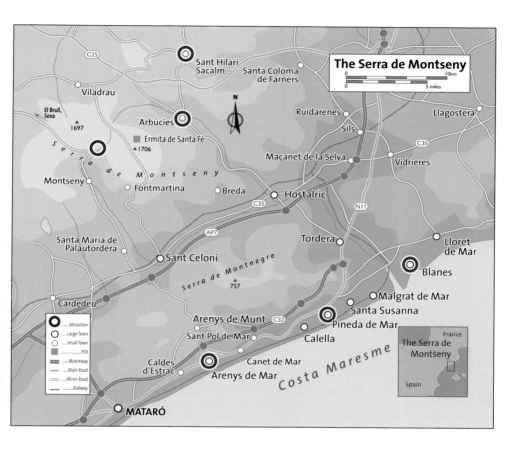

Accommodation in Arbúcies

Les Agudes € *Ctra Hostalric – St Hilari; tel: 972 860007; fax: 972 162381; www.hotellesagudes.com.* A good base for hiking in the area, with views of the peaks of Montseny.

ARENYS DE MAR

Riera Pare fita 31; tel: 937 922601; www.arenysdemar.org

The principal fishing port of the Costa Maresme began life in the 14th century as the sailors' quarter of the nearby village of Arenys de Munt. Now, like so many towns on the coast, it has outgrown the original village to become a sizeable summer resort, though fishing and ship-building are just as important as tourism. The town is centred on the Rambla, a promenade running inland from the sea along a dried-up riverbed. The parish church of **Santa María** has been remodelled in

Fresh produce is available daily at the Modernist-style covered market. A large weekly market takes place on the Rambla on Saturday mornings and fish auctions are held in the harbour on weekday afternoons.

Baroque style with a fine 18th-century altarpiece by Pau Costa; another interesting building, the neoclassical Xifré hospital, contains a museum of lacemaking, a local industry.

Arenys de Mar virtually merges along the coast with **Caldes d'Estrac**, a spa town since Roman times. The present-day spa was built in 1818 on the site of the original Roman baths; in the late 19th century it became a fashionable resort for the Barcelona aristocracy, whose handsome Modernist mansions can be seen along the promenade.

Accommodation and food in Arenys de Mar and vicinity

Jet €€ *Carrer Riera, Caldes d'Estrac; tel: 937 910651; fax: 937 912754; email: info@hoteljet.net; www.hoteljet.net.* This large, three-star hotel is centrally located and is just 300m from the beach. Extras include a tennis court, pool, Wi-Fi and private garage.

Hispania €€€ *Carrer Real 54; tel: 937 910457.* The Rexach sisters serve top-quality Catalan cuisine using fresh local ingredients, with an emphasis on seafood. The *crema catalana* here is the best you will taste anywhere.

BLANES

Plaça Catalunya; tel: 972 330348; email: turisme@blanes.cat; www.blanes.cat. The tourist office issues good local maps and details of self-guided walking tours.

There is a small car park down by the fishing harbour, but you are more likely to find a space along the seafront on Passeig de S'Abanell.

The boat trip from Blanes to Lloret de Mar or Tossa de Mar makes a good day out in summer.

Blanes leads a double life. In summer it is one of the Costa Brava's busiest resorts; in winter it reverts to being a workaday fishing port with a great deal of character.

A rocky outcrop, Sa Palomera, divides the beach in two and also marks the start of the Costa Brava. South of here, where the beach stretches into the distance, is where most of the tourists stay, not on the Costa Brava, whatever the brochures may say. To the north, a long seafront promenade leads around to the fishing harbour, a hive of activity on weekday afternoons. Behind the promenade, the old town has retained much of its charm, with Gothic churches and fountains and a small fishermen's chapel. Unlike some of the mega-resorts to the north, Blanes has enough of a life beyond tourism to have absorbed the summer crowds, largely getting on with its business while the holidaymakers stick to the beach.

Above the town, the gardens of **Mar i Murtra** are perched on a clifftop looking out to sea. The impressive collection includes cactus, spiny aloe and Californian palm, as well as a large Mediterranean garden with olive, pine and tamarisk trees. Some of the trees seem to grow out of the cliffs in classic Costa Brava style. A guided trail leads around the gardens, with plenty of opportunities to rest and admire the peaceful views.

Right
View over Blanes beach and
S'Abanell beach at dusk

🏛 **Jardí Botànic Mar i Murtra** € *Passeig Karl Faust 10. Open Apr, May & Oct daily 0900–1800; Nov–Mar daily 1000–1700, Sat & Sun 1000–1400; Jul–Sept daily 0900–2000.* A shuttle bus to the gardens operates every 15 minutes in summer from the seafront promenade.

🍴 **Els Pins** €, near the start of Passeig de S'Abanell, is a great place for a snack or a plate of seafood on the beach.

🛒 There is a large daily produce market on Passeig de Dintre, just behind the promenade. Fish auctions take place beside the harbour at 1700 on weekday afternoons.

🎆 An international fireworks contest takes place on the seafront from around 25 July.

Beyond the gardens, the road continues to **Cala Sant Francesc**, a sheltered cove and former tuna-fishing port with a small sandy beach and a chapel hidden in the olive groves. Another worthwhile excursion is to the 11th-century **Castell de Sant Joan**, reached by a short drive or a stiff hike from the road which leads to the gardens.

From the castle and the nearby hermitage there are sweeping views over the beach.

Accommodation and food in Blanes

Can Flores II €€ *Esplanada del Port; tel: 972 330007.* As you would expect, the fishing harbour is lined with fish restaurants and this is one of the best. In summer you can sit outside on a terrace watching the boats unload their catch.

El Ventall €€€ *Ctra de Lloret de Mar; tel: 972 332981; www.elventall.com.* One of the top restaurants in the area is situated in a country house on a wooded hillside between Blanes and Lloret de Mar. The restaurant serves Mediterranean cuisine and has a shady garden terrace.

Costa Maresme

There are tourist offices open in summer in Calella, Canet de Mar, Malgrat de Mar and Sant Pol de Mar.

The region's largest market takes place on Sunday mornings in Tordera, just inland from Malgrat de Mar.

Marineland €€€ is a waterpark featuring dolphin and penguin shows as well as thrilling water-based rides, including the popular Black Hole and Canyon River. It is situated between Blanes and Malgrat de Mar. *Tel: 937 654802; www.marineland.es. Open daily Apr, Sept & Oct 1000–15.30; May & Jun 1130–1830; Jul & Aug 1100–1830.*

The 'marshy coast' between Blanes and Arenys de Mar is very different in character from the rest of the Catalan coast, with long, flat sandy beaches separated from new 'urbanisations' by a busy highway and railway line. The first town, **Malgrat de Mar**, merges into the resort of **Santa Susanna** along a pleasant pine-shaded promenade. From here the N11 passes through **Pineda de Mar**, where fishing boats are washed up on the beach; **Calella**, a large seaside resort; **Sant Pol de Mar**, an old-fashioned holiday resort with a small marina; and **Canet de Mar**, with Modernist houses and a long seafront promenade.

Accommodation and food on the Costa Maresme

Gran Sol €€ *Ctra N11, Sant Pol de Mar; tel: 937 600051; fax: 937 600985; email: gran.sol@euht-santpol.org; www.hotelgransol.info.* This comfortable hotel is situated at the top of **Sant Pol de Mar** village overlooking the sea. Open all year, it has facilities including tennis courts and a swimming pool.

Sant Pau €€€ *Carrer Nou 10, Sant Pol de Mar; tel: 937 600662.* Inspirational cooking with two Michelin stars and a welcoming atmosphere. Try strawberry gazpacho followed by scallop brochettes.

Sant Hilari Sacalm

Pl. Dr Robert, Edifici Can Rovira; tel: 972 869686; www.santhilari.cat

This spa town is sometimes known as *la font de Catalunya* on account of its numerous medicinal springs. The mineral water bottled here, especially Font Vella and Fontdor, is sold all over Spain. The town is also the setting for a traditional religious procession each Good Friday, when actors perform the Vía Crucis ('Way of the Cross') in the streets.

Serra de Montseny

Reserva de la Biosfera de Montseny The main information office for the natural park is at Fontmartina (*tel: 938 475102*). There are also information centres at Santa Fe, Arbúcies, Viladrau and Campins.

Opposite
The beach at Blanes

The beauty of these hills, of almost mythical significance to Catalans, lies in the variety of habitats within a small area. The lower slopes are covered in beech, cork and oak; higher up are forests of pine and juniper. It is said that every ecosystem from the Mediterranean to northern Europe can be found within the 310 sq km of the natural park. Wild boar, otters and red squirrels are all abundant, along with red frogs and Pyrenean newts. Peregrines and booted eagles fly overhead, and the mountains are the last remaining habitat of the white-flowered saxifrage. You can spend days walking on the network of well-marked trails and climbing to the highest summits – but even if you only have a day to spare, it is worth driving through this range for some of the best mountain scenery south of the Pyrenees.

Accommodation and food in Serra de Montseny

L'Avet Blau € *Santa Fé de Montseny; tel: 938 475100.* This small hotel is in a very peaceful setting at the heart of the natural park, beside the former hermitage of Santa Fé. There are several good walks nearby, including a stroll to a lake and mountain spring.

Can Barrina €€ *Ctra Palautordera, Montseny; tel: 938 473065; fax: 938 473184; www.canbarrina.com.* A large country house with a swimming pool in its gardens and tremendous views of the sierra, this hotel near the village of Montseny has a restaurant featuring herb-influenced local cuisine.

Sant Marçal €€ *Ctra Santa Fé; tel: 938 473043; www.hotelsantmarcal. com.* This rustic sanctuary beside a Romanesque chapel has just 12 rooms and a restaurant serving mountain dishes. There are inspiring valley views from the terrace.

Can Fabes €€€ *Carrer Sant Joan 6, Sant Celoni; tel: 938 672851; www.racocanfabes.com.* Santi Santamaría uses the freshest local produce to create his highly individual Catalan cuisine. His signature dishes include roast kid caramelised with mountain sage. The restaurant is situated in an attractive cottage with stone walls, wooden floors and plenty of antiques. Very expensive, but an unforgettable experience.

Suggested tour

Total distance: 145km.

Time: It is best to allow at least 4 hours.

Links: From Blanes, the coast road leads north to the start of the southern Costa Brava route (*see pages 192–3*) at Tossa de Mar. From Viladrau and Arbúcies there are easy connections to the fast C25 to Vic (*see page 218*).

Start on the seafront in **BLANES** ❶, heading away from the harbour. Shortly after passing the Bar Els Pins on the beachfront promenade, fork right to leave the resort. When you reach a main road, turn left towards **Malgrat de Mar**. Before long you will find yourself on the N11, a dreary road choked with lorries and summer tourist traffic. This is the start of the **COSTA MARESME** ❷ and there are various opportunities to leave the road and drive down towards the beaches at **Santa Susanna** and **Pineda de Mar**. After **Calella**, the road swings left to become a coastal corniche, travelling through **Sant Pol de Mar** and **Canet de Mar** on its way to **ARENYS DE MAR** ❸.

Turn right through the centre of the town, travelling along the Rambla before beginning the short ascent to the village of **Arenys de Munt**. Now begins the climb into the woods of the Montnegre mountain range. Eventually the road reaches the A7, which is the Barcelona to Girona motorway. Pass beneath the motorway and continue into **Sant Celoni** ❹, where you follow signs through the town to Santa Fe de Montseny.

Be prepared for a difficult drive, as well as some spectacular scenery. This is a roller-coaster ride with panoramic views as you climb ever higher through the forests and pass through narrow gateways formed by the overhanging rocks. The temperature can drop by as much as 10°C as the road climbs 1,000m through a dozen different ecosystems. After 22km (though it can feel like a lot more) you reach **Ermita de Santa Fé** ❺, where there is an information centre and a network of waymarked walks as well as a small hotel.

Detour: A few kilometres north of Sant Celoni, an alternative route passes the natural park information office at **Fontmartina** on its way to Santa Fé. Taking this road, there is the opportunity of a further detour along a well-maintained track to **Turó de l'Home**, Montseny's highest peak.

From Santa Fé the road continues to the chapel of **Sant Marçal**, perched on the side of the Matagalls ridge. The views become more open as you start to descend, looking down over wooded valleys towards the plain of Vic. At the end of the road, it is worth a brief detour to the left to visit the charming spa town of **Viladrau** ❻. For

Below
Sa Palomera rock in Blanes

the main route, turn right, then right again at the junction to follow a pretty river valley to **ARBÚCIES** ❼.

Drive through the village and exit on the main road to Barcelona. After about 8km, turn right on a bumpy road to reach **Breda** ❽, a village notable for its pottery shops and its Romanesque church tower. Passing through Breda, you drop down to a main road and turn left towards **Hostalric** ❾, a small town dominated by its castle. The C35 goes past the fortified town walls; continue on this road, then bear right to cross over the motorway, following the Tordera valley and passing the busy market town of **Tordera** ❿ on your way back to Blanes.

Below
Arenys de Mar

Also worth exploring

An alternative route from Sant Celoni follows the Tordera river and travels through the sturdy village of **Montseny** on its way across the range. Although this road does not climb to the highest peaks, there are good views of the entire sierra as it traverses the plain.

After Montseny, the road rises to a pass from where a steep hike leads to the region's second peak, Matagalls. The road then descends to **El Brull**, a small village with a castle and a Romanesque church, before reaching **Seva** where you can turn right for Viladrau.

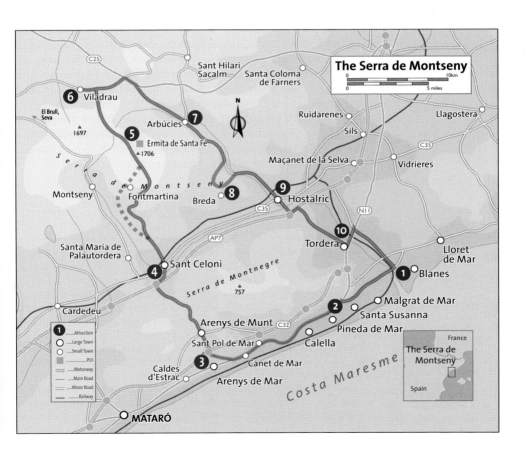

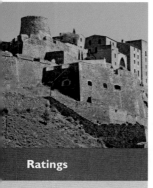

The heart of Catalonia

Ratings

Festivals	●●●●●
Art	●●●●○
Churches	●●●●○
Scenery	●●●●○
Food	●●●○○
Historical sights	●●●○○
Museums	●●●○○
Children	●●○○○

The geographical and cultural heart of Catalonia is situated between the mountains and the sea, in the sparsely populated Pyrenean foothills dotted with solid, historic towns. This is where you most hear the Catalan language, and come across *sardana* dancers holding hands in a church square. It is also where the traditional fiestas are celebrated with the greatest relish, extravagant spectacles featuring costumed giants, monsters and devils, fireworks and folk dancing, all thrown together in an exhilarating blend of pagan and Christian ritual with sheer Catalan exuberance. In medieval times this was a borderland between Muslim and Christian territories; its history can be seen in the walled towns and castles, one of which has been turned into an atmospheric place to stay. The region also contains a wealth of Romanesque art, both in its churches and in the museums at Vic and Solsona.

BERGA

🛈 *Calle Ángeles 7; tel: 938 221384; email: info@turismeberga.cat; www.turismeberga.cat*

🏛 **Sant Quirze de Pedret** € *Open Sat & Sun 1100–1400 (also 1700–1900, Jul–Sept).*

⚫ The **Corpus Christi festival** begins on the Thursday after Trinity Sunday, usually in early June. A **mushroom festival** takes place on the first Sunday of October.

The capital of the Berguedà county is an industrial and cattle-raising town with a well-preserved medieval centre. For three days each June the city goes wild at the Corpus Christi or Patum festival, so-called because it is opened by a drummer banging out *pa-tum, pa-tum* to announce the event. On the evening of Corpus Christi, a mock battle takes place between Turks and Christians on horseback; it is followed by frenzied dances featuring angels, devils, fire-breathing monsters, dwarfs, giants and a crowned eagle, the symbol of Berga. This is one of the most traditional and spectacular festivals that you are ever likely to see in Catalonia.

There is little of tourist interest in the city itself, but there are two interesting churches on the outskirts. **Sant Quirze de Pedret**, reached by a Gothic bridge to the east of town, has been restored to something like its 10th-century appearance. This is one of the few pre-

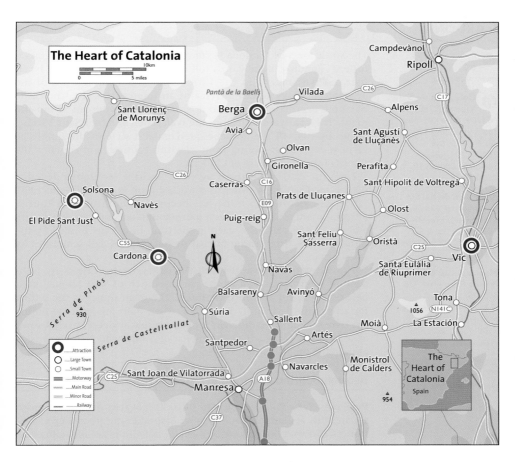

The Heart of Catalonia

10km
0   5 miles

Campdevànol
Ripoll
Panta de la Baells
Vilada
Alpens
Sant Llorenç de Morunys
Berga
Avia
Sant Agusti de Lluçanès
Olvan
Gironella
Perafita
C26
Caserras
Sant Hipolit de Voltregà
Solsona
Prats de Lluçanes
Navès
Olost
El Pide Sant Just
Puig-reig
Sant Feliu Sàsserra
Oristà
Cardona
Navàs
Santa Eulàlia de Riuprimer
Vic
Serra de Pinós
930
Balsareny
Avinyó
Tona
1056
Súria
Sallent
Moià
La Estación
Serra de Castelltallat
Artés
Santpedor
Santa Joan de Vilatorrada
Navarcles
Monistrol de Calders
The Heart of Catalonia
Manresa
Spain
954
C37

Attraction
Large Town
Small Town
Motorway
Main Road
Minor Road
Railway

Sala €€€ *Passeig de la Pau 27; tel: 938 211185; www.restaurantsala.com.* The chef, Miquel Márquez, is known as the king of the wild mushroom and uses every opportunity to incorporate local mushrooms and truffles into his modern Catalan cuisine. During the autumn he offers a special mushroom menu, which may even include mushroom ice cream.

Right
Festive dragon

Romanesque churches to survive in Catalonia, with typical features such as Arabic horseshoe arches. The original frescoes are now in museums in Solsona and Barcelona, but they have been skilfully reproduced on the walls by Emili Julià.

West of Berga, **Nostra Senyora de Queralt** is a Marian shrine on the site of a cave where the Virgin is said to have appeared. A 14th-century statue of Our Lady is worshipped inside the modern church, and there are marvellous mountain views from the terrace.

CARDONA

ℹ *Avda Rastrillo 1; tel: 938 692798; www.cardona.cat*

ℹ **Colegiata de Sant Vicenç €** *Tel: 938 684169. Open Oct–May Tue–Sun 1000–1300, 1500–1730, Sun 1000–1300; Jul–Sept Tue–Sun 1000–1330, 1500–1830.*

Montanya de Sal €€€ *Ctra de la Mina; tel: 938 692051. Open Sept–Jun Tue–Fri 1000–1500, Sat & Sun 1000–1800; Jul & Aug daily 1000–1800.*

Museu de Sal € *Carrer Pompeu Fabra 4; tel: 938 692475; www.salcardona.com. Open Mon–Fri 1100–1400, 1500–1800, Sat & Sun 1000–1400, 1700–1800.*

☀ The **Festa Major** and *corre bou* takes place in September.

The small town of Cardona is completely dominated by its medieval fortress, standing proudly on a hill above the town. It was built by an heir of Charlemagne in the 11th century, and though few of the original buildings survive it remains an impressive sight. The castle has now been converted into a *parador* where you can spend the night. The courtyard leads into the collegiate church of **Sant Vicenç**, begun in 1040 in the Romanesque-Lombard style of the time. The crypt is even older, dating from the 10th century, and contains the tombs of the early Dukes of Cardona.

From the castle walls there are views over the **Montanya de Sal**, a deep-veined salt mine which was worked from Roman times to 1990. Since its closure, the mine has become something of a tourist attraction and a visit includes a journey into an underground gallery where you can see the staggering spectrum of colours formed by the mineral veins. The nearby **Museu de Sal** features salt sculptures by Josep Arnau.

The old part of town, beneath the castle, retains one of its 14th-century gateways as well as the parish church of Sant Miquel, built between the 11th and 18th centuries. The main square is the setting for a colourful festival in September, when bulls are let loose during the *corre bou* and a young man is placed inside a wicker basket known as a *cargolera*, to be left at the mercy of a bull who rolls the basket around the square with its horns.

Accommodation and food in Cardona

Perico € *Plaça Vall 18; tel: 938 691020.* Located on a quiet town square, this restaurant has a busy grill specialising in sausages, pigs' trotters and wild boar, as well as several Italian dishes, including beef carpaccio.

Parador Castell de Cardona €€ *Tel: 938 691275; fax: 938 691636; email: cardona@parador.es; www.parador.es.* This hilltop castle is one of the most atmospheric places to stay in Catalonia. Some of the rooms have four-poster beds, there are splendid views over the town and the mountains, and the restaurant serves top-quality Catalan and Spanish cuisine.

SOLSONA

ℹ *Ctra de Bassella 1; tel: 973 482310; email: turisme@ turismesolsona.com; www.elsolsonesinvita.com*

Solsona is a very Catalan town, with strong traditions, a zest for festivals and a charming medieval nucleus. The best way into the old town is through the Portal del Pont, one of three surviving gateways from the original ramparts. This leads directly to the **Catedral**, with a single nave in Catalan Gothic style and a Romanesque belfry and

Catedral *Open daily 1000–1300, 1600–2000. Free.*

Museu Diocesà € *Plaça de Palau; tel: 973 482101. Open Tue–Sat 1000–1300, 1600–1800 (May–Sept 1630–1900); Sun 1000–1400.*

Museu del Ganivet €
Travesia Sant Josep 9; tel: 973 481569. Open Oct–Apr Tue–Sat 1000–1300, 1600–1800, Sun 1000–1400; May–Sept Tue–Sat 1000–1300, 1630–1700, Sun 1000–1400.

A market is held in Plaça Major on Friday mornings.

The **Festa Major**, beginning on 8 September, features parades of giants, dwarfs and mythical animals, as well as *sardana* dancing, fireworks and the legendary *trabucaires*, dressed in medieval costume, who fill the air with smoke by firing their ancient rifles.

apses. A 12th-century figure of the Virgin of the Cloister, carved out of black stone, is venerated in a side chapel off the south transept. Behind the cathedral, the **Museu Diocesà** is situated inside the bishop's palace, with views down over the cathedral cloister. The museum has a particularly fine collection of Romanesque art, as well as a vivid 10th-century fresco from Sant Quirze de Pedret, showing a bearded worshipper (perhaps representing God) with arms outstretched inside a circle. Look out, too, for several fine Gothic altarpieces and some remarkable modern salt carvings, not just of famous buildings but of sausages, tomatoes and cheese.

The main square, Plaça Major, leads into Carrer Llobera, where another museum, **Museu del Ganivet**, is devoted to the local knife-making industry, with a gruesome display of knives, scissors and dental instruments. At the end of this street there is another old town gate. Bear right just before the gate and cross the square to reach Carrer del Castell. This street leads past the 16th-century town hall into Plaça de Sant Joan, a delightful square with several timber-framed houses (look for the wooden heads carved into the beams) and a 15th-century Gothic fountain with a chapel on top.

Food in Solsona

La Cabana d'en Geli €€ *Ctra de Sant Llorenç 35; tel: 973 483582.* This 18th-century farmhouse restaurant on the outskirts of the town features Catalan meat and game dishes. Seasonal specialities include wild boar casserole, and partridge with wild mushrooms. Vegetarians can opt for the tasty goat's cheese and pear salad.

Right
Jaume Ferrer Bassa's *Last Supper*, Museu Diocesà, Solsona

VIC

ℹ *Ciutat 4 1;*
tel: 938 862091;
email: turisme@vic-cat;
www.victurisme.cat

🏛 **Catedral** € *Plaça de la Catedral; tel: 938 864449. Open daily 1000–1300, 1600–1900.*

Museu Episcopal € *Plaça Bisbe Oliba 3; tel: 938 869360; www.museuepiscopalvic.com. Open Oct–Mar Tue–Fri 1000–1300, 1500–1800, Sat 1000–1900, Sun 1000–1400; Apr–Sept Tue–Sat 1000–1900, Sun 1000–1400.*

Museu de l'Art de la Pell *Carrer Arquebisbe Alemany 5; tel: 938 833279. Open Tue–Sat 1100–1400, 1700–2000, Sun 1100–1400. Free.*

🍴 There are several bars on and around Plaça Major offering good-value set lunches.

🛒 A market is held in Plaça Major on Tuesday and Saturday mornings. The **Mercat del Ram** is a large traditional country market on the Saturday before Palm Sunday.

To buy the local sausages, seek out the delicatessens on Carrer dels Argenters, in the corner of Plaça Major.

Conservative, industrious and gently restrained, Vic is considered by many Catalans to be the essence of Catalonia. Although it has grown into a sizeable provincial city, the main area of interest lies in the historic centre, enclosed by the *ramblas* on the site of the old town walls. At the heart of the city is the enormous **Plaça Major**, also known as El Mercadal because of the markets which have taken place here for over a thousand years. The square itself is like a history of Catalan architecture, with Gothic, Renaissance, Baroque and Modernist buildings linked by the uneven arches around their base. On Saturday mornings it becomes a huge open-air market, with stalls selling fruit, vegetables, flowers, live chicks, books, pottery, kitchen gadgets and cheap clothes, as well as the *fuet* and *botifarra* sausages for which Vic is renowned.

From the town hall in one corner of the square, you can follow a well-marked *ruta turística* around the old town. The walk takes about an hour and you can pick up a map and route notes at the tourist office in the town hall. Among the highlights are a Romanesque bridge, a section of the 14th-century walls and the portico of a 2nd-century Roman temple which stood undiscovered for centuries inside the Montcada palace.

The walk also passes the **Catedral**, a neoclassical pile enclosing the original Romanesque belfry and crypt. Inside the cathedral, your attention is immediately drawn to the murals by Josep María Sert covering most of the walls. Sert's earlier paintings were destroyed during the Civil War and these replacements were unveiled just days before his death in 1945. The paintings, full of theatrical intensity and powerful symbolism, link the injustice suffered by Christ with that experienced by Catalonia at the hands of Spain. Sert is buried in the cathedral cloisters, which contain elements from both Gothic and Romanesque periods.

The **Museu Episcopal** has one of the most complete collections of Catalan Romanesque art. Among the items to look out for is an altarpiece from Vall de Ribes showing St Michael and the Devil weighing souls. A second museum, **Museu de l'Art de la Pell**, is devoted to the local tanning industry and features leather artefacts from around the world.

Accommodation and food in Vic

Cardona 7 €€€ *Calle Cardona 7; tel: 938 863815*. The seasonal menu uses local produce, and has an extensive wine cellar and cigar menu. The restaurant is in a 16th-century house located in the historic district of Vic.

N H Ciutat de Vic €€€ *Passatge Can Mastrot; tel: 938 892551; fax: 938 891447; email: nhciutatdevic@nhhotels.com; www.nh-hotels.com*. The top

Above
Plaça Major, Vic

hotel in town is situated just outside the historic centre. Facilities include car parking plus tennis, squash, sauna and gym.

Parador de Vic-Sau €€€ *Paratge Bac de Sau; tel: 938 122323; fax: 938 122368; email: vic@parador.es; www.parador.es.* A modern *parador* built in the style of a Catalan farmhouse overlooking the Sau reservoir. From the swimming pool there are wonderful views of the lake and the Montseny mountains. The hotel is situated 15km from Vic, beyond the village of Tavernoles.

The *sardana*

Stumble across a Catalan festival or wander into a village square on Sunday after church and you are likely to see people dancing the *sardana*. This delightful traditional dance, described by Catalan poet Joan Maragall as 'a magnificent moving ring', is performed by men and women holding hands alternately around a circle. The music is provided by an 11-piece orchestra known as a *cobla*. Banned under Franco because of its Catalan associations, the *sardana* has since been revived and the circle is said to represent the unity of the Catalan people. Above all, this is a democratic dance; the movements are easy to learn, and anyone can join in.

Suggested tour

Total distance: 107km.

Time: 2½–3 hours. The longer route over the Coll de Jou only adds 10km but you should allow an extra 30 minutes.

Links: From Berga you could head north on the C16, travelling through the Cadí tunnel (toll payable) to join the Cerdanya route (*see pages 150–1*) at Bellver de Cerdanya.

Start in **CARDONA ❶**, dropping down from the town centre to join the C55 in the direction of Solsona. This good, fast road climbs gradually towards **El Pi de Sant Just** before descending through the olive groves to **SOLSONA ❷**. From Solsona there is a choice of routes to the village of **Sant Llorenç de Morunys ❸**, a prosperous alpine resort whose population of 900 makes it the second town of Solsona county. The quickest route is on the road which forks right on the way out of Solsona, twisting and tunnelling through the Cardener gorge with magnificent views over the Llosa del Cavall reservoir. At the end of this road, turn left to enter Sant Llorenç. The village sits at the centre of the Lord valley and is the entry point for several places of interest to the north – the source of the Cardener, the ski resort of Port de Comte and the highest golf course in Catalonia.

Detour: Alternatively, take the old road from Solsona to Sant Llorenç de Morunys, crossing a wild, lonely mountain range and looking down over the ravines as you climb to the **Coll de Jou**. Be aware that this mountain pass may be closed in winter. At Coll de Jou you can turn right to return to the main route at Sant Llorenç.

The journey from Sant Llorenç to Berga follows a winding road along the southern slopes of the Sierra del Cadí, effectively the southern edge of the Pyrenees. This is a remarkably scenic drive, but you need to take care as the road is narrow, the bends frequent and intense concentration is required. Shortly before Berga, a zigzagging road to the left climbs steeply to the sanctuary of Nostra Senyora de Queralt, which is worth a brief detour if only for the mountain views. Return to the main road and continue in the direction of Berga.

Turn right at the T-junction and pass through the centre of **BERGA ❹**, following signs to Solsona. The road climbs gently at first through rolling countryside before reaching a plateau near **L'Espanyola ❺**. When the road forks, keep straight ahead to return to Cardona, whose castle looms up invitingly in the distance as you approach.

Also worth exploring

The north of Berguedà county has several interesting villages that can be combined in a scenic drive along the southern slopes of the Cadí range. They include **Gósol**, in the shadow of the Pedraforca mountain, where Picasso spent the summer of 1906 and where a **museum** features reproductions of his work; **La Pobla de Lillet**, where there is a garden designed by Antoni Gaudí; and **Castellar de N'Hug**, where the source of the Llobregat river, which divides Catalonia in two, has become something of a pilgrimage spot for Catalans. All of these can be reached from the C16 or via a long circuitous route from Sant Llorenç de Morunys.

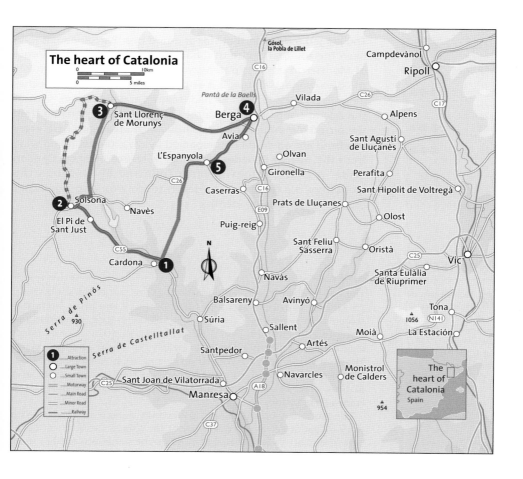

Montserrat and wine country

Ratings

Scenery	●●●●●
Wine	●●●●●
Geology	●●●●○
Nature	●●●●○
Walking	●●●●○
Historical sights	●●●○○
Museums	●●●○○
Children	●●○○○

Ask any Catalan bride where she would like to be married and she will probably choose the monastery at Montserrat. The jagged mountain that stands guard over Barcelona has long been the spiritual centre of Catalan nationalism, and the Virgin of Montserrat its most potent symbol. Pilgrims queue up to kiss the dark wooden statue; it is said that any woman who touches her will be blessed with a child. Many Catalan women, such as the operatic soprano Montserrat Caballé, take their name from the sacred mountain. The weddings which take place here every weekend are no doubt accompanied by *cava*, the sparkling wine from the nearby Penedès vineyards, a source of great Catalan pride. A tour of the vineyards followed by a visit to the monastery is a good way to get in touch with two significant aspects of the Catalan identity.

MONTSERRAT

🛈 Monasterio de Montserrat
Tel: 938 777701;
www.montserratvisita.com.
Open Mon–Fri 0730–1930,
Sat & Sun 0730–2030 (until
1930 Nov–Mar).

The saw-toothed sandstone pinnacles that rose out of the sea between 25 and 50 million years ago form perhaps the most instantly recognisable symbol of Catalonia. Ten kilometres long, 5km wide and rising to a height of 1,236m, the 'serrated mountain' appears much bigger than it really is as it climbs steeply out of the Llobregat plain. The mountain inspired a Wagner opera and it has given its name to a Caribbean island. It also plays a key role in the Catalan psyche, as a historic place of pilgrimage and a centre of resistance during the Franco dictatorship.

The monastery on the mountainside owes its fame to a legend. The story is that St Peter placed a statue of the Virgin, carved by St Luke, here after Christ's death. For many years the statue was hidden from the Moors, then in 880 it was rediscovered by shepherds who were led to a cave by angelic voices and heavenly light. The local bishop tried

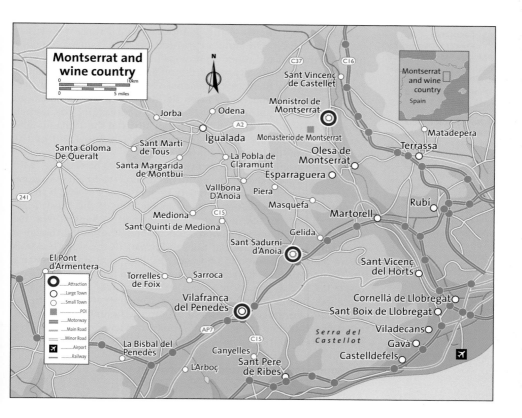

Montserrat and wine country

0 |————| 10km
0 |————| 5 miles

N

Jorba
Odena
Monistrol de Montserrat
Sant Vincenç de Castellet
C37
C16
Montserrat and wine country
Spain

Igualada
A2
Monasterio de Montserrat
Matadepera
Santa Coloma De Queralt
Sant Marti de Tous
Olesa de Montserrat
Terrassa
Santa Margarida de Montbui
La Pobla de Claramunt
Esparraguera
241
Vallbona D'Anoia
Piera
Masquefa
Martorell
Rubi
Mediona
C15
Sant Quinti de Mediona
Gelida
Sant Sadurni d'Anoia
Sant Vicenç del Horts
El Pont d'Armentera
Torrelles de Foix
Sarroca
Vilafranca del Penedès
Cornellá de Llobregat
Sant Boix de Llobregat
Viladecans
Serra del Castellot
Gava
AP7
C15
La Bisbal del Penedès
Canyelles
Castelldefels
L'Arboç
Sant Pere de Ribes

○ Attraction
○ Large Town
○ Small Town
■ POI
▬ Motorway
— Main Road
— Minor Road
✈ Airport
— Railway

ⓘ The information office is in Plaça de la Creu, across from the cable-car station. *Tel: 938 777701; www.montserratvisita.com*

ⓟ A charge is made for bringing a vehicle on to the site. Discounted longer-term parking is available for guests staying in the hotel.

ⓥ Virgin of Montserrat *Access to the Virgin is available at the monastery.*

to move the statue, but it refused to budge, a sure sign from God that the Virgin was to be worshipped at Montserrat. A chapel was built to house the statue and a Benedictine monastery was established. Although the monastic buildings were destroyed by Napoleon's troops in 1811, the Benedictine community is thriving again today.

The present church is Renaissance in style, completed in 1592 but with a 20th-century Plateresque façade. In a small chapel behind the altar, pilgrims queue to touch the statue which, despite the legend, actually dates from the 12th century. Known as 'La Moreneta' ('the little dark one'), and worshipped as the patron saint of Catalonia, the Virgin is carved in the style of the early Black Madonnas, further blackened by candle smoke over the years. The silver throne in which she sits rests on a polished stone from the mountain. The statue is protected by an oval glass, but there is a small niche through which pilgrims can place their hands. Should you wish to join in, the ritual is to kiss or touch the Virgin's right hand, which holds a sphere representing the world, while opening your other hand out to the infant Jesus.

Escolania
www.escolania.net. The choir sings Mon–Fri at 1300, Mon–Thur at 1845 and Sun at 1200, except on holidays. The main Mass is at 1200 on Sun.

Museu de Montserrat
€€ Plaça de Santa Maria; tel: 938 777777. Open Mon–Fri 1000–1700, Sat & Sun 0930–1900.

Santa Cova The holy grotto is open daily from 1015–1630 in winter; 0915–1730 in summer. The cable car runs every 20 minutes 1000–1745 in summer; in winter, at weekends 1100–1655.

Sant Joan The cable car to Sant Joan runs every 20 minutes 1000–1900 in summer 1100–1630 in winter.

Pilgrimages

The biggest pilgrimages to Montserrat take place on 27 April and 8 September.

A boys' choir, the Escolania, founded in 1223, sings twice a day inside the church. On Sundays and festival days, *sardana* dancing, human pyramids and other expressions of Catalan culture take place in the courtyard, where parts of the original Gothic cloister remain. From the balcony there are tremendous views over the Llobregat river basin. The nearby museum, **Museu de Montserrat**, has a superb art collection, with paintings by El Greco, Caravaggio, the French Impressionists and all the leading Catalan artists of the 19th and 20th centuries. There are also displays of archaeology and of the iconography of the Virgin of Montserrat.

The hills around the monastery provide excellent walking, with several well-marked paths. The entire mountain was declared a natural park in 1987; it shelters a wide variety of flora as well as wild boar and mountain goats. The easiest walk is on the Way of the Cross, a 20-minute stroll from the monastery. The descent to **Santa Cova**, the cave where the statue was found, takes around 30 minutes, though it is possible to take a funicular railway for part of the way. The walk passes Modernist sculptures by Gaudí and Puig i Cadafalch depicting the mysteries of the Rosary before reaching an 18th-century chapel inside the sacred cave. More serious walkers can take the funicular to the upper station at Sant Joan, where a 20-minute walk leads to the **Sant Joan hermitage** and a 1-hour hike to the summit at Sant Jeroni, Montserrat's highest point. On a clear day the views from here stretch from Mallorca to the Pyrenees.

Accommodation and food in Montserrat

Abat Cisneros €€ *Plaça del Monestir; tel: 938 777701; www.montserratvisita.com.* After the day-trippers have left, Montserrat is a very different place. The monastery hotel has a choice of three-star accommodation or a pilgrim-type hostel next door. The restaurant serves excellent Catalan food. A bonus is watching the sun rise over the mountain – but remember to take a coat, even in summer.

SANT SADURNI D'ANOIA

This small town has only one claim to fame, but what a claim it is – this is the home of *cava*, Catalonia's sparkling wine. Some 90 per cent of all *cava* is produced here at more than 100 cellars, ranging from huge international companies to small family-run firms and local farmers' co-operatives.

It all began in 1872, when Josep Raventós produced the first bottle of *cava* using the French *méthode champenoise*. Raventós was the heir to an important wine dynasty, created in 1659 when Miquel Raventós married Anna de Codorniu – who continues to lend her name to one of the very best sparkling wines. Although the dynasty is now split,

Codorniu €
Signposted from the road to Igualada. Tel: 938 913342. Open Mon–Fri 0900–1700, Sat–Sun 0900–1300. Visits by appointment only.

Freixenet € *Carrer Joan Sala 2; tel: 938 917096. Open Mon–Thur 1000–1300 and 1500–1630. Visits by appointment only. Free.*

Mirador de les Caves €€€ *Ctra de Ordal; tel: 938 993178; www.miradorcaves.com. This elegant restaurant on a hillside to the south of town has views over the vineyards to the distant peaks of Montserrat. The cooking is based on local ingredients – seafood with cava, and duck from the Penedès farms.*

Below
Sant Sadurni d'Anoia

with Josep María Raventós producing *cava* under his own name, **Codorniu** remains the biggest name in *cava* and one of the leading producers of sparkling wine in the world. The Spanish royal family is among their regular customers. The vast Codorniu cellars, designed by the Modernist architect Puig i Cadafalch, are undoubtedly the most interesting to visit – a cathedral of brick, stone and stained glass beneath barrel-vaulting and parabolic arches. The tour includes a thrilling ride around the 200,000 sq m of underground cellars and a thorough explanation of the *cava* production process. Tours are also available at **Freixenet**, the biggest exporters of *cava*, whose cellars are located beside the railway station on the edge of town.

Cava

Cava is a wine for celebrations, at a much more affordable price than French champagne. It owes its origins to the *phylloxera* plague of the late 19th century, which devastated the Catalan vineyards and forced winemakers into new experiments. Traditionally made from the local grape varieties, Parellada, Macabeo and Xarel.lo, it is fermented once in steel tanks and a second time in the bottle, where it is aged for up to five years. Recently, more and more producers have started to use the Chardonnay grape to create a premium *cava*. Codorniu, for example, uses Chardonnay in its Anna de Codorniu and traditional grapes in its Ne Plus Ultra brand. Besides the well-known producers, you should look out for *cavas* from smaller companies such as Juvé i Camps, Mas Tinell and Josep María Raventós.

VILAFRANCA DEL PENEDÈS

*Carrer de la Fruita 13;
tel: 938 181254;
email:
turisme@ajvilafranca.es;
www.ajvilafranca.es*

The capital of the Alt Penedès district was founded in the 12th century in an effort to attract Catalan settlers to an area newly recovered from the Moors. It soon became an important commercial centre, with tax-free privileges (*vilafranca* means 'free town') and several fine Gothic

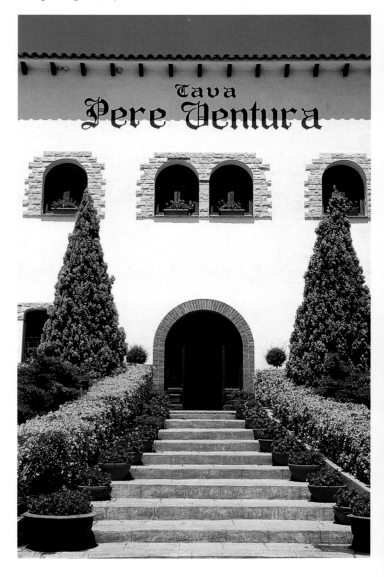

Right
A Vilafranca winery

Vinseum € *Plaça Jaume I; tel: 938 900582. Open Tue–Sat 1000–1400, 1600–1900, Sun 1000–1400.*

Torres € *Finca El Maset, Pacs del Penedès; tel: 938 177487; www.torres.es. Open Mon–Fri 0900–1700, Sat 0900–1800, Sun 0900–1300. Telephone in advance to arrange a visit.*

Primary market day is Saturday. The area is known for its ducks, hens and turkeys, sold at the large poultry fair, **Fira del Gall**, on the last Saturday before Christmas. Several other themed markets run throughout the week.

A wine fair, **Firavi**, is held in April every two years (next one in 2013).

The **Festa Major** begins on 29 August and features fireworks, dancing dragons, stick dances and one of Catalonia's best displays of *castells* or human pyramids (*see page 266*). *www.festamajor.info*

mansions. Although there is evidence of a wine industry in the area since Roman times, it was not until the end of the 18th century that grapes began to replace cereal as the main crop. The town is now the major centre of production for Penedès wines which, along with *cava*, are considered the best in Catalonia.

Vilafranca today is a busy, industrious town with a lovely old Gothic centre. Modernist buildings line the *ramblas*, leading to the heart of the old town on Plaça de la Vila, scene of a lively Saturday market. There are several interesting churches nearby. The chapel of Sant Joan has been turned into an art gallery, while Sant Francesc has a fine Gothic altarpiece attributed to Lluís Borrassá and a collection of sculptures in the cloister. Behind the town hall, the **Basílica de Santa María** is a 15th-century Gothic church with a single nave and a polygonal apse. The crypt contains a sculpture group by the Modernist sculptor Josep Llimona.

Facing the basilica, the **Vinseum** is housed in the 12th-century palace of the kings of Aragón. This is a combination of museums, with sections on local archaeology, geology, ornithology and fine art, but of most interest is the extensive wine museum. There are Greek and Roman amphorae dating back to the 4th century BC, as well as underground cellars and a reconstructed tavern where you can taste the local wines.

The best-known producer, **Torres**, is situated 3km outside the town at Pacs del Penedès. The cellars here produce some 22 million litres of wine and 4 million litres of brandy annually, much of it exported to more than 100 countries. Their top red wines, using single-estate Cabernet Sauvignon from the Torres family vineyards, have consistently been ranked alongside the leading clarets from Bordeaux. Sadly, on a tour of the cellars you do not get to taste the best wines, but they are available for sale at a very reasonable price.

If you are visiting Torres, you might as well continue along this road to the hamlet of **Sant Martí Sarroca**, where there is a ruined castle and a 12th-century Romanesque church.

Accommodation and food in Vilafranca del Penedès

Cal Ton €€ *Carrer Casal 8; tel: 938 903741.* Tucked down a side street, this upbeat modern place serves tasty, imaginative dishes.

Casa Joan €€ *Plaça de l'Estación 8; tel: 938 903171.* Traditional Catalan cooking in an old-fashioned building opposite the railway station. The restaurant tends to get very busy at lunchtimes but is closed in the evenings except on Saturday.

Pedro III El Grande €€ *Plaça del Penedès 2; tel: 938 903100; fax: 938 903921; email: info@hotelpedrotercero.com; www.hotelpedrotercero.com.* If you want to stay the night, this three-star hotel is centrally located and has comfortable air-conditioned rooms.

Suggested tour

Total distance: 122km.

Time: 2½–3 hours.

Links: Vilafranca del Penedès is also featured on the Golden Coast route (*see pages 250–51*).

From **VILAFRANCA DEL PENEDÈS** ❶, take the C243, a minor road which passes through the heart of the wine-growing area with the jagged ridge of Montserrat looming up ahead. All along this road are vineyards and small *bodegas* offering *cava* for sale. After 12km you reach **SANT SADURNI D'ANOIA** ❷, where signs point the way to numerous cellars. It is best to check first with the tourist office about visiting, as many small wineries offer very limited touring hours.

Once the non-drivers have fully satisfied their taste buds, continue on the C243 to reach the small summer resort of **Gelida**, with a ruined castle and a pre-Romanesque church. This stretch of the road is particularly scenic, with Montserrat ever present in the distance, sometimes hazy, sometimes forming a clear silhouette against the blue sky. As the road bends left to pass under the AP7 motorway, turn right following signs to the centre of **Martorell** ❸.

This busy commuter town contains a remarkable Roman bridge, **Pont del Diable**. The so-called Devil's Bridge has been heavily reconstructed, but it is still one of the most important Roman sites in Catalonia. The bridge across the River Llobregat formed part of the great Roman Vía Augusta and was an essential link on the road from Girona to Tarragona.

Arriving in Martorell, you soon reach the N11, the Barcelona to Lleida highway. Head towards Lleida, but keep a lookout for the exit to Manresa on the C16. This road soon begins to climb, and again you see Montserrat in the distance, drawing you ever closer and dominating every view.

At the little village of **Monistrol de Montserrat**, turn left to follow the snaking road up to **MONTSERRAT** ❹.

After visiting the monastery, take the left-hand fork, passing the hermitage of Santa Cecilia on your way around the mountainside. At the next junction, turn left, following signs for Barcelona. After another 1km, take the minor road to your right, twisting down through the forested slopes to join the N11 in the direction of Lleida. After a brief stretch of fast dual carriageway, take the exit for Igualada Est ('east'), skirting the leather town of **Igualada** ❺ to reach the C15. Turn left to pass **La Pobla de Claramunt**, dominated by its hilltop castle, and continue on this road all the way back to Vilafranca.

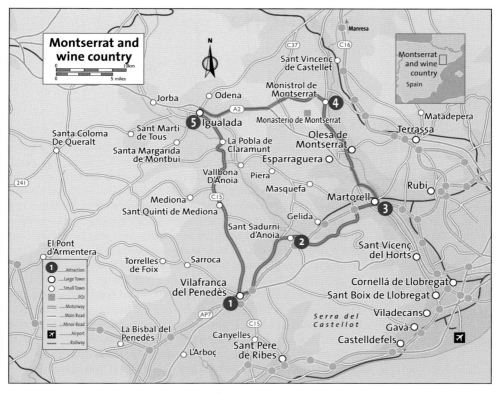

Getting out of the car

Shortly before Monistrol de Montserrat, the cable car from **Aeri de Montserrat** offers the most spectacular approach to the monastery, a terrifying five-minute ride up a sheer mountain slope. The cable cars leave every 15 minutes between 1000 and 1830 in summer, and rather less frequently in winter. Another way up to the monastery is by rack railway.

Also worth exploring

North of Montserrat on the C16, **Manresa** is an industrial town at the confluence of the Cardener and Llobregat rivers. It is dominated by its huge Gothic basilica, Santa María de la Seu, which stands on a hilltop above the Cardener. Other sights are the Pont Vell, a Gothic bridge across the Cardener, and La Cova de Sant Ignasi, the holy cave where the founder of the Jesuits, Ignatius of Loyola (*see pages 78–9*), is said to have stayed and engaged in spiritual exercises on his way to Montserrat.

Barcelona

The world is waking up to what Catalans have known for a long time, that their city by the sea is one of the most stylish in Europe. Regional autonomy, and the awarding of the Olympic Games to Barcelona in 1992, gave a huge boost to the Catalan capital. Previously derelict areas have been transformed by ambitious urban renewal schemes and the city has become a showcase for modern architecture, much as it was a century ago when Antoni Gaudí and the Modernists were running riot in the Eixample. A key project was the development of the Poble Nou district for the staging of the Universal Forum of Cultures in 2004. A new marina, Port Forum, has been built alongside the site, while Toyo Ito's dramatic Porta Fira twisting tower blocks, built in 2009, serve as a symbolic and innovative gateway to the airport. In many ways this is a city that looks in on itself, with its petty political squabbles, self-conscious Catalan nationalism and constant desire to be better than Madrid; at the same time it looks outward to the world, embracing a cosmopolitanism unknown elsewhere in Spain and proudly claiming the title of 'capital of the Mediterranean'.

Plaça de Catalunya 17-S, down the steps; tel: 932 853832; www.barcelonaturisme.com. Ayuntamiento, Plaça Sant Jaume I; tel: 932 853832; Estació de Sants, Plaça Països Catalans s/n; tel: 932 853832; Palau Robert, Passeig de Gràcia 107; tel: 932 388091; email: info@barcelonaturisme.com. Open daily 0900–2100.

El Prat Airport *Tel: 934 784704 (Terminal A) and 934 780565 (Terminal B).*

General information

There are further offices on the ground floor of the city hall in Plaça Sant Jaume and in the railway station, Estació de Sants, with regional tourist offices in the Palau Robert, Passeig de Gràcia and at the airport. Multilingual tourist information officers, in distinctive red jackets, can be found in the street in Las Ramblas and the Gothic quarter.

Arriving and getting around

Barcelona is the one place in Catalonia where you should be wary of taking a car. Driving and parking in the city is a nightmare, and foreign-registered cars are often targeted by thieves. Unless you are

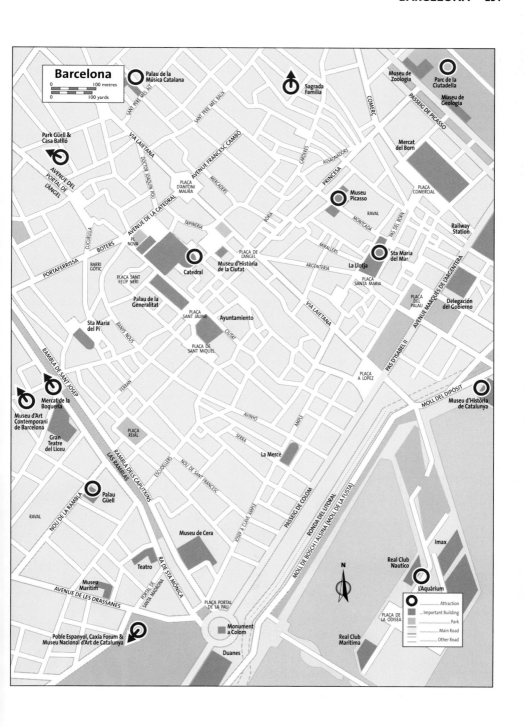

Barcelona

0 ——— 100 metres
0 ——— 100 yards

Palau de la Música Catalana

Sagrada Família

Museu de Zoologia

Parc de la Ciutadella

Museu de Geologia

Park Güell & Casa Batlló

PASSEIG DE PICASSO

COMERC

VIA LAIETANA

AVENUE FRANCESC CAMBÓ

SANT PERE MÉS ALT

SANT PERE MÉS BAIX

CARRERES

ASSAONADORS

Mercat del Born

AVENUE DEL PORTAL DE L'ANGEL

DOCTOR JOAQUIN POU

PLAÇA D'ANTONI MAURA

MERCADERS

PRINCESA

PLAÇA COMERCIAL

TAPINERIA

BORIA

Museu Picasso

RAVAL

MONTCADA

PAS DEL BORN

Railway Station

CUCURULLA

PL NOVA

AVENUE DE LA CATEDRAL

PLAÇA DE L'ANGEL

MIRALLERS

Sta Maria del Mar

PORTAFERRISSA

BOTERS

BARRI GÒTIC

Catedral

Museu d'Història de la Ciutat

ARGENTERIA

La Llotja

PLAÇA SANTA MARIA

AVENUE MARQUÉS DE L'ARGENTERA

PLAÇA SANT FELIP NERI

Palau de la Generalitat

PLAÇA SANT JAUME

Ayuntamiento

VIA LAIETANA

PLAÇA DEL PALAU

Delegación del Gobierno

Sta Maria del Pi

BANYS NOUS

PLAÇA SANT MIQUEL

CIUTAT

PAS D'ISABEL II

RAMBLA DE SANT JOSEP

PLAÇA DE SANT MIQUEL

PLAÇA A LÓPEZ

TERRAN

Mercat de la Boqueria

Museu d'Art Contemporani de Barcelona

AVINYÓ

AMPLE

MOLL DEL DIPOSIT

Museu d'Història de Catalunya

Gran Teatre del Liceu

PLAÇA REIAL

SERRA

La Mercè

LAS RAMBLAS

RAMBLA DELS CAPUTXINS

ESCUDELLERS

NOU DE SANT FRANCESC

PASSEIG DE COLOM

Palau Güell

NOU DE LA RAMBLA

RAVAL

JOSEP A CLAVÉ AMPLE

RONDA DEL LITORAL (MOLL DE LA FUSTA)

MOLL DE BOSCH I ALSINA (MOLL DE LA FUSTA)

Imax

Museu de Cera

Real Club Nautico

RA DE STA MÓNICA

Teatro

PORTAL DE SANTA MADRONA

N

L'Aquàrium

Museu Marítim

AVENUE DE LES DRASSANES

PLAÇA PORTAL DE LA PAU

⬤ Attraction
▢ Important Building
▢ Park
Main Road
Other Road

Poble Espanyol, Caxia Forum & Museu Nacional d'Art de Catalunya

Monument a Colom

PLAÇA DE LA ODISEA

Real Club Maritima

Duanes

Tours

Among the various joyrides available are the open-top Bus Turístic which offers an excellent hop-on-and-off service in summer from Plaça de Catalunya, covering virtually every major attraction in the city, funicular rides to Montjuïc and Tibidabo, the cable car over the harbour from Barceloneta to Montjuïc, and the *golondrinas* boat cruises which leave from the foot of Las Ramblas.

staying at a hotel with its own garage, leave your car outside the city and arrive by public transport. If you are flying out of Barcelona, the best option is to visit the city at the end of your holiday after returning your hire car to the airport.

An excellent local train service connects the airport with the city centre, taking around 30 minutes to reach Plaça de Catalunya. This square is at the heart of the main area of tourist interest, and most places are within walking distance. It is also a useful connection for the Metro, the city's efficient underground system. You can buy single-ride Metro tickets, but a one-day, three-day or five-day pass may be better value. Another option is the Barcelona Card, available at tourist offices and giving free travel on the Metro and local buses, as well as various museum discounts, for one, two or three days.

FC Barcelona

Barcelona's biggest football club is so much more than a team – it is a symbol of Catalan pride and success. Matches against Spanish rivals Real Madrid assume the status of internationals. When 'Barça' are playing, the city stops work, the bars fill up and victory is greeted with celebrations on the Ramblas and the hooting of car horns across the city. Numerous foreign players have been attracted to Barcelona, among them Johan Cruyff, Diego Maradona, Gary Lineker, Lionel Messi and Ronaldo. The club were European champions in 1992, 2006 and 2009. An impressive seven Barça players were included in the Spain squad that won the 2010 World Cup. Their Camp Nou stadium is the largest in Europe, and the attached club museum is a must-see for all football aficionados; the extensive exhibits include a quirky life-sized model of an old-fashioned dressing room.

Museu del Futbol Club Barcelona €€ *Carrer d'Aristides 53L; tel: 934 963699; www.fcbarcelona.es. Open Mon–Sat 1000–1800, Sun 1000–1430.*

Below
Gaudi's Casa Batllo

Licensed taxis, painted black and yellow, are a quick way of getting about. A list of fares is posted inside the taxi. Always make sure that the meter is turned on.

Barcelona's areas

Barcelona's sights can be divided into areas. Some are worth a two-hour stroll around; other areas warrant at least a day.

Las Ramblas is the most famous street in Spain, an outdoor theatre with a 24-hour cast of florists and newspaper vendors, performance artists and portrait painters, pickpockets, prostitutes and bemused tourists beneath the plane trees. Beside the non-stop activity, highlights include the Boquería market and the Liceu opera house, destroyed by fire in 1994 and reopened in 1999.

To one side of Las Ramblas, the **Barri Gòtic** or so-called Gothic quarter is the oldest part of the city, with traces of Barcelona's Roman walls as well as the medieval royal palace. The cathedral is situated here, and the narrow lanes are the best part of the city for strolling, with backstreet cafés and small specialist shops.

Raval, on the far side of Las Ramblas, was previously known as the 'Chinese quarter' even though it has never had a Chinese population. This was the city's red-light district, a warren of filthy streets and seedy bars. The slums have been cleared and a *rambla* has been built in an attempt to give the Raval a new image, but vestiges of the past remain. Cutting-edge architecture, including a new contemporary art museum, is the most visual sign of the changes sweeping the area.

Ribera, the former merchants' quarter to the east of the Barri Gòtic, has become one of the most fashionable areas of the city. This is where you will find the Picasso Museum, in a street of Renaissance and Gothic palaces, art galleries and champagne bars.

Montjuïc, the former Jewish cemetery on a hill overlooking the city, was transformed by the hosting of the 1929 World Fair. More recently it was the site of the 1992 Olympic stadium. The opening of a botanic garden on the city's former rubbish dump marked the first stage in an ambitious plan to turn Montjuïc into Barcelona's Central Park. Two of the city's finest museums are situated here.

The **Eixample** is Barcelona's 19th-century extension, built on a grid system outside the confines of the old city. The development of the Eixample coincided with the rise of the Modernisme movement, and the area is well endowed with works by Gaudí and others. Beyond the Eixample, a funicular ride leads to the funfair at Tibidabo, with its spectacular views over the city.

The area that has seen most changes over the past decade has been the waterfront district around the old fishermen's village of **Barceloneta**. It is now possible to follow a seafront promenade from the foot of Las Ramblas to the Olympic Village, where skyscrapers and stunning modern architecture look down over the beach.

Sights

It would be impossible to do justice to Barcelona within the scope of this chapter, so what follows is a brief guide to the main museums and attractions. If you plan to explore Barcelona in depth, detailed guides are available at tourist offices and shops in the city.

L'Aquàrium

One of the largest aquaria in Europe has more than 300 species on display. It is part of a waterfront entertainment complex that includes a giant-screen Imax cinema, a shopping mall, and several restaurants, bars and discos.

Caixa Forum

One of Barcelona's many art museums featuring changing themed exhibitions of contemporary art ranging from Renoir to Picasso. The museum itself is housed in an old textile mill and is an architecturally interesting combination of modern and Modernisme elements.

Casa Batlló

A colourful fantasy house by Gaudí in which there are few straight lines. From the wavy façade to the roof in the form of a dragon's back, it is a work of originality throughout.

L'Aquàrium €€€
Moll d'Espanya, Port Vell; tel: 932 217474; www.aquariumbcn.com. Metro: Drassanes or Barceloneta. Open daily 0930–2100. Closes at 2130 at weekends and at 2300 in Jul & Aug.

Caixa Forum *Avda Marquès de Comillas 68; tel: 934 768600. Metro: Espanya. Open Tue–Sun 1000–2000. Free.*

Casa Batlló and Casa Milà €€ *Passeig de Gràcia 49 and 92; tel: 932 160306 and 934 845900. Metro: Diagonal. Open daily 1000–2000.*

Above
Montjuïc

Catedral and Museum
€ *Plaça de la Seu (Barri Gòtic); tel: 933 42860. Metro: Jaume I or Liceu. Open daily 1000–1230, 1715–1845.*

Fundació Antoni Tàpies
€€ *Carrer Aragó 255 (Eixample); tel: 934 870315. Metro: Passeig de Gràcia. Open Tue–Sun 1000–2000.*

Fundació Joan Miró €€
Parc de Montjuïc; tel: 934 439470; www.bcn.fjmiro.es. Open Tue–Sat 1000–1900 (Thu until 2130), Sun 1000–1430; Jul–Sept 1000–2000.

Museu d'Art Contemporani
€€ *Plaça dels Àngels 1 (Raval); tel: 934 120810; www.macba.es. Metro: Catalunya or Liceu. Open Mon & Wed–Fri 1100–1930, Sat 1000–2000, Sun 1000–1500. In summer, open Thur until 2130. Half-price admission on Wed.*

Museu d'Història de Catalunya
€€ *Palau del Mar (Barceloneta); tel: 932 254700; www.mhcat.net. Metro: Barceloneta. Open Tue–Sat 1000–1900 (Wed until 2000), Sun 1000–1430.*

Museu d'Història de la Ciutat
€€ *Plaça del Rei; tel: 933 151111; www.museuhistoria.bcn.es. Metro: Jaume I. Open Tue–Sat 1000–1400, 1600–1900 (1000–2000 in summer), Sun 1000–1500.*

Right
Lichtenstein's *Barcelona* on Passeig de Colón

Casa Milà
This apartment block designed by Gaudí has been nicknamed 'La Pedrera' ('the quarry'). Climb up to the curving rooftop gallery for views over the city, and visit the loft, with its parabolic brick arches, where an exhibition tells the story of Gaudí's life and times.

Catedral
The Gothic cathedral was begun in 1298. The crypt contains the relics of the 4th-century Santa Eulàlia, patron of the city. Look out for the flock of geese in the cloisters. There is *sardana* dancing in the cathedral square on Sundays at 1200.

Fundació Antoni Tàpies
The work of the abstract artist Antoni Tàpies is displayed in this museum, in a former Modernisme publishing house designed by Domènech i Montaner. A twisted wire sculpture, typical of Tàpies' style, adorns the roof.

Fundació Joan Miró
The avant-garde painter Joan Miró was born in Barcelona and this museum shows a representative sample of his work. Among Miró's public works are a mural at Barcelona airport and a pavement mosaic on Las Ramblas.

Museu d'Art Contemporani de Barcelona
This stunning museum by the American architect Richard Meyer displays art collections from the 1940s onwards. It is the centrepiece of the urban renewal project that is transforming the Raval.

Museu d'Història de Catalunya
This splendid museum in the former naval palace combines history, politics and entertainment in an interactive journey through Catalonia's past, complete with videos, Civil War posters and reconstructions of old buildings.

Museu d'Història de la Ciutat
The exhibits here uncover the various layers of Barcelona's history as you stroll through the underground Roman city, visit the former royal palace, climb a medieval skyscraper, and then round off your visit with a multimedia show.

Museu Marítim €€
Avda de les Drassanes;
tel: 933 429920;
www.museumaritimbarcelona.
org. Metro: Drassanes. Open
daily 1000–2000.

**Museu Nacional d'Art
de Catalunya** €€ Palau
Nacional (Montjuïc); tel: 936
220360; www.mnac.es.
Metro: Espanya. Open
Tue–Sat 1000–1900, Sun
1000–1430.

Museu Picasso €€ Carrer
Montcada 15 (Ribera);
tel: 932 563000;
www.museupicasso.bcn.es.
Metro: Jaume I. Open
Tue–Sun 1000–2000.

**Palau de la Música
Catalana** € Carrer Palau de
la Música; tel: 902 442882;
www.palaumusica.org. Metro:
Urquinaona. Open Tue–Sun
1000–1530. Guided tours
only.

Palau Güell Carrer Nou de
la Rambla 3; tel: 933 173974;
www.palauguell.cat. Metro:
Liceu or Paral.lel. Open
Tue–Sat 1000–1430 (until
1800 in summer). Free.

Parc Zoològic €€€
Parc de la Ciutadella;
tel: 932 256780;
www.zoobarcelona.com.
Metro: Barceloneta. Open
daily 1000–1900 in summer;
1000–1700 in winter.

Casa Museu Gaudí €
Park Güell (Eixample); tel: 932
193811. Metro: Vallcarca or
Lesseps. Open daily Apr–Sept
1000–2000; Oct–Mar
1000–1800.

Museu Marítim
The former royal shipyards have been turned into a maritime museum, with displays on the history of seafaring including model ships, maps and a life-size replica of a galley.

Museu Nacional d'Art de Catalunya
This museum, housed in the Palau Nacional built for the 1929 World Fair, contains the most complete collection of Catalan Romanesque and Gothic art. The Romanesque frescoes, recovered from Pyrenean churches, are unrivalled anywhere in the world.

Museu Picasso
The Picasso Museum, housed in several Gothic palaces, contains many of the artist's earliest works, painted while he was living in Barcelona. Later work includes Carnival posters, bullfighting etchings and studies of Velázquez's Las Meninas.

Palau de la Música Catalana
The concert hall designed by Domènech i Montaner is one of the triumphs of Catalan Modernist architecture, a fantasy of mosaics, stained glass and Egyptian columns. The guided tours are informative and entertaining; if you can, see a concert here.

Palau Güell
One of Gaudí's earliest projects was this mansion off Las Ramblas, commissioned by his patron Eusebi Güell. During the Civil War, it became the anarchist headquarters. The tiled chimneys on the rooftop are emblematic of Gaudí's style.

Parc de la Ciutadella
Barcelona's favourite park contains the Catalan parliament building, as well as the Modern Art Museum and a zoo which contains a variety of animals and offers popular dolphin shows. The park, with its Modernista pavilions, makes a good place for a sunset stroll.

Park Güell
Gaudí gave free rein to his imagination at this unfinished garden city, with dragon staircases, fairy-tale witches' houses and playful mosaic park benches. The summer house is now a museum.

Poble Espanyol
Buildings from all over Spain are re-created at this 'Spanish village', built for the 1929 World Fair. Highlights include a medieval gateway from Avila, an Andalusian village street and a Catalan monastery.

Sagrada Família
Gaudí's acknowledged masterpiece is this unfinished cathedral, which he began in 1883 and was still working on when he was run over by a tram in 1926. The work continues, and the atmosphere resembles a building site more than a church. The Passion façade has recently been completed with controversial sculptures by Josep Subirachs.

Poble Espanyol €€
*Avda Marquès de
Comillas (Montjuïc);
tel: 935 086300;
www.poble-espanyol.com.
Metro: Espanya. Open
summer Mon 0900–2000,
Tue–Thur 0900–0200,
Fri–Sat 0900–0400, Sun
0900–midnight; varies at
Christmas.*

Sagrada Família €€€
*Calle Mallorca 401
(Eixample); tel: 932 073031;
www.sagradafamilia.org.
Metro: Sagrada Família.
Open daily 0900–1800
(0900–2000 in summer).*

Santa María del Mar
*Plaça Santa María (Ribera).
Metro: Jaume I; tel: 933
102390. Open daily
0900–1330, 1630–2000.
Free.*

Santa María del Mar

This beautiful Gothic sailors' church has the proportions of a cathedral and is full of space and natural light. Concerts are often held here, and it is also a favourite place to get married.

Modernista architecture

The architectural movement of Modernisme, a Catalan version of Art Nouveau, flourished in Barcelona in the last decade of the 19th century and the first decade of the 20th. Its leading proponents were Antoni Gaudí, Josep Puig i Cadafalch and Lluís Domènech i Montaner. Modernisme has been described as 'fairy-tale Gothic' for the way in which it took classic forms (a deliberate throwback to Catalonia's Golden Age) and reinvented them in flamboyant style using mosaics, wrought iron and stained glass. It was also closely linked with Catalan nationalism, whose symbols, such as flags and St George, crop up regularly. The most famous stretch of Modernista architecture in Barcelona is the *Mançana de la Discòrdia* ('Block of Discord') on Passeig de Gràcia, where buildings by the three leading architects are found on a single block. One of these, Domènech i Montaner's Casa Lleó Morera, is the starting point for the *Ruta del Modernisme*, an itinerary taking in some 50 Modernista buildings. A single ticket includes a guidebook, half-price entry to seven attractions, and tours of the Palau Güell and Palau de la Música Catalana.

Accommodation and food

*Tapas bars have taken off in Barcelona, particularly at the lower end of Passeig de Gràcia and along the new waterfront promenade. One popular chain, **Tapasbar**, has bars at Port Vell and in the Olympic Village. Another trend is for Basque-style bars serving pintxos on pieces of bread. One of the best is **Irati** (Carrer Cardenal Casanyas 17) off the Ramblas, which is always heaving in the early evening.*

Barcelona's accommodation ranges from five-star hotels to backpackers' dives, but it is often difficult to find a room. The tourist office beneath Plaça de Catalunya has a hotel reservation and information service (*tel: 932 853832*).

Los Caracoles €€ *Carrer Escudellers 14; tel: 933 023185; email: caracoles@versin.com; www.loscaracoles.es.* This rustic cellar restaurant in the backstreets of the Gothic quarter is a Barcelona institution, offering spit-roast chicken, roast suckling pig and the speciality, grilled snails.

El Emperador €€ *Plaça Pau Vila; tel: 932 210220.* One of several terrace restaurants on the ground floor of the old naval palace, this is a good place to eat fresh seafood with a view of the harbour.

Mesón de Castilla €€ *Carrer Valdoncella 5; tel: 933 182182; fax: 934 124020; email: hmesoncastilla@teleline.es; www.mesoncastilla.com.* Ideally situated near the top of the Ramblas, this old-fashioned hotel has antique Castilian furniture and some charming Modernista touches.

Set Portes €€ *Passeig d'Isabel II 14; tel: 933 193033; email: reservas@7portes.com.* The oldest restaurant in Barcelona maintains its 19th-century atmosphere, serving classic Catalan rice and fish dishes to appreciative diners.

Arts €€€ *Passeig de la Marina 19; tel: 932 211000; fax: 932 211070; www.ritzcarlton.com.* This skyscraper overlooking the Olympic harbour remains the city's most fashionable address with stunning views and luxurious rooms and boasting every amenity – including a full spa and the option of a private butler.

Can Cortada €€€ *Avda de l'Estatut de Catalunya; tel: 934 272315; www. gruptravi.com/cortada.* This 16th-century farmhouse on the outskirts of the city is a favourite meeting place for politicians, who come to savour its traditional Catalan cuisine.

España €€€ *Carrer Sant Pau 9; tel: 933 181758; fax: 933 171134.* An additional appeal of this cutting-edge hotel is the splendid restaurant designed by the architect Domènech i Montaner.

Neri €€€ *Carrer de Sant Sever 5; tel: 933 040655; www.hotelneri.com.* This historic mansion is now a stunning, fashionable hotel which couples original architectural elements with colourful modern design.

Entertainment and nightlife

There is always something going on in Barcelona – check the listings in local newspapers, and in the free English-language tourist magazines (try *Metropolitan* and *See Barcelona*; it is also worth looking at *Barcelona Business*, although not so much for entertainment listings). Keep an eye out for posters advertising theatre or musical events. If you get the chance, you should go to a concert at the Liceu opera house (*tel: 934 859900*) or the Palau de la Música Catalana (*tel: 932 957200*). Another special night out is the Tablao de Carmen flamenco show at the Poble Espanyol on Montjuïc (*tel: 932 289530; closed Mon*). This is not tourist kitsch, but authentic flamenco dancing on the spot where the famous gypsy dancer, Carmen Amaya, first performed for Alfonso XIII in 1929. Look out, too, for *nuevo flamenco*, a Catalan version of flamenco with Latin and reggae influences.

Below
Las Ramblas

🍴 The best area for bar-hopping is along the waterfront, from Port Vell to the Olympic Village. Although the centre of gravity has shifted firmly towards the port, the Eixample retains its share of designer bars, such as the famous **Nick Havanna** (*Carrer de Rosselló 208*) and the fairground-themed **La Fira** (*Carrer de Provença 171*). The top nightclub is **Otto Zutz**, in an old factory north of the Eixample (*Carrer Lincoln 15*). Other popular places are **Catwalk** (*Carrer de Ramón Trias Fargas 2–4; www.clubcatwalk.net*), **Duvet** (*Carrer Corsega 327*) and **Luz de Gas** (*Carrer de Muntaner; www.luzdegas.com*).

Nightlife revolves around the bars and clubs, many of which do not get going until well after midnight. Fashions come and go, but perennial favourites, open throughout the day, are **Café de l'Opera** (*Rambla 74*), an old-style coffee house with dark wood and panelled mirrors, and **Els Quatre Gats** (*Carrer Montsió 3*), a café and restaurant once favoured by Picasso and other artists.

Another classic is **Marsella** (*Carrer Sant Pau 65*), which opens at 2200 nightly, serving potent absinthe to a cast of characters in one of the last vestiges of the old Raval. **El Xampanyet** (*Carrer Montcada 22*) is a popular *cava* bar near the Picasso Museum; two doors along, **Palau Dalmases** is a cocktail bar set in a Baroque palace, with live opera on Thursday nights.

Shopping

The biggest department store, **El Corte Inglés**, dominates Plaça de Catalunya. It is open from Monday to Saturday, 1000–2100. Most of the upmarket fashion stores are to be found in the Eixample, especially along Passeig de Gràcia, Rambla de Catalunya and Avda Diagonal.

For a quirkier shopping experience, head south from Plaça de Catalunya along Passeig Portal de l'Àngel, with clothes and shoe shops and another branch of El Corte Inglés. This leads into the heart of the Barri Gòtic, where small, specialist shops sell hats, fans, toys, chocolate, avant-garde art, offbeat fashions and South American jewellery and clothes. The best area is in the narrow alleyways between the cathedral and Las Ramblas, especially Carrer Portaferrissa, Carrer del Pi and Carrer Banys Nous. Carrer La Palla has numerous antique shops. For footwear, seek out **La Manual Alpargatera** (*Carrer Avignyó 7*) for its huge range of rope-soled espadrilles, and **Sole** (*Carrer Ample 7*) for sturdy leather sandals and boots.

Barcelona's biggest market, **Mercat de La Boquería**, is situated in a 19th-century hall on Las Ramblas. Besides fresh fruit, vegetables, meat and fish, this is a good place to stock up on picnic food such as bread, cheese, ham, sausages, fig cake, olives and olive oil.

Suggested walks

Time: These walks are designed to take a leisurely half day, though they could easily spill over into a day with a lunch stop and visits to museums.

Route 1: Start at the foot of **LAS RAMBLAS**, by the monument to Christopher Columbus. Walk slowly up the Ramblas, savouring the atmosphere of this unique 1,500m-long street. There are numerous opportunities for diversions, especially into the **BARRI GÒTIC** to your right, but eventually you arrive at the top of the street, marked by a fountain, Font de Canaletes. This is where football fans gather after a game; it is said that whoever drinks from the fountain will return to Barcelona. Ahead of you, the large open space of **Plaça de Catalunya**, with its gardens and sculptures, is the nearest thing the city has to a main square. It also marks the divide between the old city and the 19th-century **EIXAMPLE**.

Route 2: Go down to the Eixample Metro station and take line L1 to Espanya, emerging on **Plaça d'Espanya** beside an old bullring that is being converted into a commercial and leisure centre. Ahead of you, through the twin Venetian towers erected for the 1929 World Fair, an avenue leads up towards **MONTJUÏC**. The fountains along here are illuminated on summer evenings, creating a splendid spectacle. Save your legs and climb on to one of the escalators which lead up to the Palau Nacional, home of the **MUSEU NACIONAL DE L'ART DE CATALUNYA**. Behind the palace, more escalators lead to the **Estadi Olímpic** ('Olympic Stadium'); look into the stadium, then walk down the hill to the **FUNDACIÓ JOAN MIRÓ**.

Now take the funicular railway or walk down to the **Paral.lel** district, where little remains of the seedy glamour which made this the music-hall and cancan capital of Barcelona. From here, Carrer Nou de la Rambla leads through the edge of the **RAVAL**, the old red-light district, where the occasional shop selling sexy underwear sits incongruously beside another selling Communion dresses. Gaudí's **PALAU GÜELL** is at the end of this street, which leads back into Las Ramblas. Cross over Las Ramblas into **Plaça Reial**, an arcaded square whose lampposts were Gaudí's very first commission in the city. The square is attractive but it is not a place to linger as it has a slightly brooding atmosphere, with drug dealers and other unsavoury characters standing around on the corners.

Route 3: Start at the foot of **LAS RAMBLAS**, by the monument to Christopher Columbus, and cross the wooden walkway to reach **Port Vell**, a good place for a *tapas* lunch by the sea. If you want to extend your walk, you can continue along the waterfront, through the fishermen's quarter of **BARCELONETA** and along its magnificent beach. Eventually this leads to the **Vila Olímpica**, built on the site of a former shanty town to house the athletes in the 1992 Olympics. The village is dominated by its twin skyscrapers and by Frank Gehry's giant golden fish sculpture looking down over the marina. From here you can take the Metro, retrace your steps along the waterfront, or walk back towards the centre through the **PARC DE LA CIUTADELLA**.

The Golden Coast

Ratings

Beaches	●●●●●
Children	●●●●●
Nightlife	●●●●○
Restaurants	●●●●○
Museums	●●●○○
Scenery	●●●○○
Towns/ villages	●●●○○
Historical sights	●●○○○

Many people consider the Costa Daurada the poor cousin of Catalonia's *costas* as it has traditionally appealed to the lower end of the tourist market. Campsites and concrete apartments predominate here, and so far there have only been limited attempts to follow the Costa Brava upmarket. As British and German tourists begin to look elsewhere, the Russians are taking their place, drawn by the endless beaches and the attractions of cheap sun, sea and sand. Salou in summer is a perfect illustration of the excesses of package tourism, but not everywhere on the Costa Daurada is like this. Cambrils and Sitges are also popular holiday centres, but they retain a great deal of atmosphere, the one as a fishing village, the other as a bohemian resort. And just behind the coast, as always, the old towns and villages survive, virtually untouched by the tourist invasion.

CAMBRILS

ℹ *Passeig de les Palmeres; tel: 977 792307; email: tur@cambrils.org; www.cambrils.org*

⚓ Boat trips leave the harbour several times daily in summer for Salou. There are also occasional trips to L'Ametlla de Mar (see page 270).

🏛 **Parc de Samá €** *Ctra de Montbrió. The park is open during daylight hours.*

Cambrils would make a pleasant destination at any time of year, but it is particularly attractive in winter and early spring when Salou is shut down and the town can revert to its original occupation as a fishing port. There are few experiences more enjoyable than a walk around the harbour walls at dusk, as the fishermen unload their catch and the daily auction takes place. The restaurants by the harbour, famed for their fresh seafood, serve huge platters of crayfish, clams and crabs to gourmets from Barcelona and beyond. Large-scale tourist development is mostly restricted to the outskirts of the town, along the road to Salou. There are several good beaches here, some wide and sandy, others smaller and shaded with pines. The old town, set back from the harbour, is a typical Catalan town of golden stone houses and green shutters around a 17th-century church.

Further inland, on the road to Montbrió, **Parc de Samá** is an attractively landscaped garden with Modernisme fountains and towers, built around the neo-colonial palace of the Marquis of Marianao.

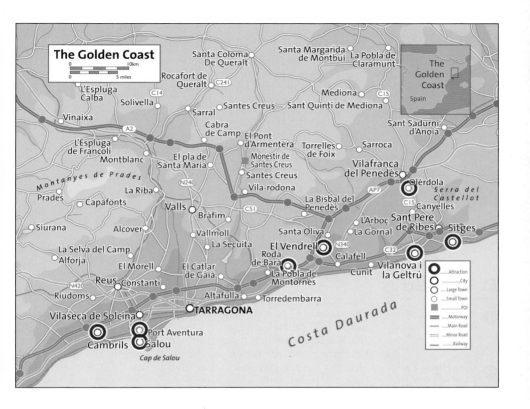

The Golden Coast

Accommodation and food in Cambrils

The covered market on Plaça del Pòsit, behind the harbour, is good for picnic food. For something more special, try **La Cuina del Marino** (see right) or **Degust** (Rambla Jaume I).

A weekly street market is held on Wednesday mornings.

Napoli € *Passeig Miramar 11; tel: 977 360656.* This genuine Italian trattoria on the seafront offers pizzas from a wood-fired oven as well as luscious desserts including vodka and *cava* sorbets.

La Cuina del Marino €€ *Carrer Pau Casals 23; tel: 977 793141.* Come here for gourmet takeaway food, such as paella, fish casserole, Basque-style cod, sole meunière, spit-roast chicken and garlic rabbit, all prepared to order.

Posito de Pescadores €€ *Pescadors 23; tel: 977 361741.* You need to queue at lunchtime to get into this bustling fishermen's bar, serving fresh seafood, paella and *tapas* in the old fishermen's hall beside the market.

Princep €€ *Narcis Monturiol 2; tel: 977 361127; fax: 977 363532; email: informacione@hotelprincep.com; www.hotelprincep.com.* What this hotel lacks in sea views it makes up for in location, a stone's throw from the fishing harbour. The rooms are comfortable and well furnished, and the restaurant serves exquisite seafood.

Can Bosch €€€ *Rambla Jaume I 19; tel: 977 360019*. Regarded as Cambril's best eatery, this celebrated fish and seafood restaurant near the port is the place for a memorable meal. Reservation always recommended, essential at busy times.

Joan Gatell €€€ *Passeig Miramar 26; tel: 977 366782; email: joangatell@aeht.es*. This famous seafood restaurant has been in the same family since 1914, serving simple but classic dishes such as *arròs marinera* (rice and seafood soup) and *caldereta de bogavante* (lobster casserole). There is also a six-course gastronomic menu. The dining terrace enjoys harbour views.

Rincón de Diego €€€ *Carrer Drassanes 7; tel: 977 361307*. A small, eclectic seafood restaurant just behind the harbour, known for its highly personal contemporary Catalan cuisine.

EL VENDRELL

Avda Brisamar; tel: 977 680010; email: turisme@elvendrell.net; www.elvendrellturistic.com

Casa Museu Pau Casals € *Carrer Sta Anna 2; tel: 977 665642. Open Tue–Fri 1000–1400, 1700–1900 (1800–2000 in summer); Sat 1100–1400, 1700–2000; Sun open morning only.*

The capital of the Baix Penedès district is a busy little market town with a solid Catalan atmosphere. The cellist Pablo Casals (1876–1973) was born here, though his opposition to Franco and commitment to Catalan nationalism meant that he spent much of his life in Puerto Rico and never returned to Catalonia after the Civil War. His family home in the fishermen's quarter of Sant Salvador is now the **Casa Museu Pau Casals**; it contains his first cello, as well as his collection of paintings and an auditorium where concerts are held. The museum is situated in the most appealing part of town, with fishing boats on the beach and fish restaurants on the promenade.

Accommodation and food in El Vendrell

A weekly market takes place on Fridays.

Europe San Salvador €€ *Carrer Llobregat; tel: 977 684041; fax: 977 684743.* This large seaside hotel is open from Easter to October and has facilities including tennis courts and an outdoor pool.

El Molí de Cal Tof €€ *Ctra Santa Oliva 2; tel: 977 662651.* A rustic Catalan restaurant with a fireplace at the centre serving classic dishes such as grilled snails and *xató*, the spicy local fish salad.

Meridien Ra Beach Hotel & Spa €€€ *Avinguda Sanatori 1; tel: 977 694200.* This luxurious seafront hotel offers all the comforts that typify the Meridien chain, including a glossy new spa specialising in thalassotherapy.

OLÈRDOLA

Museu Arqueològic de Olèrdola €
Tel: 938 901420. On the C15 between Canyelles and Vilafranca del Penedès. Site open Mar–Oct daily 1000–1400, 1500–2000; Oct–Feb Tue–Fri 1000–1400, 1500–1600, Sat & Sun 1000–1600.

This strategic hilltop site was inhabited from the Bronze Age through to the Roman occupation and again in late medieval times, when it played a key role in the Christian defence of Catalonia. Much of the site has still to be excavated, but you can see an Iberian rock dwelling from the 2nd century BC as well as a Roman cistern and parts of the Roman wall. From the later occupation there is a pre-Romanesque church, the remains of a medieval castle and some 10th-century anthropomorphic-shaped tombs, carved out of the rock in the shape of the human body. There is also a small **archaeological museum**.

PORT AVENTURA

There is ample car parking at Port Aventura. The park can also be reached by bus, train or road train from nearby resorts.

Port Aventura €€€
Autovia Salou/Vila-Seca Km2; tel: 902 202220; www.portaventura.co.uk. Open Apr–mid-Jun & Oct daily 1000–2000; mid-Jun–mid-Sept daily 1000–2400.

Left
Casa Museu Pau Casals

The purists may scoff that it has nothing to do with Catalonia, but this theme park makes a great day out – especially with kids. The park is divided into five themed areas, purporting to represent China, Mexico, Polynesia, the Wild West and a Catalan fishing village. Each contains a mixture of live entertainment, children's activities, restaurants, shops and white-knuckle rides. Inevitably some of the cultures get stereotyped and distorted, but there is no doubting the quality of the displays. The shows feature Chinese acrobatics, Mexican music and Polynesian dancing, while thrill rides include swingboats, the popular Tutuki Splash and the Dragon Khan roller coaster, dominating the park with its eight loops and 100kph drop.

During the summer, Port Aventura can get extremely crowded, so it is best to arrive early and plan your day carefully. You can pick up a leaflet of show times at the entrance, and waiting times for the most popular rides are displayed around the park. The queues tend to be shorter at lunchtime and late in the day.

Caribe Aquatic Park €€
Tel: 902 202220;
www.portaventuradirect.com.
Open Mon–Sat 0900–2200,
Sun 1000–1800.

Each of the themed areas has its own restaurants offering regional food. **Es Racó de Mar**, near the entrance, serves traditional Catalan cuisine.

Universal Mediterranea, owners of Port Aventura, has also opened **Costa Caribe**, a waterpark, in the same area. Attractions include waterslides, a lazy river, a wave pool and a large covered area, which stays open all year long.

RODA DE BARÀ

For more on Roman Catalonia, see Tarragona (*pages 252–9*).

The N340 coast road follows the course of the Vía Augusta, which once linked Tarragona to ancient Rome. All that remains is an imposing triumphal arch, **Arc de Barà**, dating from the 2nd century AD. The traffic no longer passes beneath the arch, which stands on an island in the middle of the road, but close your eyes and you can imagine chariots driving through. The nearby 'urbanisation' of Roda de Barà has a pair of pretty beaches backed by tamarisk trees.

Food in Roda de Barà

Below
Sculpture on the waterfront, Salou

La Bota €€ *Ctra N340; tel: 977 801101.* The restaurant beside the arch features Catalan home cooking, making full use of rustic ingredients such as pigs' trotters, pork sausages and snails. In summer you can eat on a large outdoor terrace.

SALOU

Passeig Jaume I 4;
tel: 977 350102;
email: pmtsalou@salou.org;
www.salou.org

The tourist capital of the Costa Daurada first became fashionable at the beginning of the 20th century, when wealthy visitors from Barcelona built their villas on the promenade. Since then it has grown to become one of the largest resorts in Spain, with a winter population of just 11,000, but up to half a million visitors in summer. The attraction is the long sandy beach, which shelves gently into the sea, offering safe swimming as well as every kind of watersport. Behind the beach, a palm-lined promenade leads to the harbour, where a funfair offers old-fashioned rides. Elsewhere, Salou in summer is a high-energy mix of discos, foreign bars and sunburnt bodies from every corner of Europe.

Salou may look like a thoroughly modern town, but it has an important place in Catalan history. A statue on the promenade reveals that it was from here that Jaume I, the Conqueror, sailed in 1229 to capture the island of Mallorca for the kings of Aragón.

Boat trips leave the harbour several times daily in summer for Cambrils. There are also occasional trips to Tarragona (see pages 252–9).

A street market is held in Vía Roma on Monday mornings, and a craft market takes place every evening in summer in the **Masia Catalana**, a reproduction Catalan farmhouse on Avda Carles Buigas.

Accommodation and food in Salou

Tahiti € *Avda Carles Buigas 9; tel: 977 380339.* The spit-roast chicken that comes with a huge plate of chips, is definitely the thing to order at this busy restaurant on the main tourist shopping street. Great value, but no outdoor tables or sea views.

Cap Salou €€ *Cala de la Font 1; tel: 977 371985; fax: 977 370301; email: info@besthotels.es; www.besthotels.es.* Unlike the centre of the resort with its long, flat beach, the headland of Cap Salou features pine woods and rocky coves. This mega-hotel overlooking the sea has 465 rooms and facilities including tennis, swimming and mini-golf.

Albatros €€€ *Carrer Bruselles 60; tel: 977 385070.* Fresh Catalan market cuisine, with an emphasis on fish, is served at this small terrace restaurant above the Capellans cove.

SITGES

Sinia Morera 1; tel: 938 103428; www.sitgestur.com

There is free parking along the seafront, though your best bet is to park close to the Hotel Terramar and walk along the promenade.

Museu Cau Ferrat € *Carrer de Fonollar; tel: 938 940364. Open mid-Jun–Sept daily 1000–1400, 1700–2100; Oct–mid-Jun Tue–Sat 0930–1400, 1530–1830, Sun 1000–1500.*

Museu Maricel del Mar € *Carrer Fonollar. Opening times and phone as Museu Cau Ferrat.*

Museu Romàntic € *Carrer Sant Gaudenci; tel: 938 942969. Opening times as Museu Cau Ferrat.*

If you plan to visit more than one museum, it is worth buying a combined entrance ticket.

This cosmopolitan beach resort has long attracted a different kind of tourist, ever since it became the meeting place for a group of Modernista painters in the late 19th century. Artists still come, fashionable Barcelonans flock here at weekends, and gay tourists are drawn by its tolerant lifestyle – especially in February, when Rio comes to Sitges with extravagant Carnival parades and outrageous costumes.

The setting is magnificent, a succession of small beaches in the shadow of La Punta, a rocky bluff overlooking the harbour. The headland is dominated by the 16th-century parish church, reached by a flight of steps from the promenade. Behind here is the oldest and most appealing part of town, with narrow streets, whitewashed cottages, flower-filled balconies and chic galleries, boutiques and bars.

The painter Santiago Rusiñol (1861–1931) spent many years in Sitges and his home on La Punta is now the **Museu Cau Ferrat**. Rusiñol built the house out of two fishermen's cottages, adding Gothic and Modernista touches and naming it *ferrat* after his collection of wrought iron. The museum contains paintings by Rusiñol and by Picasso and El Greco among others.

The **Museu Maricel del Mar**, next door, has an eclectic collection which includes Romanesque murals, Gothic paintings and a large display of Catalan Modernista art. Among the artists featured are Santiago Rusiñol, Ramon Casas and members of the Catalan Luminist school, who were drawn to Sitges by the intensity of its light. The old dining room has a set of murals, *Allegories of the World War*, by Josep María Sert, while the belvedere features modern Catalan sculpture and picture windows looking out to sea. Across the street, the **Palau Maricel**, on the site of an old hospital, is occasionally open on summer evenings for concerts and guided tours.

Sitges is known for its colourful festivals, both traditional and modern. **Carnival** (*opposite*) takes place over the week leading up to Ash Wednesday, usually in February. On the Sunday following Carnival there is a **vintage car rally** from Barcelona to Sitges. The Sunday after **Corpus Christi** in June is marked by religious processions and 'flower carpets' in the streets, while the **Festa Major**, around 23–24 August, features dragons, giants, firecrackers and stick dancing.

Carrer 1 de Maig, running back from the seafront, is known as the 'street of sin' because of its many designer bars and clubs, where loud salsa, Brazilian and *nuevo flamenco* music can usually be heard late into the night.

Below
Sitges

The **Museu Romàntic**, in an 18th-century town house, has Romantic-era furniture and an outstanding collection of dolls.

Accommodation and food in Sitges

Eguzki € *Carrer Sant Pau 3; tel: 938 110320*. A lively Basque *tapas* bar where the *pintxos* are laid out along the counter for you to help yourself. To settle your bill, simply count the number of cocktail sticks on your plate.

Al Fresco €€ *Carrer de Pau Barrabeig 4; tel: 938 940600*. Enjoy tasty Asian-inspired cuisine at this centrally-located restaurant with its bright fresh décor and friendly service.

Romàntic €€ *Carrer Sant Isidre 33; tel: 938 948375; fax: 938 948167; email: romantic@hotelromantic.com*. A charming hotel situated in three 19th-century villas furnished with antiques and modern art. Breakfast is usually served in the peaceful, shady garden.

San Sebastián Playa €€ *Carrer Port Alegre 53; tel: 938 948676; fax: 938 940430; email: hotelsansebastian@hotelsansebastian.com; www.hotelsansebastian.com*. Modern hotel with neoclassical touches facing a smaller beach beyond the headland of La Punta.

Terramar €€ *Passeig Marítim 80; tel: 938 940050; fax: 938 945604; email: hotelterramar@hotelterramar.com; www.hotelterramar.com*. This large, modern beach hotel, open from May to October, is situated 2km from the centre at the end of the promenade.

Maricel €€€ *Paseo de la Ribera 6; tel: 938 942054; www.maricel.es*. Chef Ferran Sancho delivers an exquisite array of Mediterranean cuisine in a lovely seaside setting.

VILANOVA I LA GELTRÚ

ℹ *Passeig del Carme, Parc de Ribes Roges;* tel: 938 154517; email: turisme@ving.es; www.villanova.org. The tourist office is situated in a park close to the beachfront promenade. In winter it is only open at weekends.

P There is plenty of parking down on the seafront, from where it is a short walk to the town centre.

🏛 **Museu del Ferrocarril** € *Plaça d'Eduard Maristany;* tel: 938 158491. Open Tue–Fri & Sun 1030–1430, Sat 1030–1430, 1600–1830.

🛍 A market is held on Saturday mornings.

🎭 **Carnival** (see below) begins on the Thursday before Lent.

Despite outward appearances, the capital of the Garraf county is a pleasing, very Catalan town with a delightful *rambla*, a pair of good beaches and a local atmosphere which amply rewards a two-hour stroll. More industrial and a lot less pretty than Sitges, Vilanova nevertheless attracts many people as a more authentic introduction to the region. The main beach stretches beyond the seafront promenade; there is a second beach by the lighthouse behind the fishing port. From the harbour, Rambla de la Pau leads into the heart of town, culminating at the parish church; near here, pedestrian shopping streets fan out from a palm-lined main square. Appropriately located next to the train station, the **Museu del Ferrocarril** (Railway Museum) offers visitors of all ages a fascinating glimpse of traditional steam trains, and includes the largest collection of the 'puffers' in Europe.

Accommodation and food in Vilanova i la Geltrú

César €€ *Carrer Isaac Peral 8; tel: 938 151125; fax: 938 156719; www.hotelcesar.net.* Open all year, this charming hotel has a heated swimming pool and a beautiful garden facing the beach.

El Groc €€ *Rambla Principal 3; tel: 938 141737.* This restaurant in the centre of town serves stylish modern Catalan cuisine, such as duck with orange or roast salmon with bacon.

Peixerot €€€ *Passeig Marítim 56, Urbanización Ibersol; tel: 938 150625.* Famous fish restaurant at the foot of the Rambla with large, bright windows looking across to the port. It serves classic Catalan seafood dishes, including *arròs negre* (rice with squid ink), fish baked in salt, and *pica-pica*, a selection of fish starters.

Carnival

The riotous pre-Lenten Carnival probably goes back to Roman times and the Bacchanalian festivities heralding the arrival of spring. In Franco's time, Carnival was banned but the people of Sitges went on celebrating nevertheless. The precise nature of Carnival varies throughout Catalonia but usually includes parades of floats and fancy dress, which in Sitges take on a hedonistic and gay character. The biggest parades in Sitges take place on the Sunday before Lent and late at night on Shrove Tuesday. There are also separate parades for children over the weekend. Carnival officially begins with the arrival of Carnestoltes, the Carnival king, the previous Thursday, and ends on Ash Wednesday with the traditional 'burial of the sardine', signifying the end of winter. Although Sitges attracts the bigger crowds, many people prefer the more traditional festivities at Vilanova i la Geltrú, which begin on the Thursday with a *xatonada* – a communal feast consisting of the typical local *xató* salad of endives, salt cod and tuna. The weekend is marked by masked balls, parades and a huge 'battle of sweets', and Carnival ends with the mock funeral of Carnestoltes, burnt at the stake as punishment for his licentious ways.

Suggested tour

Total distance: 171km.

Time: 3 hours.

Links: You can join the Montserrat and wine country route (*see pages 228–9*) at Vilafranca del Penedès, or the Cistercian monastery route (*see pages 267–9*) at Tarragona (*see pages 252–9*). From Cambrils the N340 continues along the coast to the start of the Ebro Delta route (*see pages 277–9*) at L'Hospitalet de l'Infant.

Start on the beach at **SITGES ❶**, heading away from the old town until you reach the Hotel Terramar, where you turn right to join the Tarragona road. Turn left here and continue to **VILANOVA I LA GELTRÚ ❷**, passing the Barcelona casino on your right. Arriving at Vilanova, follow signs to the port and park down by the harbour for a stroll along the promenade or a walk into the town centre.

Leave Vilanova on the C31, signposted to Tarragona. This follows the coast through a succession of fishing villages, most of them turned into summer resorts.

Cunit is the first village in Tarragona province and it therefore marks the start of the Costa Daurada proper. It is as good a place as any to get out of your car for a bracing walk along the beach. After **Segur de Calafell**, take the ring road around **Calafell** to reach **EL VENDRELL ❸**, where you could make a short detour to see Pablo Casals' house on the beach at Sant Salvador.

From El Vendrell, the N340 continues to Tarragona. After 8km you reach **RODA DE BARÀ ❹**, marked by the Roman arch in the middle of the road. Continue through **Torredembarra** and **Altafulla**, a pair of charming villages each dominated by a ruined castle. The road now becomes a coastal corniche, with sea views to your left as you approach **Tarragona** (*see pages 252–9*). You can plunge into the heart of the city or escape around the ring road, but either way you need to look out carefully for signs to Salou.

Arriving in **SALOU ❺**, turn left to reach the sea, with the main tourist district to your left. Drive along the beachfront and continue past the harbour for another 7km, crossing a marshy shoreline to reach **CAMBRILS ❻**. Turn inland here to join the A7 toll motorway in the direction of Barcelona, continuing for 66km and leaving at junction 30 near **Vilafranca del Penedès**.

From Vilafranca, take the C15 to return to the coast, passing vineyards and the archaeological site at **OLÈRDOLA ❼**. Just before **Canyelles ❽**, dominated by its medieval castle, veer right towards **Sitges**, travelling through the valleys of the Garraf mountains on a narrow road which snakes between the hills.

Getting out of the car

If you want to stretch your legs, the coastal towns on this route all have fine sandy beaches and seafront promenades. A good summer excursion is the short boat trip from Salou to Cambrils – or if you have children with you, a ride on the miniature road train around Salou.

Also worth exploring

North of Sitges, the C31 hugs the coastline on its way to the airport at Barcelona. This is the Costa del Garraf, named after the nearby mountain range, and a traditional weekend retreat for the people of Barcelona.

The main town, **Castelldefels**, has a seemingly endless beach as well as a yacht marina at **Port Ginesta** and the remains of a fortified old town. Unfortunately, the scenic drive along the coast is somewhat spoiled by the presence of a large cement factory at **Garraf**.

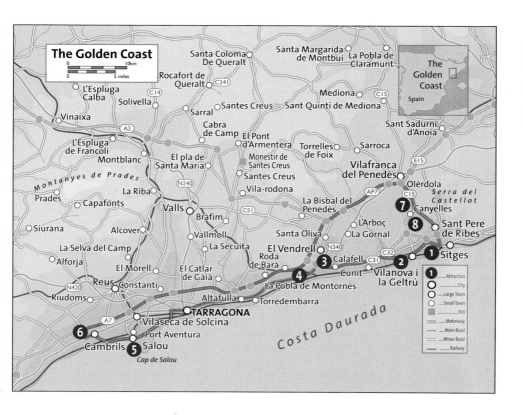

Tarragona

ⓘ *Carrer Major 39; tel: 977 250795; turisme.tgna@altanet.org.* There is also a Catalan government tourist office off the Rambla Nova at Carrer Fortuny 4. *Tel: 977 233415; email: ot.tarragona.ctc@gencat.net; www.catalunyaturisme.com*

⇄ It is best to visit Tarragona by train or bus. The railway station is by the seafront, a 20-minute walk from the centre. The bus station is close to Plaça Imperial Tarraco, the city's central crossroads.

The belching chimneys of the petrochemical industry that surround modern Tarragona give little clue to the history of this ancient Roman port. This was imperial Tarraco, chosen by the Romans after the Punic Wars as the capital of their western Mediterranean empire and the base from which they extended their conquest of the Iberian peninsula. Julius Caesar and several Roman emperors visited Tarragona, and Pontius Pilate was born in the city – at that time one of the richest in Europe. Today, as the capital of the Costa Daurada, Tarragona is thriving once more. It has wide avenues, parks and an atmospheric fishermen's quarter, El Serralló, where smacks are tied up in the harbour and fishermen sit in the sun mending their nets. However, the main reason for visiting Tarragona is still to see the Roman remains, which continue to be uncovered with each passing year.

Sights

Amfiteatre

The Roman amphitheatre was built at the start of the 2nd century AD outside the walls of the city, overlooking the sea. The central arena is surrounded by tiered seats, some of them carved out of the rock. This was the setting for various violent spectacles, including gladiator contests, fighting with wild animals and the martyrdom of Christians. In AD 259, Bishop Fructuosus of Tarraco and two of his deacons were martyred here following a decree from the emperor Valerian. During the Visigothic era, a basilica with a horseshoe-shaped apse was erected inside the arena in commemoration of Fructuosus; it was later replaced by a Romanesque church, parts of which remain. You can wander around the arena, sit on the benches and walk through the door where the gladiators once entered. Beneath the arena, excavations have uncovered a shrine with a wall painting of Nemesis, protector of gladiators and hunters.

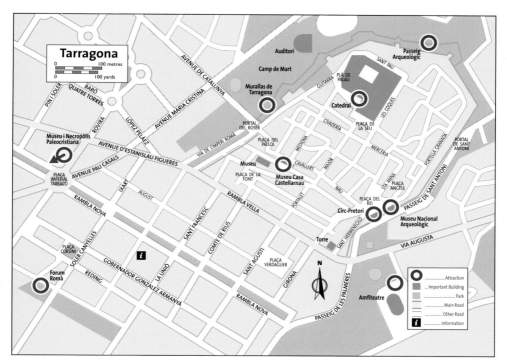

Tarragona

0 ___ 100 metres
0 ___ 100 yards

Auditori
Camp de Mart
Passeig Arqueològic
Muralles de Tarragona
Catedral
PORTAL DEL ROSER
PLAÇA DE LA SEU
PLAÇA DEL PALLOL
Museu i Necròpolis Paleocristiana
Museu
PLAÇA DE LA FONT
Museu Casa Castellarnau
PLAÇA IMPERIAL TARRACO
Circ-Pretori
PLAÇA DEL REI
Museu Nacional Arqueològic
Torre
PLAÇA CORSINI
PLAÇA VERDAGUER
Forum Romà
Amfiteatre
PORTAL DE SANT ANTONI

AVENUE DE CATALUNYA · AVENUE MARIA CRISTINA · ROVIRA · LÓPEZ PELAEZ · AVENUE D'ESTANISLAU FIGUERES · AVENUE PAU CASALS · IXART · AUGUST · RAMBLA NOVA · SOLER · CANYELLES · GOBERNADOR GONZALEZ ARMANYA · LA UNIÓ · REDING · SANT FRANCESC · COMTE DE RIUS · RAMBLA VELLA · SANT AGUSTI · GIRONA · RAMBLA NOVA · PASSEIG DE LES PALMERES · SANT HERMENEGILD · VIA AUGUSTA · PASSEIG DE SANT ANTONI · MERCERIA · MAJOR · CAVALLERS · NAU · PORTALET · STA. ANNA · PLAÇA ANGELS · PORTELLA GRANADA · GUITARRA · CIVADERIA · MEDIONA · PLA DE PALAU · LES COQUES · SANT PAU · PIN I SOLER · BARÓ · QUATRE TORRES · VIA DE L'IMPERI ROMÀ

○ .... Attraction
■ .... Important Building
■ .... Park
— .... Main Road
— .... Other Road
i .... Information

P Arriving by car, head for Plaça Imperial Tarraco (it is almost impossible to miss it) and park in one of the underground car parks.

🏛 Amfiteatre € *Parc del Miracle; tel: 977 242579; www.museutgn.com. Open Easter–Sept 0900–2100, Sun 0900–1500; winter 0900–1700, Sun 1000–1500. Closed Mon.*

Catedral € *Plaça de la Seu; tel: 977 238685. Open Jun–mid-Oct Tue–Sat 1000–1900; mid-Nov–mid-Mar Mon–Sat 1000–1400; at other times Mon–Sat 1000–1300, 1600–1900. Closed Sun, except for services.*

Catedral

The cathedral, built between the 12th and 14th centuries, is a fine example of the transition from Romanesque to Gothic styles. It is approached by an impressive flight of steps, leading to the carved Gothic portal representing the Last Judgement. A second doorway leads into the cloister, with its peaceful garden of orange trees, from where a Romanesque portal gives access to the church. The cathedral, built on the site of a mosque and before that a Roman temple, is dedicated to Santa Tecla, the patron of Tarragona. According to tradition, she was the first Christian martyr and is said to have accompanied St Paul on a journey to Tarragona. Her story is told in the 15th-century Gothic altarpiece by Pere Joan, and in the reliefs in the chapel of Santa Tecla, where a concealed tomb, opened once a year, is said to hold one of the saint's arms.

Circ-Pretori

Parts of the Roman circus and *praetorium* ('governor's residence') have been combined into a single precinct which forms a branch of the city history museum. The circus, built in the reign of Domitian in the 1st century AD, was where chariot races were held. The original site was much larger but most of it has been built over, and the remains that you see were only discovered following the demolition of a cinema.

Circ-Pretori €
Entrance on Rambla Vella or Plaça del Rei; tel: 977 230171. Open Oct–Easter Tue–Sat 0900–1900, Sun 1000–1500; Easter–Sept Tue–Sat 0900–2100, Sun 0900–1500.

Forum Romà € *Carrer Lleida. Opening times as the Circ-Pretori.*

Museu Casa Castellarnau € *Carrer Cavallers 14; tel: 977 242220. Open Oct–Easter Tue–Sat 0900–1900, Sun 1000–1500; Easter–Sept Tue–Sat 0900–2100, Sun 0900–1500.*

Murallas de Tarragona € *Avda Catalunya s/n; tel: 977 245796. Access from Via de l'Imperi Romà. Open Apr–Sept Tue–Sat 0900–2100, Sun 0900–1500; Oct–Apr Tue–Sat 0900–1700, Sun 1000–1500. Closed Mon.*

Museums and Roman sites

All of these are closed on Mondays. A single ticket, available at the tourist office or any of the sites, gives access to the amphitheatre, Roman forum, circus, praetorium and Roman walls, as well as the Museu Casa Castellarnau and a modern art museum. The ticket is free to under-16s and to anyone in possession of a ticket to Port Aventura (see page 245). The archaeological museum and Roman necropolis can also be visited on a combined ticket.

Three of the original Roman arches survive, along with some steps and tiered seats. An exhibition in the 14th-century Torre de les Monges ('Nuns' Tower') describes the history of the circus and its restoration. From here, you walk through underground tunnels to reach the praetorium, dominated by a tall tower whose rooftop gives fine views of the city. Popularly known as 'Pilate's tower' and built during the 1st century AD, this was the palace of the emperors Augustus and Hadrian and was later remodelled by the kings of Aragón. The museum contains a number of Roman antiquities, including a 3rd-century sarcophagus recovered from the seabed. Its exquisite reliefs recount the myth of Hippolyte, crushed by the wheels of his chariot after his horses were frightened by a sea monster.

Forum Romà

You need to be a keen archaeologist, or at least have a vivid imagination, to appreciate a visit to the old Roman forum. This was once the nerve centre of Tarragona's political, religious and commercial life, with temples, shops and offices, as well as the magistrates' court. All that remain are the plinths of the columns that once supported a portico, together with the entrance to a 1st-century basilica and various fragments of stone inscriptions.

Murallas de Tarragona

Although they have been extensively remodelled over the years, the Roman walls of Tarragona are the only remaining monument from the earliest days of the Roman republic. At one stage they stretched for 4km to the port, but only a small section around the old town survives. According to tradition, they were built by the Scipio brothers in the 3rd century BC – hence the motto *Tarraco Scipionum Opus* ('Tarraco is the work of the Scipio brothers'), first coined by Pliny. The walls were constructed on massive Cyclopean bases which led many to conclude that they had come from an earlier Iberian settlement, though the letters from the Iberian alphabet seen along one stretch are probably the marks of the stonemasons employed by the Romans. For a close-up view, take this pleasant 'archaeological walk' (**Passeig Arqueològic**) through the gardens beneath the walls. The walk follows a path between the original Roman wall and an 18th-century fortification built by the British during the War of the Spanish Succession. It ends close to the Torre del Minerva, a Roman watchtower, where part of a relief of the goddess Minerva can be seen.

Museu Casa Castellarnau

The Habsburg emperor Charles V is said to have stayed in this Gothic mansion, remodelled in the 18th century by the wealthy Castellarnau family. Among the exhibits are period furniture and paintings, and a re-creation of an old pharmacy. A recent addition is a tapestry by Joan Miró, given to the city of Tarragona in gratitude for the care his daughter received following a car accident. The museum hardly merits

Above
Tarragona's Roman amphitheatre

🛈 **Museu Nacional Arqueològic** € *Plaça del Rei 5; tel: 977 236209. Open Oct–May Tue–Sat 0930–1330, 1530–1900, Sun 1000–1400; Jun–Sept Tue–Sat 0930–2030, Sun 1000–1400. Free Tue.*

a special visit, but as it is included on the Tarragona museums pass you might as well drop in – especially if you feel like a change from Roman remains.

Museu Nacional Arqueològic

Although it does not have the atmosphere of the authentic Roman sites, this museum, housed in a modern building with a Roman inscription across its façade, is an essential stop on any tour of ancient Tarraco. Among the objects discovered in and around the city are

Can Llesques €, in Plaça del Rei, serves numerous varieties of *llesca*, toast rubbed with tomato and topped with everything from salted anchovies to spinach and Catalan sausage.

There is a religious procession involving fishing boats on 16 July in the fishing port of El Serralló to mark the feast of **Mare de Déu del Carme**. The city's big festival, **Santa Tecla**, is on 23–4 September, when the *castellers* build their human pyramids in the Plaça de la Font.

Markets

A large indoor food market takes place on weekday mornings in Plaça Corsini, close to the Rambla Nova. Flowers are sold along Rambla Nova itself, and there is a street market on Tuesdays and Thursdays. On Sunday mornings, a bric-a-brac and antiques market is held on the cathedral steps. Weekday afternoons see a lively fish auction in El Serralló following the return of the fishing fleet.

Roman pottery, coins, jewellery, bronze lamps, fertility aids and funerary sculptures. There are remains of several buildings and epigraphs from Roman temples. The collection of Roman mosaics is outstanding, the most complete in Catalonia. Look out for the beautiful mosaic of the head of Medusa, and another which shows the fish and sea creatures of the region in intricate detail.

Museu i Necròpolis Paleocristiana

This late Roman burial ground on the banks of the Francolí river was discovered early in the 20th century when a tobacco factory was being built. More than 2,000 graves have been found here, giving an overview of funerary art from pagan through to Visigothic times. The tombs range from simple wooden coffins and others recycled from fragments of amphorae, to elaborate stone sarcophagi with sculpted decoration and mosaic lids. A large number are preserved *in situ* and others are on display in the accompanying museum, along with archaeological finds from the site and an exhibition on the Roman way of death. Bishop Fructuosus, martyred in the amphitheatre, is among those believed to have been buried here.

Accommodation and food

Pulvinar € *Carrer Ferrers 20; tel: 977 235631.* A pizzeria which proudly preserves a good section of masonry and pavement from the Roman circus. The menu includes several vegetarian options.

Aq €€ *Carrer de les Coques 7; tel: 977 215954.* A sophisticated modern restaurant, serving traditional dishes with an innovative twist.

Husa Imperial Tarraco €€ *Paseo Palmeras s/n; tel: 977 233040; fax: 977 216566; email: hotelimperialtarraco@husa.es; www.husa.es.* The top hotel in town also has the best location, with marvellous views over the amphitheatre and out to sea. Facilities include private parking and a pool.

Lauria €€ *Rambla Nova 20; tel: 977 236712; fax: 977 236700; email: info@hlauria.es; www.hlauria.es.* Because most people stay in the nearby resorts there is a shortage of good accommodation in Tarragona, but this family-run hotel on the main promenade makes a reasonable choice. The top-floor rooms have sea views, and there is a small pool in the courtyard.

Les Voltes €€ *Carrer Trinquet Vell 12; tel: 977 230651.* Parts of the vaults of the Roman circus can be seen inside this busy restaurant, which serves Catalan meat and seafood dishes.

Palau del Baró €€€ *Carrer Santa Anna 3; tel: 977 241464.* Catalan cuisine in the setting of a baronial palace, with antique furniture and a romantic garden patio.

Suggested walk

Length: 8km.

Time: 3 hours, plus time for visits. Allow a full day.

Begin at **Plaça Imperial Tarraco** ❶, a huge modern roundabout where the main roads into the city converge. You can pick up a map at the information booth at the top of the **Rambla Nova**. This wide thoroughfare, a busy shopping street lined with cafés and florists, has a pleasant pedestrian promenade along its centre. Stay on this road for almost 2km until it runs out at the **Balcó del Mediterrani** ❷, a mirador overlooking the sea, the **AMFITEATRE** ❸ and the small beach, **Platja del Miracle**. Beside the mirador is a statue of Roger de Llúria, the Catalan admiral who led the invasion fleet of Menorca in 1287.

Turn left here along **Passeig de les Palmeres**, a popular early evening promenading spot. Landscaped gardens fall away to the sea on your right and the tall square tower of the old Roman praetorium looms up ahead. Turn left again along **Rambla Vella**, once the Vía Augusta, passing one of the entrances to the **CIRC-PRETORI** ❹. Turn right at Carrer Portalet to reach **Plaça de la Font**, a busy lunchtime square of open-air cafés and restaurants on the site of the old Roman circus. The town hall stands at one end of the square, where the chariots used to enter.

Climb up through the heart of the old town to reach **Carrer Major**, with its jewellers, antiques and pastry shops. At the top of this street you reach the cathedral steps. After visiting the **CATEDRAL** ❺, descend the steps and turn right into the heart of the old Jewish quarter, with its narrow lanes of balconies and shutters, sunlight, shadows and golden stone. Eventually you will arrive at **Plaça del Pallol**, a peaceful Gothic square. From here, **Portal del Roser**, the western gateway to the Roman city, leads to the start of the **PASSEIG ARQUEOLÒGIC** ❻, a promenade beside the Roman walls.

The walk ends on the outside of the walls, close to the **Portal de Sant Antoni** . Follow the walls until they run out, then turn right into **Plaça del Rei**, whose outdoor cafés make a good place to stop for a drink or an ice cream. On one side of the square is the **MUSEU NACIONAL ARQUEOLÒGIC** ; on the other, the Circ-Pretori. Follow the steps down to Passeig de les Palmeres and retrace your steps along Rambla Nova.

Also worth exploring

If you have developed a taste for Roman Tarragona, there are two sites worth visiting on the outskirts of the city. The **Pont de les Ferreres** is a Roman aqueduct built during the reign of Augustus, 4km north of Tarragona on the Valls road (*see route on pages 267–8*). At **Centcelles**, 5km from Tarragona and reached through the village of Constantí, there is a 4th-century mausoleum with some well-preserved Roman mosaics. *Open Tue–Sat 1000–1330, 1500–1730 (Jun–Sept 1000–1330, 1600–1900), Sun 1000–1330.*

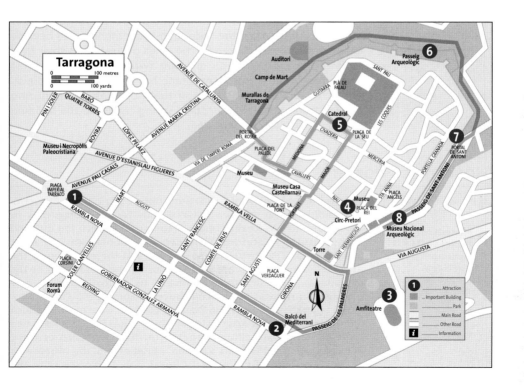

The Cistercian monastery route

Ratings

Churches	●●●●○
Festivals	●●●●○
Scenery	●●●●○
Towns/villages	●●●●○
Wine	●●●●○
Mountains	●●●○○
Children	●●○○○
Museums	●●○○○

Away from the coast, the interior of Tarragona province is a beguiling mixture of vineyards, orchards, lush valleys and winding mountain roads. The area is known as the Cistercian Triangle, on account of the three Cistercian monasteries (Poblet, Santes Creus and Vallbona de les Monges) founded by Count Ramón Berenguer IV in the mid-12th century. It was Ramón's marriage to Petronilla of Aragón which brought about the union of the two states, paving the way for Catalonia's Mediterranean expansion and the Reconquest of New Catalonia – the area around Tarragona which had remained under Moorish control. After the Reconquest, the monasteries became Christian fortresses, chosen by the kings of Aragón as their final resting place. This region also has two of Catalonia's most appealing small towns. Montblanc has retained its medieval ramparts, while Valls is the spiritual home of two enduring Catalan traditions – the *calçotada* spring feast and the building of human *castells* (*see page 266*).

MONESTIR DE POBLET

ℹ️ *Passeig Abat Conill 9; tel: 977 872247.*

🏛️ **Monestir de Poblet** €€ *Tel: 977 870089; www.poblet.cat. Guided tours daily 1000–1230, 1500–1630 (until 1800 Jun–Sept). Mass is daily at 0800 and on Sun at 1000, 1300.*

This walled complex of monastery buildings, named after the surrounding poplar groves, was founded by Ramón Berenguer IV in 1150 to give thanks for the Catalan Reconquest. Between the 13th and 15th centuries, Catalonia's Golden Age, Poblet was the most important spiritual centre in the country and the pantheon of the Aragonese kings. Ransacked in 1835 during the dissolution of the monasteries, it has since been restored to its original use and is now the largest inhabited Cistercian monastery in Europe.

You enter through the Porta Daurada ('Golden Gate'), whose gilded bronze doors commemorate a visit by Philip II in 1564. This leads to a large square, Plaça Major, where you find the 12th-century Romanesque chapel of Santa Caterina. Ahead of you, the twin towers of the 14th-century Porta Reial ('Royal Gate') give access to the monastery proper and lend it a fortress-like appearance. Beyond the gate, the beautiful Romanesque cloisters have an octagonal fountain

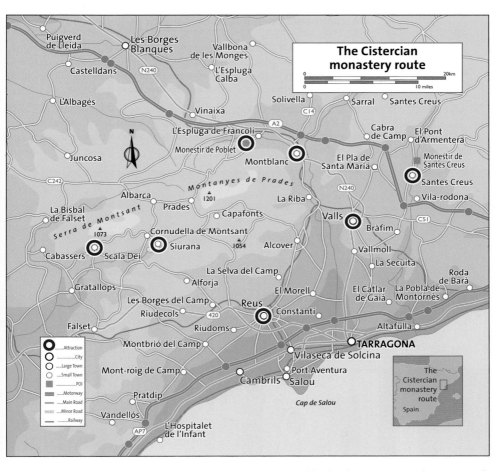

pavilion at their centre, probably built over an earlier Moorish fountain. Around the cloisters are spread out the various monastery buildings, including the refectory, the library and the chapterhouse where the former abbots of Poblet are buried. From the upper cloister, reached from the monks' dormitory, there is an excellent view of four towers, arranged left to right across the skyline in a chronological history of architectural styles – Romanesque, Gothic, Renaissance, Baroque.

The monastery church dates from the 12th century but also features a range of styles. Look out for the fine Renaissance altarpiece, carved in alabaster by Damián Forment. It is flanked by the tombs of the kings of Aragón, buried here between 1196 and 1479. The tombs, badly damaged during the 19th century, were remodelled in the 1950s by the sculptor Frederic Marès.

Accommodation and food in Monestir de Poblet

Hostal Fonoll € *Ramón Berenguer IV; tel: 977 870333; fax: 977 871366; www.hostalfonoll.com.* This simple *pension*, just outside the entrance to the monastery, offers basic accommodation or better rooms with private bath. There is also a bar and restaurant with terrace.

Masia del Cadet €€ *Les Masies de Poblet; tel: 977 870869; fax: 977 870496; www.masiadelcadet.com.* Small, secluded hotel and restaurant in a restored 15th-century farmhouse with comfortable bedrooms and lovely views.

Below
Monestir de Poblet

MONESTIR DE SANTES CREUS

🛈 **Monestir de
   Santes Creus €**
*Tel: 977 638329.
Open summer Tue–Sun
1000–1330, 1500–1900;
closes in winter at 1730.*

Less celebrated than Poblet and no longer inhabited by monks, the monastery of Santes Creus nevertheless enjoys the best setting in the Cistercian triangle, overlooking the Gaiá valley at the end of a long village street. It was established in the 12th century soon after Poblet, and populated with monks from southern France. You enter through the main courtyard, with the abbot's palace on your right and the

Grau € *Carrer Pere III 3; tel: 977 638311.* If you fancy staying the night in the village, this hostel beside the monastery makes a peaceful spot. It also serves good Catalan food.

solid façade of the monastery church ahead. The church, begun in 1174 in the form of a Latin cross, is built in transitional Romanesque-Gothic style. Although most of the Aragonese kings were buried at Poblet, the church contains the tombs of Pere III and Jaume II, enclosed in 14th-century Gothic pavilions. The superb cloister features flamboyant Gothic capitals carved with plant and animal motifs, while the so-called Old Cloister, in complete contrast, has low, unadorned arches around a central fountain.

MONTBLANC

ⓘ *Antiga Església de Sant Françesc; tel: 977 861733.*

Ⓜ **Museu de la Conca de Barberà €** *Carrer Josa 6. Open Tue–Sat 1000–1300, 1600–1900 (Jun–Sept 1700–2000); Sun 1000–1400.*

Ⓐ A market is held on Friday mornings.

Ⓢ The festival of **Sant Jordi** takes place on or around 23 April each year.

With its cobbled lanes, Gothic houses and arcaded main square, Montblanc is one of Catalonia's most pleasing small towns. What makes it even more special is that it is still enclosed by its well-preserved medieval ramparts, considered Catalonia's finest example of medieval military architecture. Two-thirds of the original walls are intact, along with 32 square towers and two portals. According to tradition, St George slew the dragon at the Portal de Sant Jordi, and his legend is re-enacted each year during a week of festivities in which actors in medieval costume perform on the walls.

In the 14th century this was one of Catalonia's most influential towns; the Corts Catalans, Europe's first form of parliamentary government, met in the church of Sant Miquel. The history of the area is told at the **Museu de la Conca de Barberà**, in a 13th-century town house near the Gothic church of Santa María. A branch of the museum, in the chapel of Sant Marçal, contains a collection of religious art donated by the sculptor Frederic Marès. Montblanc is the capital of the wine-producing Conca de Barberà district, and some Modernista wine cellars, designed by Gaudí's disciple Cesar Martinell, can be seen close to the railway station outside the town walls.

Accommodation and food in Montblanc

Ducal € *Carrer Francesc Macià 11; tel/fax: 977 860025.* This simple hotel in the centre would make a comfortable base for a one-night stay.

Cal Colom €€ *Carrer Civaderia 5; tel: 977 860153.* An intimate restaurant, hidden in an alley off the main square, serving good, fresh Catalan cuisine.

Les Espelmes €€ *Ctra N240, Coll de Lilla; tel: 977 601042.* The views stretch to the sea from the terrace of this restaurant, on a mountain pass between Montblanc and Valls. The restaurant serves classic Catalan cuisine with an emphasis on grilled meat, and is always packed out with local families for Sunday lunch.

REUS

ℹ️ *Sant Joan 34; tel: 902 362000; email: infoturisme@reus.net; www.reus.net/turisme.* The tourist office organises guided walks around the Modernista trail between July and September. *Mon–Sat 1200 (in Spanish and French), 1800 (in English and Catalan).*

🏛️ **Museu Comarcal Salvador Vilaseca €** *Raval de Santa Anna 59; tel: 977 345418; www. reus.net/museus.* Open *Tue–Sat 1000–1400, 1700–2000; Sun 1100–1400.*

Teatre Fortuny *Plaça Prim 4; tel: 977 315730 (ticket office).* Performances of theatre and music from October to June.

🛒 The central covered food market is open on weekday mornings and is reached by following the Modernista trail from the tourist office. A large street market takes place near here on Mondays and Saturdays.

The industrial and market town of Reus appears to have little immediate interest and by the time you have negotiated its complicated one-way system and found somewhere to park you may wonder why you bothered – but it is worth persevering in order to see its superb collection of Modernista architecture. Antoni Gaudí grew up here and, though he has not left any buildings to his home town, his influence is plain to see. The tourist office has devised a *Ruta del Modernisme* which can be followed by using a map or by renting an audio tour. Among the more interesting buildings are Casa Navàs, designed by Lluís Domènech i Montaner, with stained glass, mosaics and a handsome porticoed façade, and Casa Laguna by Pau Monguió, a tiny house squeezed above a narrow shopfront on Carrer de Monterols. Also worth seeing are the **Museu Comarcal Salvador Vilaseca**, mostly devoted to local archaeology, and the **Teatre Fortuny**, a restored 19th-century opera house named after a local painter, which is once again busy between October and June.

Accommodation and food in Reus

Casa Coder € *Plaça Mercadal 16; tel: 977 340707.* Old-style café, founded in 1790, serving breakfasts, *tapas*, sandwiches, pasta and pizzas.

Hotel Gaudi €€ *Raval de Robuster 49; tel: 977 345545; www.gargallohotels.es.* A modern hotel in a central location with excellent facilities and comfortable rooms with Wi-Fi. Prices can drop by up to a third if you reserve via the website.

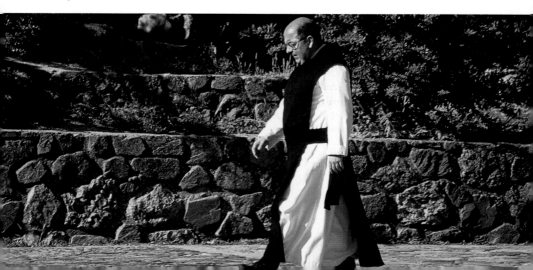

SCALA DEI

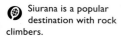 **Reial Cartoixa de Scala Dei** € *Carni de la Cartoixa*; tel: 977 827006. Open Tue–Sat 1000–1330, 1500–1700 (Jun–Sept 1000–1330, 1600–1900), Sun 1000–1330.

The Priorat vineyards of Tarragona province have established a growing reputation, but the first vines in this area were cultivated by monks at Scala Dei. This was the first Carthusian monastery in Spain, founded by Alfonso II of Aragón in 1162. After its dissolution, it stood in ruins for many years, but it has recently been restored and can now be visited.

SIURANA

Siurana is a popular destination with rock climbers.

This isolated hamlet is perched on a precipice, offering magnificent views over the Siurana valley. The village, known as 'the balcony of the Priorat', was the Moors' last stronghold in Catalonia before they were finally defeated in 1153. You can see the ruins of the Arab castle and also a Romanesque church, but the main attraction is just wandering among the houses and gazing down at the artificial lake far below. There are two excellent *casas rurales* in town.

VALLS

La Cort 61; tel: 977 612530; email: turisme.valls@ altanet.org; www.ajvalls.org

A market is held on Wednesday and Saturday mornings, with an antiques market in El Pati on the first Saturday of the month. The *calçotada* market takes place in El Pati on Sundays from February to April.

The capital of the Alt Camp district has two interesting churches and an atmospheric Jewish quarter, but it is best known throughout Catalonia as the home of two very different traditions. The *calçotada* is a spring feast that originated in Valls and is now held across Catalonia. *Calçots* are spring onions the size of leeks, cooked over vine cuttings until they are black; the skin is peeled off and the rest gradually lowered into the mouth after being dipped in *romesco* sauce, a tasty local mixture of hazelnuts, almonds, tomato, garlic and olive oil. Lamb chops and sausages are grilled over the embers, and the meal is accompanied by copious quantities of wine or *cava*. Everyone wears a bib to avoid getting covered in sauce. A *calçotada* feast, with *calçot*-eating competitions, is held on the last Sunday in January; for the next three months, *calçots* are grilled in the main square on Sundays at the annual *calçotada* market.

The other tradition is the building of human *castells* (*see page 266*), which takes place at the town's main festivals between June and October. This, too, is a custom that has spread throughout Catalonia, but the *castellers* of Valls are still among the best. A monument to the *Xiquets de Valls* (the teams of human castles) by the sculptor Josep Busquets can be seen in one of the town squares and there are plans to build a museum of *castells*.

The festivities usually take place in Plaça del Blat, in front of the town hall. Near here is the Gothic church of Sant Joan, begun in 1569.

Opposite
Cistercian monk, Poblet

From the town hall, Carrer de la Cort leads to the main square, El Pati, passing the **Capilla del Roser**, where mosaics covering the two side walls show scenes from the battle of Lepanto between Christians and Turks in 1571.

Accommodation and food in Valls

Félix € *Ctra de Tarragona Km17; tel: 977 609090; fax: 977 605007; email: felixhotelsa@infonegocio.com; www.felixhotel.net.* Situated to the south of town, this hotel has a pool in the garden and a busy restaurant where *calçots* are usually on the menu.

Masía Bou €€€ *Ctra de Lleida; tel: 977 600427; email: restaurant@masiabou.com.* This famous restaurant is credited with popularising the *calçotada* feast. You can eat *calçots* here as a starter for most of the year, but for the full works come between February and April. In summer you can eat on a terrace beneath the trees.

Festivals in Valls

The *castells* season begins on 23 June, during the **Festa Major**, which also features giants, devil dancing and fireworks spread over three days of festivities. There are more *castells* on 10 September, the eve of Catalonia's national day, and the season climaxes at the festival of **Santa Ursula**, held on 21 October or the following Sunday. Winter festivals include **Tres Tombs** in January, when horses and carts parade through the streets, and the **Mare de Déu de la Candela** (Candlemas) on 2 February, which every ten years becomes the main festivity of the year in fulfilment of an ancient oath. The **Festa de la Calçotada** takes place on the last Sunday in January.

Castells

The tradition of building human *castells* or pyramids dates back to the 18th century but has recently seen a revival as part of the wider Catalan renaissance. Like the *sardana* dance, the *castells* are deeply symbolic and to many they represent a powerful metaphor for the Catalan spirit. Some of the feats are truly remarkable as well as highly dangerous, involving as many as nine storeys of men; to watch them rise step by step from their base, supported by a sea of hands in the crowd, is an unforgettable experience. The tower is always crowned by a small child, known as an *enxaneta*, who raises his arm to signify completion. *Castells* are built at several Catalan festivals, particularly in Valls, Vilafranca and throughout Tarragona province, but their fame has spread far and wide. A biannual *castells* championship is held in the bullring at Tarragona, and *castellers* from Valls have performed in Chicago and Milan.

Above
Courtyard of Santa María,
Montblanc

Suggested tour

Total distance: 164km. The detour through the Priorat vineyards will add around 30km.

Time: 4 hours, plus visits to the monasteries.

Links: This route links up with the Golden Coast route (*see pages 250–51*) at Tarragona.

Begin in **Tarragona** ❶ (*see pages 252–9*) by taking the N240, signposted towards Lleida from the roundabout at Plaça Imperial Tarraco. Just outside the city, as you pass beneath the motorway and the road narrows to single lanes, look out for the signpost to the **Pont**

de les Ferreres on your right. This impressive Roman aqueduct, built in the 1st century AD, is also known as the Pont del Diable ('Devil's Bridge'). You can reach it by a short walk through the pine woods; if you have a head for heights you can even take a walk along the top.

Continue on the N240 to **VALLS** ❷. Just before you enter the town, keep right on the ring road and take the C51 in the direction of El Vendrell, passing through a rural landscape of almond and olive groves. Soon after **Alió**, turn left towards the **MONESTIR DE SANTES CREUS** ❸, which looms up ahead. After visiting the monastery, continue to **El Pont d'Armentera**, passing terraced vineyards above the River Gaiá, then turn left towards **El Pla de Santa María**. The road travels through a thickly wooded landscape before dropping to a plain and returning to Valls through its drab industrial outskirts.

Turn right on the ring road to return to the N240, climbing steeply over the **Coll de Lilla**, where farmhouse restaurants offer traditional Catalan cooking with inspiring views. At the top of the pass, make sure to get out of your car to look down over the valley and the distant sea. The road now winds down the mountainside to MONTBLANC ❹.

Shortly after Montblanc, take the left turn towards Poblet through the village of **L'Espluga de Francolí**, whose attractions include a museum of rural life and some splendid Modernista wine cellars. The road continues to the **MONESTIR DE POBLET** ❺. Leaving the monastery, follow signs to Prades, twisting and turning through a spectacular mountain landscape with vineyards on the lower slopes and wild olives higher up. **Prades** is an attractive village built of red stone, with an unusual spherical fountain in its main square. The road now climbs to the hilltop village of **Albarca**, where you turn left to drop down into the valley with the ridge of the Sierra de Prades on your left. You soon reach **Cornudella de Montsant**, another pretty medieval village, where a newly paved road gives access to the dramatically perched hamlet of **SIURANA** ❻, 6km away.

Detour: At this point you could make a worthwhile detour into the **Priorat** wine region, home to some of Catalonia's strongest and most highly prized red wines. The steeply terraced vineyards cling to slaty grey slopes and it is difficult to believe that anything much can grow here, but they produce some of the finest wines in Spain. The best place to begin a short tour is by taking the minor T702 to the right, 5km beyond Cornudella de Montsant. This leads to **SCALA DEI** ❼, from where you can return via **Porrera** to complete a round trip. The route is extremely scenic, but the driving exhausting, with numerous hairpin bends.

The main route follows the C242 over the **Coll de Arbolí** before dropping down through **Alforja** and **Les Borges del Camp** to join the N420 to **REUS** ❽ and Tarragona.

Also worth exploring

Vallbona de les Monges € *Tel: 977 330567. Open Tue–Sat 1030–1330, 1630–1845, Sun 1200–1330, 1630–1845 (1745 in winter).*

The third of the great Cistercian monasteries, **Vallbona de les Monges**, lies 18km north of Montblanc and is reached by taking the C14. It was founded in 1157 for a community of Cistercian women and is still inhabited by nuns. The cloisters here contain Romanesque and Gothic elements, while the church is an example of transitional Gothic architecture. Among the tombs are those of Queen Violante of Hungary (wife of Jaume I of Aragón) and her daughter.

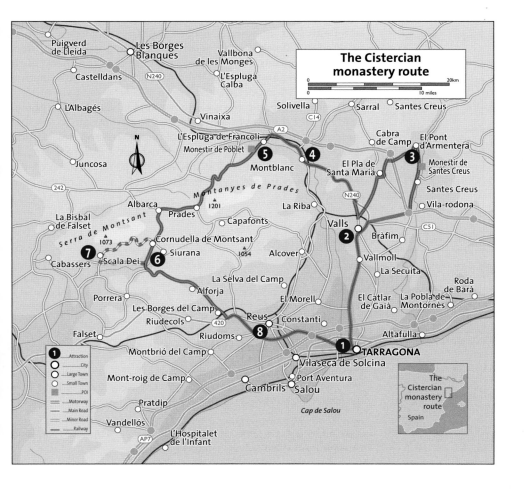

The Ebro Delta

Ratings

Nature	●●●●●
Scenery	●●●●○
Beaches	●●●○○
Castles	●●●○○
Children	●●●○○
Food/wine	●●●○○
Villages	●●●○○
Walking	●●●○○

Where the Costa Daurada runs out, the River Ebro flows into the sea across a watery landscape of salt marshes, rice fields and lagoons. The Ebro Delta is the largest area of wetland in Catalonia and one of the most important in Europe. Flamingos, herons and waterfowl are among the many birds attracted here, and much of the delta is now a protected nature reserve. Just as important, though, is the area's human history. For centuries, people have exploited this landscape for fishing, hunting and the harvesting of everything from salt to leeches; these days it is the source of Catalonia's rice crop. Inland, the towns of the Ebro valley bear the scars of a different sort of human history. In the 1930s, this was the scene of some of the fiercest Civil War battles, when the peaceful waters of the Ebro ran with blood.

L'AMETLLA DE MAR

ⓘ *Carrer Sant Joan 55; tel: 977 456477; www.ametllademar.org*

⊙ The festival of **Sant Pere Pescador**, patron saint of fishermen, is held on 29 June.

The small summer resort of L'Ametlla de Mar is also a working fishing port with smacks tied up in the harbour and a fish market on weekday afternoons when the fleet comes in. There is a small beach here, and a handful of rocky coves where the pine woods reach almost to the sea. The streets behind the harbour have a pleasant village feel.

Accommodation and food in L'Ametlla de Mar

L'Alguer €€ *Carrer Trafalgar 21; tel: 977 456124; email: restaurantalguer@ restaurantalguer.com.* The best place to sample the local seafood is at the terrace of this restaurant on the harbourside promenade.

Bon Repòs €€ *Plaça Catalunya 49; tel: 977 456025; fax: 977 456582; email: hbonrepos@teleline.es; www.bonrepos.com.* This old-fashioned family hotel is open only in summer.

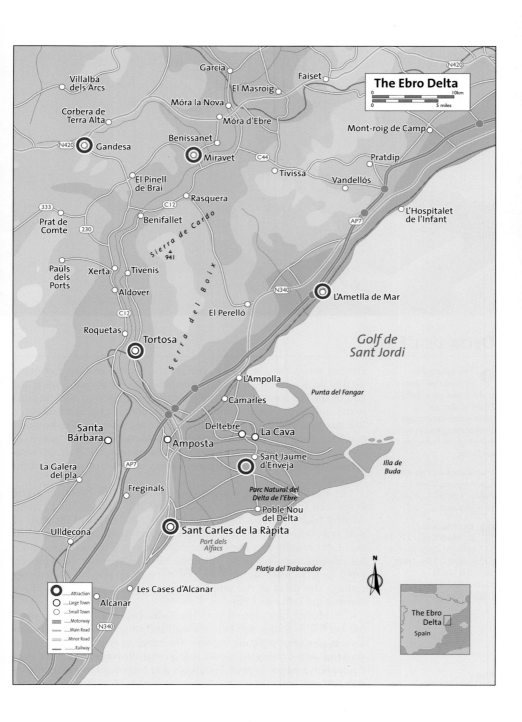

The Ebro Delta

Villalba dels Arcs

Garcia

Faiset

N420

El Masroig

Móra la Nova

Corbera de Terra Alta

Móra d'Ebre

Mont-roig de Camp

N420   Gandesa

Benissanet

Miravet

C44

Pratdip

El Pinell de Brai

Tivissa

Vandellós

L'Hospitalet de l'Infant

333

Rasquera

C12

Prat de Comte

230

Benifallet

Sierra de Cardó

AP7

▲ 941

Paüls dels Ports

Xerta

Tivenis

Serra del Boix

N340

L'Ametlla de Mar

Aldover

El Perelló

C12

Roquetas

Tortosa

Serra del Boix

Golf de Sant Jordi

L'Ampolla

Camarles

Punta del Fangar

Santa Bárbara

Deltebre

La Cava

Amposta

Sant Jaume d'Enveja

Illa de Buda

La Galera del pla

AP7

Parc Natural del Delta de l'Ebre

Freginals

Poble Nou del Delta

Ulldecona

Sant Carles de la Ràpita

Port dels Alfacs

N

Platja del Trabucador

Attraction
Large Town
Small Town
Motorway
Main Road
Minor Road
Railway

Les Cases d'Alcanar

Alcanar

N340

The Ebro Delta

Spain

DELTA DE L'EBRE

ⓘ The main park
information centre is
at the Ecomuseu (*below*).
There is also an
information centre and
birdwatching museum in
the village of Poble Nou
del Delta.

The nearest tourist office
is in Amposta. *Avda Sant
Jaume 1; tel: 977 703453;
www.ebre.com*

🅷 **Ecomuseu**
*Dr Martí Buera 22; tel:
977 489679. Open Mon–Fri
1000–1400, 1500–1800,
Sat 1000–1300,
1500–1800, Sun
1000–1300.*

Above
Ebro Delta fisherman

Driving across the Ebro Delta, you get the strange sensation of being
neither on water nor on land. Formed by a rise in the sea level at the
end of the last Ice Age, the delta consists mostly of reed beds and flat
marshland under continuous threat of flooding. This is a landscape
like nowhere else in Catalonia, a place of huge skies, endless horizons
and long, empty beaches. In winter the fields turn a muddy brown; in
spring and summer, after the rice has been planted, they fill with
water, turning the roads into causeways and the inhabitants into
islanders.

The best place to get an introduction to the delta is at the
Ecomuseu in the main town of Deltebre. The museum, in a typical
country house, features displays on the flora and fauna of the delta as
well as a short outdoor walk through the Ebro Delta in miniature. On
this brief circuit you see rice fields, fruit trees, a bird hide and a
fisherman's hut. This is no substitute for a walk in the delta proper,
but it helps to whet the appetite. You can pick up maps and advice for
touring the delta at the attached information centre for the **Parc
Natural del Delta de l'Ebre**.

Considering how close it is to the Costa Daurada beaches, tourism
has been slow to develop here, though the villagers see ecotourism as
a valuable source of future income. The range of activities ranges from
walking and cycling to horse riding and birdwatching. The bird
population reaches its peak in October and November as migrant birds
pass through and others settle in for the winter. More than 300 species

The boat trips leave from outside the Casa Nuri restaurant, hourly in summer and at 1230 and 1530 daily in winter.

Mosquitoes

Although the mosquitoes are no longer malarial, they can still be a nuisance in summer and it is a good idea to wear insect repellent, especially at dusk.

have been spotted here, 60 per cent of all those found in Europe. Flamingos, with their unmissable pink plumage, are a common sight, along with thousands of ducks and coots. Black-winged stilts feed on the rice fields in summer. If you are lucky, you might see a night heron or the rare Audouin's gull. For the best chance of seeing birds, come early in the morning or just before dusk.

It would be possible to spend days here, but on a brief visit head for the area known as Riumar and follow signs to the *desembocadura* ('river mouth'). From a landing stage opposite the isle of Buda, boats make regular cruises towards the mouth. Near here is the start of a waymarked walk, *Itinerari de Garxal*, which leads through a typical delta landscape to a mirador overlooking a beach. The walk is very straightforward and takes about an hour. Beach-lovers should check out some of the other beaches, such as Platja dels Eucaliptus on the southern side, more like an ocean beach with its huge expanses of white sand – though remember that the currents can be dangerous here and you need to be confident to swim.

Accommodation and food in Delta de l'Ebre

Casa Nuri €€ *Ctra de les Goles; tel: 977 480128.* Popular with day-trippers, this restaurant stands on a busy tourist corner where the boats leave for the river mouth and the souvenir shops sell packets of the local rice. The restaurant serves classic delta dishes such as paella, *arròs a banda* (rice and seafood stew) and local eels.

Delta Hotel €€ *Camino L'Illeta; tel: 977 480046; www.dhgroup.es.* Comfortable hotel with restaurant and all the facilities. Open year-round.

GANDESA

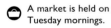

Avda Catalunya; tel: 977 420910; www.gandesa.altanet.org

A market is held on Tuesday mornings.

During the Battle of the Ebro in 1938, General Franco directed Nationalist operations from a command post in the hills overlooking Gandesa. These days the site is marked by a memorial. The town contains several fine Gothic mansions, and the parish church has a 13th-century Romanesque doorway. Gandesa is the capital of the Terra Alta wine-producing district, and the wine co-operative, designed by César Martinell with parabolic brick arches and a turreted roof, is a superb example of Modernista architecture.

Accommodation and food in Gandesa

Piqué € *Vía Catalunya 68; tel: 977 420068; fax: 977 420329.* The only hotel in Gandesa is situated near the entrance to the town and has a restaurant known for its regional cuisine. Rooms without air conditioning are cheaper.

MIRAVET

Pottery

Miravet is known for the quality of its pottery, especially its pitchers. You can watch them being made in the 'potters' quarter' on the edge of the village.

This picturesque village on the north bank of the Ebro shelters beneath a rocky outcrop crowned by an ancient fortress. The castle, built by the Moors, was given by Ramón Berenguer IV to the military order of the Knights Templar, who built a Romanesque chapel inside its walls. In 1308, the last Templars in Catalonia were finally beheaded here after resisting the orders of Pope Clement V to disband. You can walk up to the castle for views over the river and the village.

The River Ebro

The longest river in Spain rises in the Cantabrian mountains and flows into the sea some 746km later in Catalonia. This is the only one of Spain's major rivers to empty into the Mediterranean rather than the Atlantic; it is also the river from which the Iberian peninsula takes its name. Travelling through La Rioja, Navarra and Aragón on its way to Catalonia, the Ebro seems to provide a natural barrier between the plains of Castile and the southern Pyrenees – perhaps, too, between the people of central Spain and the various independent-minded peoples of the northeast.

Above
Miravet

SANT CARLES DE LA RÀPITA

Plaça Carles III 13;
tel: 977 744624;
email: turisme@larapita.com;
www.larapita.com

A market takes place
on Saturday mornings.

Sheltering inside the natural harbour of Els Alfacs, this elegant seaport was founded by Carlos III in the 18th century when much of the Ebro Delta was uninhabitable due to the presence of malarial mosquitoes. Fishing is still the biggest industry here. Restaurants and *tapas* bars by the harbour sell local prawns, clams, date mussels and eels, and a lively auction takes place when the fishing fleet returns on weekday afternoons.

Accommodation and food in Sant Carles de la Ràpita

Miami Can Pons €€ *Passeig Maritim 18; tel: 977 740551*. This famous seafood restaurant is now in the third generation of the Pons family, and is still producing the original classics such as fresh prawns and *suquet* (fish casserole). The owners have a hotel in the same street, the Hotel Miami Mar, open from April to October (*tel: 977 745859*).

Below
Sant Carles de la Ràpita

TORTOSA

Catedral
Tel: 977 441752.
Open daily 0900–1300,
1700–2000.

A market is held on
Monday mornings.

The capital of the Baix Ebre county has seen more history than it might care to remember. Founded by the Iberians, strengthened by the Romans and held for centuries by the Moors (whose hilltop castle is now a stylish hotel), the city was captured for Catalonia by Ramón Berenguer IV in 1148. Besieged by Napoleon's troops at the start of the 19th century, Tortosa suffered its greatest tragedy in 1938, as the setting of the Battle of the Ebro. At least 50,000 Republican soldiers, including many international volunteers, lost their lives when the

ℹ️ *Plaza del Carrilet 1;*
tel: 977 449648;
www.tortosa.cat

⊙ Tortosa's biggest
festival, **Nostra
Senyora de la Cinta**,
takes place in the first
week of September.

Republicans launched a summer offensive across the Ebro to divert General Franco from his assault on Valencia. It was a defeat from which the Republican movement never recovered. A memorial in the middle of the Ebro, erected by the victorious Nationalists and built from the only surviving pillar of the old bridge, recalls the battle.

The town's history can be seen in its buildings. The Arab castle still dominates; even if you are not staying here, you should drive up for the view over the rooftops from its walls. The 14th-century **Catedral**, on the site of a mosque and before that a Roman temple, has a baroque façade, a Gothic interior and a lavish Baroque side chapel, built from local jasper and Italian marble and dedicated to Our Lady of La Cinta, the city's patron. Opposite the cathedral, the bishop's palace has a fabulous inner courtyard surrounded by Gothic arcades. It can usually be visited in the mornings. South of here, the Llotja de Mar is the former grain exchange, a Gothic building which once fixed the price of wheat across the whole of the western Mediterranean. It stands inside a park at the heart of the Eixample, the city's Modernisme quarter, with its splendid covered market and municipal slaughter-house. You can wander back up to the castle along the narrow, Moorish lanes, passing Gothic and Renaissance churches on the way, then pause for rest in the peaceful **Jardins del Príncep**, with their open-air sculpture.

Accommodation and food in Tortosa

Below
Tortosa

Parador de Tortosa €€€ *Castell de la Suda; tel: 977 444450; fax: 977 444458; email: tortosa@parador.es; www.parador.es.* For a sense of

history and wonderful views, this 10th-century castle is the only place to stay. The restaurant, with its Gothic windows, serves imaginative Ebro cuisine such as frogs' legs and eels in garlic sauce. There is a poolside terrace within the medieval walls.

Suggested tour

Total distance: 175km. The detour adds around 20km.

Time: 3–4 hours.

Links: This route starts around 15km south of Cambrils on the Golden Coast route (*see pages 250–51*).

Begin at **L'Hospitalet de l'Infant ❶**, an unexciting beach resort which owes its name to its 14th-century Gothic hospital. From here, follow the N340 coast road south, with alternating views of the sea and of the nuclear reactors at Vandellós. After 18km you reach **L'AMETLLA DE MAR ❷**, where a short diversion leads down to the port. From here, the N340 swings inland, then returns to the coast at **L'Ampolla**, where there is a small beach in the shadow of the Cap Roig headland.

Shortly after L'Ampolla, take the left turn to **Deltebre**, crossing the **DELTA DE L'EBRE** on a bumpy track which passes between the rice paddies. Continue to follow signs to Deltebre and La Cava. When you reach a roundabout, go straight ahead towards **La Cava ❸** and take the first right to reach the natural park information centre and museum. If you want to take a boat trip to the river mouth, return to the roundabout and follow signs for **Riumar**.

Once you have explored the northern half of the delta, return to La Cava, drive along its main street and take any of the turnings signposted *transbordadores* to board a car ferry across the river. The ferry lands at the village of **Sant Jaume d'Enveja**. Drive through the village until you reach a T-junction, where a right turn will take you quickly to **Amposta ❹**, the biggest town of the delta region.

Detour: For better scenery, turn left towards **Platja dels Eucaliptus**. Just before the end of the road, look out for a track on the right, signposted 'INFOSA'. This takes you along a stunning stretch of road, with the sea and the wide sandy beaches to your left, a lagoon to your right and the Sierra del Montsiá in the distance.

Before long the road divides, with a sandy track (suitable only for off-road vehicles) leading across a spit to **Punta de la Banya**, a mecca for birdwatchers. Turn right here, passing the whitewashed walled village of **Poble Nou del Delta**, founded in 1947 and now a popular destination for ecotourism. On your left is **Els Alfacs**, a huge natural harbour protecting the fishing port of **SANT CARLES DE**

Above
L'Ametlla de Mar

LA RÀPITA ❺. When you reach Sant Carles, turn right on the N340 towards Amposta.

Drive through Amposta and follow signs for **TORTOSA** ❻, reached by a bridge across the Ebro after 16km. The C12 now climbs through the Ebro valley, passing citrus orchards and olive groves. Sacks of oranges hang outside the shops in the village of **Xerta** ❼. The road travels high above the river, offering marvellous views.

Detour: Some 10km beyond Xerta, a left turn on the C43 climbs steeply into the Cavalls mountain range on its way to **GANDESA** ❽. On the way it passes **El Pinell de Brai**, a wine village with splendid Modernista cellars. At Gandesa you reach a plateau and bear right on the N420, crossing the *meseta*. **Corbera d'Ebre**, just outside Gandesa, was destroyed by Franco's troops during the Civil War and the old village has been left in ruins as a silent reminder. A memorial in the shape of a jackboot stands outside the abandoned church. Continue on this road to **Móra d'Ebre**, where you cross back to the right bank of the Ebro at **Móra la Nova**. From here you need to travel briefly south on the C12 towards Tortosa to return to the main route.

Alternatively, stay on the C12 as it crosses the river and broadly follows its course to **MIRAVET** ❾. Soon after Miravet, on the approach to Móra la Nova, turn right on the C44, climbing into the Sierra de la Creu with the Costa Daurada spread out beneath you and dropping back down to the coast at L'Hospitalet de l'Infant.

Also worth exploring

South of the Ebro Delta, the N340 coast road continues to **Les Cases d'Alcanar**, the last village in Catalonia and a chic summer resort. This fishing and seafaring village is known as the place where Colonel Antonio Tejero hatched his failed military coup in 1981, soon after the restoration of democracy. Beyond here is the start of the **Costa del Azahar** ('Orange Blossom Coast') in Valencia, whose main sight is the fortified town of **Peñíscola**. The castle here, on a rocky peninsula with the sea on three sides, was built by the Knights Templar on the site of an Arab fortress.

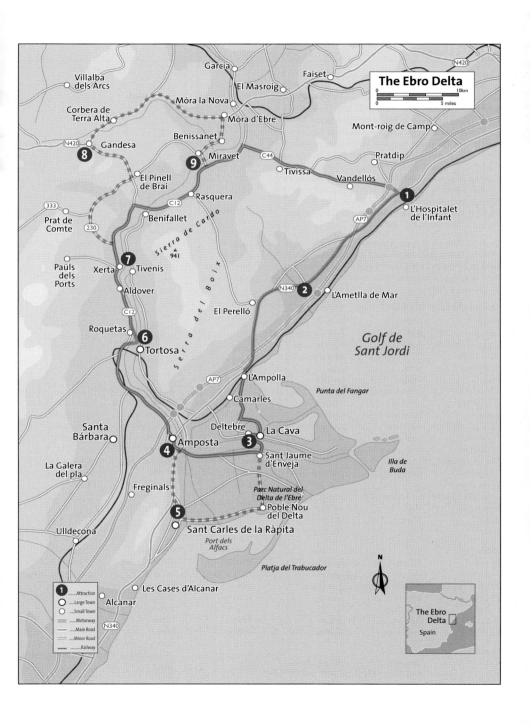

The Ebro Delta

0 _____ 10km
0 _____ 5 miles

Villalba
dels Arcs
Garcia
El Masroig
Faiset
N420
Corbera de
Terra Alta
Móra la Nova
Mont-roig de Camp
N420
Gandesa
Móra d'Ebre
8
Benissanet
Pratdip
Miravet
C44
9
Tivissa
Vandellós
El Pinell
de Brai
Rasquera
1
L'Hospitalet
de l'Infant
333
C12
AP7
Prat de
Comte
230
Benifallet
Sierra de Cardo
Pauls
dels
Ports
Xerta
7
Tivenis
941
Aldover
C12
El Perelló
N340
L'Ametlla de Mar
2
Roquetas
6
Tortosa
Sierra del Boix
Golf de
Sant Jordi
AP7
L'Ampolla
Punta del Fangar
Camarles
Santa
Bárbara
Deltebre
La Cava
Amposta
3
4
Illa de
Buda
La Galera
del pla
Sant Jaume
d'Enveja
Freginals
Parc Natural del
Delta de l'Ebre
Poble Nou
del Delta
5
Ulldecona
Sant Carles de la Ràpita
Port dels
Alfacs
Platja del Trabucador
N

1 ....Attraction
○ ....Large Town
○ ....Small Town
====== ....Motorway
_____ ....Main Road
_____ ....Minor Road
_____ ....Railway

Les Cases d'Alcanar
Alcanar
N340

The Ebro
Delta

Spain

Language

The official languages of Catalonia are Catalan (*català*) and Castilian Spanish (*castellano*). Catalan is spoken by around 65 per cent of the population and is the main language of communication outside Barcelona. Since 1980 its use has been increasingly 'normalised' in government, the media and the education system. Catalan is a Romance language, with roots in ancient Latin, sharing common features with both French and Spanish. It is also spoken in Andorra, Valencia, the Balearic islands and parts of the French Pyrenees. Many Catalan words look like their equivalents in French or Spanish but sound completely different. You should never make the mistake of referring to Catalan as a dialect of Spanish.

Castilian Spanish is spoken across Spain and is universally understood. Euskara (Basque) is widely spoken in the Basque Country and Navarra. Another local language is Aranese in the remote Catalan valleys of the Vall d'Aran.

Useful phrases

	Catalan	Spanish
Hello	hola	hola
Good morning	bon dia	buenos días
Good afternoon	bona tarda	buenas tardes
Goodnight	bona nit	buenas noches
Goodbye	adéu	adiós
Please	sisplau	por favor
Thank you	gràcies/merci	gracias
Excuse me	perdoni	perdón
Sorry	ho sento	lo siento
How much is it?	quant és?	¿cuánto es?
How are you?	com està?	¿qué tal?
Fine, thanks	molt bé, gràcies	muy bien, gracias
Do you speak English?	parleu anglès?	¿habla usted inglés?
I don't speak Catalan/Spanish	no parlo català	no hablo español
tomorrow	demà	mañana
open	obert	abierto
closed	tancat	cerrado

Days

Monday	dilluns	lunes
Tuesday	dimarts	martes
Wednesday	dimecres	miércoles
Thursday	dijous	jueves
Friday	divendres	viernes
Saturday	dissabte	sábado
Sunday	diumenge	domingo

Numbers

1	un/una	un/uno/una
2	dos/dues	dos
3	tres	tres
4	quatre	cuatro
5	cinc	cinco
6	sis	seis
7	set	siete
8	vuit	ocho
9	nou	nueve
10	deu	diez
20	vint	veinte
100	cent	cien/ciento
1000	mil	mil

Eating out

lunch	dinar	almuerzo
dinner	sopar	cena
menu	carta	carta
set menu	menú	menú
first course	primer	primero
main course	segon	segundo
dessert	postre	postre
bread	pa	pan
water	aigua	agua
red wine	vi negre	vino tinto
white wine	vi blanc	vino blanco
beer	cervesa	cerveza
the bill	el compte	la cuenta

Hotels

single room	habitació senzilla	habitación individual
double room	habitació doble	habitación doble
bath/shower	bany/duxta	baño/ducha
breakfast	esmorzar	desayuno
one night	una nit	una noche
garage	garatge	garaje
car park	aparcament	parking
swimming pool	piscina	piscina
balcony	balcó	balcón

On the road

petrol	gasolina	gasolina
unleaded	sense plomb	sin plomo
diesel	gasoil	gasóleo
motorway	autopista	autopista
airport	aeroport	aeropuerto
station	estació	estación de trenes
street	carrer	calle
avenue	avinguda	avenida
promenade	passeig	paseo
square	plaça	plaza
bridge	pont	puente
park	parc	parque
tourist office	oficina de turisme	oficina de turismo
beach	platja	playa
mountain range	serra	sierra

Index

Acknowledgements

Project management: Cambridge Publishing Management Limited
Project editor: Edward Robinson
Series design: Fox Design
Cover design: Liz Lyons Design
Layout: Cambridge Publishing Management Limited
Repro and image setting: Cambridge Publishing Management Limited
Map work: PCGraphics (UK) Ltd

We would like to thank Neil Setchfield for the photographs used in this book, to whom the copyright in the photographs belongs, with the exception of the following:

AISA/World Illustrated/Photoshot: page 217; **Authors Images/Photoshot:** page 89; **Dreamstime.com:** pages 1A and 28 (Jarroyo1982), 1B and 238–9 (Philip Lange), 13 (Marlee), 127 (Adolfo Martinez Sautua), 147 (Samuel Areny), 157 & 191 (Rafael Laguillo), 189 (Olga Langerova), 199 (Ferenc Ungor), 214 (Pasaro); **Nick Inman:** 139, 179, 204, 207, 211, 215, 258, 270; **Pictures Colour Library:** page 102; **Turespaña:** pages 76, 78, 79, 80, 81, 83, 84, 86, 90, 92, 93, 94, 96, 98, 100, 106, 109, 110, 114, 116, 118, 122, 125, 130 (both), 132, 136, 158, 159, 160, 190, 209, 212, 219, 272, 274, 275, 276, 278; **World Pictures:** pages 40B, 58A, 142, 144, 148, 149.

Feedback form

We're committed to providing the very best up-to-date information in our travel guides and constantly strive to make them as useful as they can be. You can help us to improve future editions by letting us have your feedback. Just take a few minutes to complete and return this form to us.

When did you buy this book? ....
....

Where did you buy it? (Please give town/city and, if possible, name of retailer)
....
....

When did you/do you intend to travel in Catalonia? ....
....

For how long (approx)? ....

How many people in your party? ....

Which cities, national parks and other locations did you/do you intend mainly to visit?
....
....
....
....

Did you/will you:
❏ Make all your travel arrangements independently?
❏ Travel on a fly-drive package?
Please give brief details: ....
....

Did you/do you intend to use this book:
❏ For planning your trip?   ❏ Both?
❏ During the trip itself?

Did you/do you intend also to purchase any of the following travel publications for your trip?
A road map/atlas (please specify) ....
Other guidebooks (please specify) ....

Have you used any other Thomas Cook guidebooks in the past? If so, which?

....
....

Please rate the following features of *driving guides Catalonia & the Spanish Pyrenees* for their value to you (circle VU for 'very useful', U for 'useful', NU for 'little or no use'):

The *Travel facts* section on pages 12–21	VU	U	NU
The *Driver's guide* section on pages 22–27	VU	U	NU
The *Highlights* on pages 38–9	VU	U	NU
The recommended driving routes throughout the book	VU	U	NU
Information on towns and cities, National Parks, etc	VU	U	NU
The maps of towns and cities, parks, etc	VU	U	NU

Please use this space to tell us about any features that in your opinion could be changed, improved, or added in future editions of the book, or any other comments you would like to make concerning the book:

....
....
....
....
....
....
....
....

Your age category: ❏ 21–30   ❏ 31–40   ❏ 41–50   ❏ over 50

Your name: Mr/Mrs/Miss/Ms ....
(First name or initials) ....
(Last name) ....

Your full address (please include postal or zip code):

....
....
....
....
....

Your daytime telephone number: ....

**Please detach this page and send it to: driving guides Series Editor,
Thomas Cook Publishing, PO Box 227, Coningsby Road, Peterborough PE3 8SB.**

Alternatively, you can email us at: *books@thomascook.com*